"It's going to be a revolution, Charlie. Get with it."

Dr. Timothy Leary was talking to the author of this biographical close-up, Dr. Charles W. Slack. It was 1959. Both were teaching psychology at Harvard.

It became a revolution, all right, and Leary was its high priest. He planted the seeds of the hippie movement. He promoted the use of marijuana by millions. And he preached his answer to boredom, sex, campus riots, the Vietnam War, you-name-it. His answer: hallucinogenic drugs.

Leary introduced Slack to LSD, but Slack never did get "with it." Except now and then, when his own career was slipping, he felt low, ran into Leary again, usually at some big, wild party—and became, literally, a fellow-traveler.

"Leary takes my hand. 'You must come with us to California.'"

" 'Sure, sure,' I say."

Here is the inside story of Leary's rise and fall, told through his travels with Slack, the semi-square, through Haight-Ashbury, the East Village, into exile in Switzerland.

Psychology Today calls Slack the "best-informed biographer of Leary," and in this eyewitness report Leary emerges for the first time in all the roles that made him the pied piper for the insanity of the Sixties: the drug freak, charmer, proselytizer, husband, womanizer, hedonist—a supreme free spirit to his followers, "a threat to the community" to one judge, "an insidious menace" to another.

Slack knows all these Learys. Not one of them left the last decade untouched. And not one of them is dull.

Photo: John Carr

DR. CHARLES W. SLACK, a clinical psychologist, now teaches at the University of Alabama Medical Center in Birmingham. His wife, Eileen, is superintendent of the State Training School for Girls.

Timothy Leary, the Madness of the Sixties and Me

Timothy Leary, the Madness of the Sixties and Me

by

Dr. Charles W. Slack

Peter H. Wyden/Publisher

NEW YORK

The Introduction to this book originally appeared as
"Tim the Unsinkable," in *Psychology Today*, January 1973.
(Copyright © 1973 by Communications/Research/Machines, Inc.)

Portions of Chapter 2 originally appeared in *Eye* Magazine
in different forms as "An Evening With Timothy Leary,"
Eye, March 1968. (Copyright © 1968 by Hearst Corporation.)

Playboy Interview: Timothy Leary originally
appeared in *Playboy Magazine* (copyright © 1966
by Playboy) and is used with permission.

LIBRARY OF CONGRESS CATALOG CARD NUMBER: 74–76237
MANUFACTURED IN THE UNITED STATES OF AMERICA
ISBN: 0–88326–051–4

To Eileen,
who saved my soul

Acknowledgments

I thank Corrinne Lawrence and Bart Paugh for help with the manuscript of this book. For inspiration and support at key moments, I thank Frances Slack, Dave McClelland, Roma Slack, George Harris, Gordon Slack, Rosemary Smith and Evelyn Slack. Important research facts were supplied by Hobart Spring, Frank Ferguson and Peter Whitmer. Four families made havens for me during this book: the Warner V. Slack family, the Walter E. Lewis family, the John Ohlighers and Ed and Sally Newton. My brother, Warner, has always been my closest friend, and now he is also my favorite literary critic. May other readers be absorbed by these pages as much as my relatives.

Contents

	Introduction	xi
1	Why Dr. Leary Now, April 1968	1
2	Revolt in the Second Class	34
3	Shindigs and Shades	67
4	California Separates from the Mainland	90
5	Cures and Curiosities	116
6	Upside Down	146
7	Going Downhill in New York and Beyond in the Sensational Sixties	168
8	Headlines	192
9	Journey to the End	213
10	Getting There	223
	Notes	261
	Bibliography	263

Introduction

"Nothing so disturbs a bishop as a saint in the parish," said the late Norbert Wiener. Secularly, nothing so disturbs the Establishment as a man who refuses to go through established channels. Such a man is on a level above ordinary rules of success and failure . . . or thinks he is.

All through the sixties, Timothy Leary proclaimed that he had *the* shortcut, *the* instant inside track, *the* philosopher's stone, not only for attaining liberty, happiness and life-that-seems-everlasting but also for gaining artistic creativity, political freedom and spiritual awakening —*complete* spiritual awakening. That answer: LSD and the other hallucinogenic drugs.

And nothing disturbs the dean of a college like a lecturer who quits going to class and just hands out the *ultimate* answer to his students. Yet it took Harvard three years to give Leary the ax. Anyhow, by the time he got fired, in 1963, Leary didn't care. He bounced back, to become a leader of untold numbers of mostly-young people who themselves left school to become living accusations against the reigning institutions of culture and politics. From unemployed teacher to symbol of the counter-culture. This was more like it!

Carrying on through the sixties, Leary successfully planted the seeds of the hippie movement, or at least its East Coast seedling; helped promote the use of marijuana by millions; gave LSD and other hallucinogenic drugs to hundreds; beat a couple of drug raps and, when finally arrested, convicted and sentenced, escaped from his California prison; managed to live "off the land," or at least off his wits, without much visible means of support for most of the decade; and remained continually in the public eye, all the while sharing personal acquaintance with a few of the richest people in the world and many celebrities of the arts, the theater and radical politics, that in-group which was always "on the outs" with bourgeois America, the group Tom Wolfe called "radical chic."

Less successful were Leary's attempts, in 1960, to start his own psychological association; in 1963, his own foundation; in 1965, his own religion; in 1966, his own magazine; in 1967, his own Indian tribe; in 1968, his own country; in 1971, his own "declared war on the United States," urging "not just bombing the ROTC's" but "escalate the violence . . . start hijacking planes . . . kidnap prominent sports figures and television and Hollywood people" (in order to free Bobby Seale). It is characteristic of Leary that he moves from each resounding defeat to a new idealistic view of himself and the world, thus "upleveling" (his word) failure into success. Timothy Leary is not easy to sink.

In between pronunciamentos and position papers, running for governor of California and running *from* the police of three or four countries, he dashed off several books—not all of them good, but all interesting, with slapdash pseudo-science, altisonant alliteration, terrible pot-puns on every line and panegyrics for all his turned-on celebrity friends.

Like other scandalous hedonists from de Sade to Mae West, Leary-in-fact is somewhat different from the Leary-image which he and his fans created and which his enemies, "the forces of middle-aged, middle-class America," unfittingly project onto him. Despite the derring-do of his prison escape (minimum security, mind you), Leary-in-fact is a charming, very friendly, highly intelligent, decidedly non-violent person, usually in control even when high as a kite—a good guy, pleasant con-man, wonderful host, warm human being and good conversationalist. However, in his writing and in person, in everything he says and does, eventually it seems to leak out, somehow, that he has *the* answer and you *don't*. Even between the lines of his essays and books, *he* is sexy-in-ecstasy, whereas you are anxious and impotent. He is up and you are down. Nya-nya, nya-nya. Tim is thumbing his nose at you squares. Subtly it creeps up on you. He has powerful friends and you don't, switched-on, in-crowd, celebrity friends, high-all-the-time-and-getting-away-with-it friends, zonked and paying no penalty. Infuriating, absolutely infuriating!

Anyhow, that's one impression. That's one Timothy Leary: the image. It was the image which U.S. District Judge Ben Connally had in mind when he doled out twice the minimum sentence because "He [Leary] poses a threat to the community . . . openly advocates violation . . . poses a danger. . . ." Likewise, Superior Court Judge Byron McMillan refused to set bail on Leary because of his image, calling him "an insidious menace" to society and a "pleasure-seeking, irresponsible Madison Avenue advocate of the free use of drugs." There is not a bit of doubt, then that, because of this image, Leary got a twenty-year max for possession of less than one ounce of grass. This same image-fact ambivalence showed up after his escape to Switzerland, where national authorities at first refused extradition, believing him to have been harshly sentenced in the U.S. for a minor offense, while other Swiss authorities asked him to leave because he was a bad example to youth.

The real Timothy Leary was born in Springfield, Massachusetts, in 1920, of a devout Catholic mother and a military-medico father (Eisenhower's dentist). The handsome, smart, rebellious Army brat grew into a handsome, smart, rebellious adolescent, raised largely by his mother and an aunt while his father roamed off to sea. He entered Holy Cross College in 1938 but soon dropped out. He upleveled that failure by getting appointed to West Point, where he lasted only eighteen months. At West Point he was handed the famous silent treatment for an alleged infraction of the rules. Many who knew him well then say he was innocent. In 1941 Leary showed up at the U. of Alabama, which, then as now, happened to have a strong department of psychology. *This was more like it!* Leary joined an elite fraternity (Theta Chi) and made high grades, but then bragged to his frat brothers about loving-it-up in the girls' dorm at midnight and was caught and suspended. This defeat was upleveled by enlisting in the Army as a psychologist. Leary spent the war in a Pennsylvania hospital and by 1950 had acquired his professional meal-tickets for American psychology: a Master of Science degree from Washington State University and a Doctorate in Philosophy from the University of California at Berkeley.

Leary's career from then until 1960 spans the rise of

modern clinical psychology: the hope and fervent belief that something called "the scientific method" would, someday, somehow, provide relief for the mentally ill and freedom for the rest of us from the pains of prejudice, interpersonal strife and right-wing authoritarianism.

American psychology—sturdy, statistical, functional and military-drab—had a war-time affair with some exotic intellectual and mysterious European refugees: field theory, gestalt theory and psychoanalytic theory. After the war, in love with the new theories, American psychology was ready to tackle mental illness and other social problems. The government and the rich foundations joined the fight. Money came in. *This was more like it!* With cash flowing freely from the Veterans Administration and other sources, clinical psychology began to grow exponentially; frighteningly, thought a few square traditionalists. One wag labeled it all "the leisure of the theory class" with "conspicuous assumptions."

The fifties were fast-growth heydays of clinical psychology everywhere, but Harvard and Berkeley were No. 1 and No. 2. Not surprisingly, Leary made it at both, first Berkeley and then, after a prolonged sabbatical in Spain, at the Harvard hub—the center of the clinical in-crowd. "Theory Leary," the grad students called him, a very embodiment of his own interpersonal hypotheses: unflappable with hostile patients, facile in debate with hardheads, handling authoritarian psychiatrists with disdainful aplomb, generally fearless, even reckless—the perfect clinical psychologist of 1959–60, the year the doubts crept in.

You see, when you got right down to it, nobody had been legitimately *cured.* There were no miracle methods.

Statistics showed that about one-third got better, one-third got worse and one-third remained the same—no matter what The theory was.

Furthermore, along with the rise of clinical psychology, there was an increase in mental illness, divorce, crime and delinquency. It was getting to be clear that theory had failed. And Leary *was* theory.

In the summer of 1960, beside the swimming pool of a rented villa in sunny Cuernavaca, Mexico, Leary-in-fact ate a large dose of the Indians' sacred psilocybin mushrooms. *This was more like it!*

Timothy Leary, the Madness of the Sixties and Me

1

Why Dr. Leary Now, April 1968

"This quite remarkable spring will possibly go down as the most contentious since 1848."

—John Kenneth Galbraith

"Com'on baby, light my fire."

—Jim Morrison

Confrontation

It was the spring of 1968, and Robert Kennedy was alive and well, The Beatles were still together, and everybody young was worrying about the draft. In the spring of 1968, the word "soul" was just beginning to mean "black," and black, or at least young black, was beginning to be beautiful. A movie of *Romeo and Juliet* starred two lovely teenagers, rose-petal fresh and shocking pink for the nude scene. Thousands (or so it seemed) of young-men-of-the-hour burned draft cards, demonstrated, sat-in and danced in the streets to protest the war and the draft. Hundreds (or so it seemed) of movie stars of sixteen and seventeen, radical politicians of nineteen and twenty, combination movie stars *and* radical politicians of twenty-one to twenty-nine years old spoke up brazenly at rallies and told McNamara he was a killer, told Bob Hope he was a fink.

There were dozens of beautiful, thin, wild girls-of-the-moment with long, smooth black or blond hair: rock singers, models, clothes designers, movie stars and combinations of these in one, all either living with or just-quit living with one of the young-men-of-the-hour. Gracie Slick, for example, and Janis Joplin (the latter "fire" and the former "ice") were beautiful and talented at a time when "beautiful" meant "soul" and talent was disguised as "balls" or "cheek" or "sass" and beautiful girls were "gutsy broads" or they were nothing.

Mysterious, boisterous, barrelhouse, rock star Janis Joplin was a gutsy broad. In the spring of 1968 she was living with at least one member of a rock group called "The Fugs" and that fact, together with her considerable talent for letting it all hang out and not giving a damn whatsoever for anything or anybody that "Amerika" might hold dear, made her truly a far-out counter-culture personality, or (how she hated the word) "star"— perhaps even more far-out than Jane Fonda, who was trying to get more "directly involved" in revolutionary politics.

Janis summed up the change as youth took over. "In the old days," she said in a magazine for hip young people, "there wasn't anybody like me in Port Arthur. Everybody thought I was a beatnik. It was lonely, all those feelings welling up and no one to talk to. Man, those people hurt me. I was just 'silly, crazy Janis.' It makes me happy to know that now I am making it and that they're back there, plumbers just like they were."

In other words, the only world that counted was the singing, dancing, death-defying hippie world of the young. That world included San Francisco's Haight-Ashbury, New York's East Village and practically all of lower-class London. The world that didn't count (Port Arthur) was "over thirty," watched TV (the Monkees, not The Beatles), worked at *jobs* like plumbing instead of "doing their own thing" like Janis, thought the war was "honorable" and were too old to fight anyway.

Everywhere there were signs of the dissolution of relations between young and old. The gulf was called "the generation gap." As Madison Avenue executives scrambled frantically to close the gap and update their ad images to include long hair and living together, the young radicals moved to widen it by planning riots, bomb-making and other not-so-loving moves calculated to disarm and disolve the war-mongering Middle American plumbers and their Establishment politicians. The passive resistance of the early sixties was turning to active belligerence in sixty-eight, and there was almost no possibility left for any exchange of ideas between the young and the rest. Discussion was impossible; arguments led to separation; even debate was rare. The only allowable form of communication was "confrontation." A confrontation was a scene where the young told off the old and the old mumbled incoherently.

Thus it came to pass that Peter Edmiston, under-thirty, pulled up a chair in my tiny, dirty, temporary magazine office on LaGuardia Place, East Village, Manhattan, to eat his lunch of coffee and pizza and to confront me, going-on-forty, with his values and to let me know exactly what he thought of me and my writing and everything else I might possibly be holding dear at the time.

"Anybody can tell where you professors are at," he began, dangling a pizza slice so it dripped on my manuscript. "Even the way you dress. Your pants have cuffs.

You have a tiepin on. You thought you were real up-to-date so you bought a pink and purple tie and you wore your best tiepin and all. Your black shoes are all laced up and polished so you'll go over big at the faculty meeting. Do you think your sideburns are hip? I bet you think sideburns are hip."

Now, Peter was *not* a student. Peter was the brand-new husband of the editor of the magazine that gave me the square feet I occupied, a magazine for which I had written some and wanted to write more. His wife, Susan, was willowy, quiet, vaguely spaced, but very capable of putting together a magazine every month. Peter and Susan were already a number-one young couple in the world that counted. They ate at Max's Restaurant, did their own things and knew Janis Joplin personally. Peter was the business manager for some of the most far-out personalities: poet Allen Ginsberg and the aforementioned Fugs were but two of the clients he negotiated the contracts for.

Peter had brown hair so full that you couldn't tell whether he had sideburns or not. He wore a cashmere turtleneck and his pants were belted somewhere, perhaps an inch, above the crotch with a wide tooled-leather belt about two feet long—by contrast with shoulders that stretched out sweaters. Peter Edmiston was handsome, rich, gutsy, smart, good-familied, thin, young and married to my editor.

It was not only my looks he lit into between chomps of pizza and slurps of coffee. Knowing I was a professor, he listed professors who were OK and who were not OK. Herbert Marcuse, the Freudian-Marxist, was OK; Richard Alpert, drop-out psychologist and psychedelicist, was OK. Others, including me and the rest of the Columbia faculty and administration with few exceptions, were not OK.

My international politics were probably all wrong as well.

"Young people would a thousand times rather follow a man like Ho than a man like Johnson. We *all* hope that Ho will win and that Johnson will lose."

My writing belonged to the "World's Fair of 1939."

"Allen Ginsberg is where it's at now in terms of writing. Do you know what he thinks about that piece of yours?"

I replied that I didn't care.

"Well, *we* care about everything Allen Ginsberg thinks," said Peter, meaning himself and millions of other rightly dressed, leftward-leaning, pizza-chomping, inward-looking, beautiful children. "Everything Allen Ginsberg says is important. Many people think Allen Ginsberg is a saint."

What could I say? "And Janis and Jimi Hendrix and Bob Dylan . . . saints?"

He just looked at me over the rim of his coffee container.

"What about Ken Kesey?" I asked. I had just read something about Kesey and LSD.

"Oh, do you know Ken Kesey?"

I had to admit I had only read Kesey and never actually touched the hem of his caftan. "But I do know Tim Leary," I said. "We taught together at Harvard."

"Is that so?"

"Yes."

"Well, he must have changed a lot since those days," Peter said.

"Yes," I said, "quite a bit."

"Do you get to see him much, now?"

"Oh, now and then," I replied.

Peter crumpled his pizza-pie paper in a wad and stuffed it into the empty coffee container, which overturned, sending a thin trickle of brown gunk out onto my blotter. Peter stood up to leave. On his way out the door he said, "Well, a lot of young people think Leary is God."

One who did was my pretty young research assistant at Columbia. She thought Leary was God and told me so. I found that I, a non-believer, had the unique but not particularly admirable reputation of having known but not recognized God before he was God. When I didn't introduce her to Leary, she stayed home for a week and tripped out on acid, listening to the Cream rock on the stereo. After she returned to work, she would not talk to me. "There but for the grace of God goes Slack" was all she would say.

Wherever I turned, I bumped into true believers.

A couple of Vassar girls I met in the Village said they had risked expulsion from college by breaking the parietal laws and sneaking into the Millbrook estate where Leary was living, "in order to see the face of God."

A blue and orange button was printed which read simply: "LEARY IS GOD."

But Leary wasn't alone. A few others also got the credit—especially musicians. There was a "John Lennon for God" fan club, Jim Morrison was described as an "Evil God," and so on. There was even, momentarily, a now-forgotten rock group called "The Godz."

As for Leary's own beliefs that spring, he did *not* think he was God. He belonged among those who used to think so but had gotten over it.

"*You* are God," he told me.

Identity

The first time you take LSD, it makes you think you are God. This is certainly one of the most common reactions to the drug. Proselytizing is likely to follow—with little success among those who haven't had any of the drug. As Leary wrote about his first hallucinogenic trip:

"I started doing this the day after my conversion. I rushed over to Tepoztlan [Mexico] to tell the McClellands . . . David McClelland is a Presbyterian convert to Quakerism. His shock and horror was unmistakable. If I had described the pleasure of heroin or sexual seduction of minors, he couldn't have shown more reflex dismay.

"I found myself getting poetic and dogmatic. I know it is a real reality! I know it is the Divine message! David McClelland now looked alarmed. Clinical diagnostic glances. Wow! Do I have a nut on my hands here. He was my boss at Harvard."[1]

However, when one tries to convince a person who also has had some LSD recently, the reaction is different. "Two acid-heads are better than one," Leary was fond of saying. Each tends to support the other's delusion (so that the other will support his and/or because they are both still so goofed-up that they genuinely believe each other). A mutual conspiracy of non-criticism, an I-won't-break-your-euphoria-if-you-won't-break-mine agreement, unspoken and the stronger for being silent, takes place. As a consequence of LSD, there was a lot of ego-involved spiritual rap that spring!

A problem in interpreting who now thought they were God and who didn't was the time lag in publishing. People who tried to rush into print discovered that the temporal process of publication moved at slow Earth speed. So, for example, by the time *Esquire* magazine got around to announcing, in July, that Allen Ginsberg thought he was God, the thought had passed its peak in Allen's mind by a few years. Nonetheless, the news still had a certain immediacy about it. Take this statement from Ginsberg-as-God to the operator from the telephone company, to wit:

"Hello, operator, this is God, I want to talk to Kerouac. To whom do I want to talk? Kerouac. What's my name? This is God. G-O-D . . ."

. . . or the voices quoted by Leary in *High Priest,* his book which came out later in 1968:

"Listen! Wake up! You are God! You have the Divine plan engraved in cellular script within you. Listen! Take this sacrament! (LSD) You'll get the revelation! It will change your life! You'll be reborn!"[2]

Alan Watts, who had once momentarily thought he was God but had now considerably recovered, uttered, that spring, in another book, a reminiscent explanation. LSD, he said, "may come as a shock to the kinesthetic sense, a threat to one's identity, and a disturbance to standards and habits of judgment. The individual unused to this situation may interpret it onesidedly . . . he may imagine that he is God Almighty, in charge of the whole universe."[3]

All in all, in the spring of sixty-eight it seemed as though everybody who was anybody thought he or somebody he knew was God or *had* thought so—I mean, had taken at least one cosmic-consciousness Supreme Experience acid trip and, at least for a few hours, had the decided impression that he and the Diety were One.

Pop star Donovan, reported in a hip trade-paper, said

that he was God and "had come to lead a change in the world."

Up on one of the top floors of the old Chelsea Hotel, in the gloom of early-morning after-the-concert pot haze and weird shadows moving around on the dirtiest hotel walls in New York, Mikey Hart, a drummer for the most zonked-out group at the time, couldn't answer my interview questions because, he said, *he* was God.

And over at Max's Kansas City restaurant—*the* Max's, New York's Max's, on Union Square, where the headwaiters usually *acted* like God—one of them told me, in a whisper, that he actually *was* God and could, therefore, produce a table at will.

"Never in the history of the world have we had so many, wonderful saints," said Tim Leary from his Indian teepee up near Poughkeepsie, New York.

Yes, Leary, dressed in buckskins with a beadwork headband over his graying locks, had retired with his bride of a few months, the former Rosemary Woodruff, to an Indian teepee on the grounds of the old Millbrook estate outside of Poughkeepsie. Millbrook was owned by the wealthiest of Leary's friends, William M. (Billy-Mellon) Hitchcock, direct descendant of Andrew Mellon and Tommy Hitchcock. The teepee, however, I think, belonged to Richard Alpert, the no-longer-rich son of the no-longer-president of the bankrupt New Haven Railroad. Actually, Alpert, if I remember him correctly, had a little income left at that time, but not much. Leary, I know, was quite broke.

Leary had come east from Berkeley on April 17th, hoping that a lecture fee might be in the offing to erase some long-standing West Coast debts. The fee, however, had not been forthcoming, and now he was holed up at

Millbrook, living off the land (and Billy and Dick), waiting for some inspiration as to how to pay for his and Rosemary's plane fare back to Berkeley.

The teepee-living scheme was a typical Leary solution to a financial problem. It would be most uncharacteristic for Tim to be just plain broke. Instead, he "returned to Mother Earth and lived off the land, ass off the plastic seatcovers and down on the ground where Nature wanted it to be." Tim Leary, God-of-the-moment, was among the first in freakville to have the latest hippie accessory (conspicuous consumption among the anti-consumers): an Indian teepee.

Of more practical importance was the no-rent feature of the dwelling. Of course, Billy would probably have let Tim and Rosemary stay in the house for their honeymoon if they had wanted to badly enough, but, to tell the truth, Billy was getting, well, a bit edgy about the house.

To the in-group it might be Mecca. To those high on acid, STP and the other stuff going around that spring, the ugly old stone-and-wood Millbrook mansion might be a shrine, a Holy of Holies, but to the ordinary burghers of Poughkeepsie and environs, to those high on nothing more than a few beers after a hard day at the IBM typewriter factory, this place was *very, very* spooky!

Now, people who are stoned on LSD *do* look and sound spooky. The longer they remain stoned and the more LSD they take, the spookier they look and sound. Millbrook was a big place, so a lot could go on without anybody knowing, but the occasional sights and sounds as witnessed by chance passersby were so bizarre and suggestive that the place began to develop the worst possible reputation. Naked bodies, male and female, colorfully painted, could now and then be viewed running through the oak trees. Tom-toms and acid rock could be heard at midnight, punctuated by insane shrieks. (Was that an orgasm coming over the microphone at 50 db or was it a murder, or both?)

Remember, this was only nineteen sixty-eight! Before Woodstock! Poughkeepsie's experience with freak-outs was limited. What were they running in there anyway, an opium den? That girl with the flowers glued to her forehead and no bra, she didn't look to be over fourteen years old. And the man she was with, the one with the earrings and the hairdo. If *he* wasn't some kind of a drug addict, then I don't know *what* he was. Spooky-haired weirdos telling little children to drop out of school. And the stories about experiments! Sex instruction with drugs, orgies and witch-rituals.

So, to the parochial eyes and ears of Pughkeepsie, the Gothic estate was a combination hippie whorehouse and Frankenstein castle. What *was* going on there? Who was behind this? Shouldn't someone put a stop to it?

The horror stories of Millbrook and its LSD experiments had prompted a few visits from the police and at least one formal raid, substantiating the worst fears of Hudson Valley Middle America. By spring, rumor had it that a posse was being formed and that incumbent sheriff, Larry Quinlan, didn't have much chance next election unless he closed the place down. Flack of all kinds was reaching Billy no matter where he happened to jet—all kinds of threats to bring in the board of health, and other bourgeois nonsense which could, nevertheless, cause more embarrassment to the Mellon-Hitchcocks than money could easily get rid of.

So anyhow, this way—with the teepee—Leary didn't have to ask Billy if he could stay in the house. Instead,

Tim and Rosemary just moved in somewhere on the grounds, out behind the gazebo, back of the azaleas. He and Rosemary could experience the wonderful togetherness that comes from living right with the Earth instead of above it, like people in houses do. Also, they could be on the look-out and send smoke signals in case of a raid.

Leary explained the charm of teepee living:

"In addition to the great peace that comes from being next to the earth, from which springs all life, there is the constant activity around the fire in the center of the teepee. The group activity of tending the fire is a marvelous communal experience. The tepee is architecturally perfect, developed over millions of years of structural engineering. Genius went into the design. The poles are placed just so the rain never comes in but the smoke always goes out." (Rosemary, who, as squaw, did most of the cleaning up, told me later that the smoke didn't always go out.)

Might it be boring to live in a teepee?

Leary was annoyed with me for even thinking such a thought. "Boredom," he said, "is the result of thinking itself." By "thinking" he meant mental activity which was self-conscious and not completely merged into the surround.

"You are on an ego trip, Slack. You are entirely too conscious of your own mind. You are self-conscious, self-concerned, self*ish*. In short, Slack, you are a square. Your mind has not yet been blown."

"I have a rich mental life," I said defensively.

"That's exactly what I *mean*," said Leary. "You must give up all mental life as you know it. Give it up forever. You must lose your mind. Death of the mind, *that* is the goal you must have. Nothing less will do."

Death of the mind! And that might not be the only death! LSD provides a whole new orientation toward death. It can make you think you are about to die and scare you out of your wits. Or it can make you think you have died, I mean that you are already dead, of all things, and have lived one life and are now starting on another. It can make you completely unafraid of death—a dangerous state indeed! It can make other people, who are actually alive, *seem* dead—you would swear they were in their graves. But then, actually, real-world-wise, LSD can kill you. Leary would never admit it but, let's face it, LSD could do you in for ever.

Death

Now, in the spring of sixty-eight, big-news LSD deaths, like the Manson murders, had not yet reached living color, yet the shroud of LSD death together with amphetamine/speed death and heroin/junk death and all other kinds of horrible hippie death of mind, soul and body hung over the New York counter-culture like a big wet blanket on an otherwise high time. There were deaths in the basements of old, smelly East Side tenement houses where drop-out girls from Westchester were found stabbed. There were deaths from rooftops where bad-trip purple-colored street acid caused flights of more than fancy. There were teenage lost-love suicides down in the girls' locker room at old Art and Science High, where the notes stuck to the wash-stand mirror read "Tom says I and him can never get up there together again like we were. Give my class ring to Sue. Sorry, Linda."

There were quiet, sleepy, painless, cool deaths from heroin overloads and then raging, screaming, tongue-biting, convulsive deaths from strychnine-laced street acid. All kinds of suspicious motorcycle and automobile accidents happened where breathometers showed no alcohol but red-underlidded survivors giggled instead of cried like they ought to have *if they had any idea of what they'd just done!*

Meanwhile, on the West Coast, Saint Charlie Manson (who was still a nobody) must have been discovering his version of the Great Cosmic Death Truth and, just then, been convincing Susan Denice Atkins and Sandra Pugh . . .

I would also say that, around New York City, over at Max's, and in the East Village, all the famous freaks, all the steady acid-droppers, had a touch of death about them. Acid-heads talked about Leary's "death of the mind" as though it were a desired *Ding an sich,* a state of bliss achieved only through intensive effort plus, of course, a million mikes or so of now vintage-rare solid Sandoz psilocybin or dimethyltryptamine up the old arm vein.

Some said that the quality of street acid had deteriorated. Underground acid chemist Owsley (real name Augustus Owsley Stanley, III, the Betty Crocker of illegal LSD) had quit making the good stuff, they said, and the Mafia was producing bad-trippers. Some said that *all* the underground acid factories had stopped production of LSD and that the poorer freaks who had no money and nothing stashed away were turning to amphetamines, or speed. "Speed Kills" was a slogan that began to prove accurate. Hippies who had been hyped-up too long found that they just couldn't hype down, ever! They took more and more amphetamines and spasmed themselves to a rapid fade-out. Speeedeath!

But illegal drugs were far from the major causes of death. Then as now, the Establishment could be shown to be killing more people than the Anti-Establishment. Easily proved! The tobacco industry each month figured prominently in thousands of deaths, the automobile industry (together with the liquor industry) in thousands more. The war machine, which had already killed 50,000 communists, 14,000 South Vietnamese soldiers and 13,-000 civilians since January, ground down a few hundred more each day in April. The Anti-Establishment blamed the Establishment for death: death due to the war, death due to alcohol, death due to police brutality and even death due to acid. (After all, if it were legal, it would be pure!) Compared to the thousands of deaths caused by the culture, the few hundred caused by the counter-culture seemed a paltry few . . . unless they happened to be friends of yours. And some of them were friends of mine.

Because of where I lived and how I worked, I knew several people who died in drug-related deaths that spring. Almost anyone who taught in New York knew of some. A student of a student of mine was found in his parents' suburban Connecticut swimming pool after a pot and acid weekend party. The sixteen-year-old son of a businessman I knew "fell" from a pedestrian bridge over a highway in Boston.

And these were just the scattered individuals. Hell, I knew of whole groups who died of, by or for drugs in one way or another. Take the Lords, a West Side Puerto Rican street gang I had once written about. Three Lords were killed in a car accident on the Taconic Parkway; all kinds of drugs were found in the car. Three more died directly from overloads of heroin. (I say "three," but actually I lost track of the count.) One of the Lords, Little Herman, a survivor and my informant, said he couldn't stand New York anymore. He was leaving for San Juan.

Also lost that summer were the two kingpins of the art department of the beautiful brand-new magazine I was so proud to be writing for. The magazine was richly laid out in imaginative detail. Its best photographs were brilliant. I loved the mod lettering, the strange colors and the blending of print and line. There was rarely a boring page.

I was also getting to know the chief photographer, little Michael Solden, and his girlfriend, the art director, raven-haired Judith Parker. Judith was responsible for what was called the "attitude of the book." People said gnomic Michael was "beautiful." I thought his photographs were just fine.

Before it had hardly begun, it was definitely over. Judith, the beautiful art director, and Michael, the beautiful chief photographer, were dead at the bottom of Long Island Sound.

They had been tripping out every weekend at her place on Fire Island. One Sunday night, they decided to return to Manhattan in a tiny rubber raft. A storm came up. The magazine couldn't quite right itself after that. In less than a year, it too had drowned.

There were two main kinds of deaths: those of people you knew and those shown on TV. The TV deaths divided into old, out-of-date, black-and-white deaths, like World War II, and new, on-the-spot, living-color deaths, like Tet and the siege of Khe Sanh.

There was the wonderful-world-of-color coverage of Martin Luther King's funeral, followed by National-

Guard-riot death in spotlight color as the troops moved into Chicago, Detroit and Boston. Baltimore and Pittsburgh were also under siege. To complete the death-watch circle, you could see the looters stealing color TV sets so they too could look at life.

At the top of the month, we had the Columbia riots with Stokely Carmichael and H. Rap Brown holding five buildings. Cop-battered undergraduates bled all over the lenses and yelled, "Off the pig!" Next we had the biggest nuclear blast ever detonated in the U.S., the Nevada Underground. The Nevada Underground and the Columbia Underground: "Good night, Chet."

What was the total effect of this nightly roundup death-spree on the human spirit that spring? Who knows? April was only the beginning. Soon we would have Biafra. The assassination of Robert Kennedy, the Great Mayor Daly Democratic Convention Street Holocaust in Chicago . . .

One unexpected effect of the world-wide confrontation and living-color death was that it brought us survivors together. We huddled in the gloom and tubelight waiting for the next horror news, and in the breaks we clutched for the nearest warm body. Cro-Magnons around the cave fire suffered no greater *angst* than we, that spring, around the *NBC Evening News*. Stomach cramps of omnipresent doom.

We were certain to get it sooner than we had bargained for. Pollution, Pueblo, politics and poisons. King, Kennedy, crime, Chicago. Riots, Reagan, Rhodesian hangings, revolts. The birds are dead, the fish are floating belly-up, DDT, CBW, mercury, nerve gas.

Hence, togetherness! Loving, faithful, close, terrified togetherness. The Mamas had the Papas, Peter, Paul and

Mary, Simon and Garfunkel. We had to have something to hang on to. Sonny had Cher, Romeo had Juliet. Something constant in the midst of world destruction. Joan Baez had Jack Elliot, John Lennon had Yoko Ono. Something romantic and warm to hold for a minute, to last a while at least.

Love

The sixties were a time of eros-unleashing. Free-love communes, group-marriage farm families and big-city tenement crash-pads, non-marriages of all kinds, countless varieties of *ménages à trois, quatre, cinq* and up—all proposed and tried as hip solutions to the failure of the old relationship of Mom, Dad, Sis and Buddy. Those who joined the new relationships blamed the old relationships for ills of the complex society and the deteriorating quality of life. Anyhow, by the mid-sixties, millions of Mom-and-Dad families had already broken up— Mom and Dad divorced, Sis off in a coed dorm and Buddy easy-riding the countryside on his Yamaha custom chopper.

Not the Learys, however. They were together again. The Leary family had come full circle. It had survived several splits and was now reunited. Middle-class families might be breaking up due to the pressures of the terrible sixties, but Tim, Rosemary, Susan and Jackie were, if anything, more tightly cohesive than ever before. Temporarily the group was physically apart, with the children, Jack and Susan, in Berkeley while Tim and Rosemary played Indian on the Millbrook estate, but as soon as Leary could get the money, they would all be together geographically as well as in spirit.

This reunited togetherness of the Learys was a far cry from the old Mom-Dad-Ozzie-and-Harriet unreconstructed togetherness of the middle-class fifties. On the contrary, the younger members of the Leary family had often tried to go their own ways, but had, each time, met with ego-deflating failure. Susan, for example, who was twenty years old, had tried to leave home a couple of times but did not make it on her own. Jackie took another escape route. He was often found wandering, freaked-out, about town. On Thanksgiving Day, Jackie was arrested when a Laguna Beach woman reported to the police that he was acting strangely on her front porch. The police finally brought him home, still "in dazed condition."

It was as though the Leary seedpod *wanted* to burst but atmospheric pressures were keeping it self-contained. All the attention from authorities, the arrests, the publicity and harassments were serving to unite, not separate. After a raid on Millbrook, when Jackie was arrested by Sheriff Quinlan along with Timothy and others, Leary remarked, "The family that is busted together is adjusted together."

Same went for just Tim and Rosemary as a dyad. There is no doubt that adversity drew them together, as it did all adherents of the drug-centered counter-culture, who shared one great bond—a hatred for the duly constituted government authority which threatened their freedom. Of course, a more important factor in their closeness was the shared experience of hallucinogenic states. As Leary told it to *Playboy* Magazine, September 1966:

". . . a certain kind of neurological and cellular fidelity . . . develops. I have said for many years now that in the future the grounds for divorce would not be that your wife went to bed with another man but that your wife had an LSD session with somebody else, because the bonds that develop are so powerful.[4]. . .

"One of the great purposes of an LSD session is sexual union. The more expanded your consciousness—the farther out you can move beyond your mind—the deeper, the richer, the longer and more meaningful your sexual communion."[5]

In other words, "We like to get high together," said Rosemary.

However, adversity and psychedelia were not the whole story of their romance. In addition to the insanity of their style of life, Timothy and Rosemary happened to be madly in love with each other. Their love was to be a lasting, sharing, resilient relationship. In future years they would never be apart if they could help it, and as long as they were together, threats of poverty, arrest, prison, exile and even deprivation of drugs would seem bearable.

A close friend, known to me only as Ed the Clown, who lived with them in Berkeley, described it thus:

"Rosemary and Tim just seem to fit together. Not only doing the frug at dance halls or with all the celebrities but during the day and in the morning when everybody has gone home. Tim out on the sun deck doing his yoga and Rosemary cleaning up the place after the freak-out or washing up at the kitchen sink."

Although Rosemary had had a show-business career before joining Tim, she was a domestic creature at heart and never minded such chores.

I believe it is greatly to Tim's credit that he was still capable of this deep involvement with someone who returned his trust, shared his hardships and did the dishes, because, although Timothy Leary had been in love many times in the past, none of his previous affairs, including three marriages, could be said to have been lasting—or even to have ended well.

The worst, by far, was Leary's first marriage, to the mother of Susan and Jackie. This was an unusual affair for the 1950s, involving flaunted infidelity on both sides. At the end of it, they were both to be found acting out frequently at wild *Who's Afraid of Virginia Woolf* parties, which would climax with Tim and Marianne Leary in arms not each other's. People who knew them then got the impression they were trying to drive each other crazy. The kids ran wild.

Finally, on October 22, 1955, Tim's thirty-fifth birthday, Marianne Busch Leary asphyxiated herself at 9:28 in the morning by intentionally turning on the motor in the family car and sitting there with the garage doors shut until she died. Tim went to Spain shortly thereafter. He got sick in Spain and thought he was going to die, but recovered.

On his return to Berkeley in 1957, he married his second wife, Mary (Del) Gorman, who helped him recover from his recent psychic shocks. Although he was supposed to be teaching and doing research in Berkeley, he really spent a lot of time in Mexico with Del and the children. Although there is no doubt that Del was good for Leary, the marriage didn't last many months.

When I first met Tim, in the fall of '58 at Harvard, he had just returned from Mexico/Berkeley, leaving Del in California. I don't think he was capable of believing that lasting relationships were possible, let alone desirable. With women and Leary, in those days, it was first-come, first-served. He was, however, always perfectly charming, suave, handsome and very considerate of the feelings and wishes of girls. Plenty of good-lookers came to be served.

By the time Tim had sampled LSD in the early sixties, he was willing to create the psychedelic sexual revolution all by himself:

"There is no question that LSD is the most powerful aphrodisiac ever discovered by man," he said, again in *Playboy*.

"I'm saying simply that sex under LSD becomes miraculously enhanced and intensified. I don't mean that it simply generates genital energy. It doesn't automatically produce a longer erection. Rather, it increases your sensitivity a thousand percent. Let me put it this way: Compared with sex under LSD, the way you've been making love—no matter how ecstatic the pleasure you think you get from it—is like making love to a department-store-window dummy. In sensory and cellular communion on LSD, you may spend half an hour making love with eyeballs, another half hour making love with breath. As you spin through a thousand sensory and cellular organic changes, she does, too. Ordinarily, sexual communication involves one's own chemicals, pressures and interactions of a very localized nature—in what the psychologists call the erogenous zones. A vulgar, dirty concept, I think. When you're making love under LSD, it's as though every cell in your body—and you have trillions—is making love with every cell in her body. Your hand doesn't caress her skin but sinks down into and merges with ancient dynamos of ecstasy within her."[6]

Considering Leary's appeal for women and their appeal for him, it may come as a surprise that his closest male companion during these high-balling, between-marriage, Harvard days was a young man who did not like girls at all. Richard Alpert, Ph. D., former Harvard Assistant Professor of Clinical Psychology and Research Associate in the Laboratory of Social Relations of Harvard University, was a good-looking, rich-kid, upper-middle-class, Jewish-domineering-Mama homosexual, and a real woman-hater to boot. Now, it could be that Dick Alpert provided Tim with less competition than a straight buddy would have and that that was why he picked Dick as a pal. Or, it could be that Leary's Don Juanism had that latent-homosexual, Freshman-Psychology-One, deep-dark Freudian explanation (the one that gave you comfort if you were a lousy lover and jealous of the class coxwain).

Either way, Tim liked Dick Alpert, or tried, long and hard, to like him. Tim also tried, long and hard, to *cure* Dick, and that was actually the beginning reason for the orgies.

Leary was genuinely convinced that LSD was a cure for homosexuality. All Alpert had to do was to take enough of it with enough beautiful girls around and he would straighten out. A succession of big old houses were rented in and around Boston and New York. Wild, fantastic, month-long sex parties were thrown at these "research centers," spiked by LSD, DMT (dimethyltryptamine) and psilocybin, all of which were perfectly legal at the time and were ordered directly from the drug company in the name of Harvard. In the beginning Leary actually frowned on pot and hashish (which were illegal), because they didn't fit the proper research image he was trying to maintain. The orgies were called "experiments" and the people were called "research subjects."

Later on, what the hell, science was just a game anyhow and you couldn't stop the people from bringing in pot and hash, so "game" pretenses were dropped.

The rented houses tended to get pretty banged up, what with installing Buddist altars and group-sex mattresses in the dining rooms and do-your-own murals on most of the walls. In one house, a young cult member sealed off a third-floor bedroom completely so that the only entrance was through a trapdoor in the floor, and that was covered by a prayer rug. The room had Indian religious porno—bas-relief life-sized photographs pasted over the walls. This created a nice, freaky meditation effect and was reportedly excellent for the illusion of balling temple goddesses.

Also tending to depreciate the value of the real estate was a series of regular housekeeping hang-ups. Nobody was inclined to clean the kitchen after freak-outs or orgies when they could just get high again and turn the mind around to where dirty dishes looked beautiful.

Leary and Alpert tended to use up a house in short order. Owners would be aghast when they got an inkling of what was going on. Threatened with eviction, Leary and Alpert would look around for another place. They went through three or four nice old houses.

Needless to say, Alpert was *not* cured, but became even more recalcitrant in his sexual predilections. One frequenter of the orgies described the relationship between Leary and Alpert as a "tug of war between Tim and Dick."

"The whole idea was who was going to give in. Would Leary let Dick do *it* to him or would Dick let Leary fix him up with one of the girls? Well, Leary thought he had won the battle when Dick promised he would quit homosexuality, but then Dick didn't keep his promise. He would sneak off to New York and hold little homo orgies of his own in an apartment he specially rented just off Central Park. He paid male prostitutes from the park to come up to his orgies. Well, Leary found out about it and really got mad that Dick wasn't cured. And yet, in a way, it was a point for Dick, because *his* will had prevailed over Tim's, because, really, he had no intention of changing for Leary, LSD or anyone or anything else."

Finally it was Leary who, according to this witness, gave in.

"There was a session where Tim and Dick played 'trade the goblet.' They did this to make sure each took as much acid as the other. They filled two glasses with orange juice mixed with LSD and poured the stuff back and forth between the two glasses. There must have been two or three thousand micrograms in the glasses. Then they made sure that each one had the exact same amount in his glass and then they drank it all up, looking at each other, swallow by swallow, to make sure that neither one chickened out. Leary was so high! He lost all control, although he didn't pass out. There was a big sex scene with everybody watching where he let Dick go down on him. Dick's homosexuality had won out. But it was the beginning of the end of the close relationship."

From then on, Leary specifically advised all those who might be setting up crash pads, starting their own religions, building communal settlements or otherwise creating a family or tribe not to try to mix straight and gay people. "The guys-with-gals can share one tent, but the guys-with-gurus-only must set up their own separate thing."

In between orgies, and sometimes simultaneous with

them, celebrity parties were held, to which a succession of show-biz and music-world personalities, upper-class jet-setters, writers, pop-scientists and other interesting, with-it folks were invited to try acid and have fun . . . and, of course, discover who was God at the same time. Many famous people came. The girls were unfailingly pretty and very accommodating, zonked or not. Leary himself began to be viewed as a celebrity, and this didn't hurt his chances as a lover either. Of course, it was his role as the Grand High Passer-Outer of the stuff which really made the kick-seeking chicks go for him. The whole thing, got, finally, to be a bit much even for Tim. In 1966, he complained, modestly, in *Playboy* magazine:

PLAYBOY: It's been reported that when you are in the company of women quite a lot of them turn on to you. As a matter of fact, a friend of yours told us that you could have two or three different women every night if you wanted to. Is he right?

LEARY: For the most part, during the last six years, *I have lived very quietly in our research centers.* [Italics mine!] But on lecture tours and in highly enthusiastic social gatherings, there is no question that a charismatic public figure does generate attraction and stimulate sexual response.

PLAYBOY: How often do you return this response?

LEARY: Every woman has built into her cells and tissues the longing for a hero-sage-mythic male to open up and share her own divinity. But casual sexual encounters do not satisfy this deep longing. Any charismatic person who is conscious of his own mythic potency awakens this basic hunger in women and pays reverence to it at the level that is harmonious

and appropriate at the time. Compulsive body grabbing, however, is rarely the vehicle of such communication . . .

In December 1964, three years before he met Rosemary, in a move which surprised many, Leary wed Nena
von Schlegrugge, a perfect-featured, perfect-everything
girl-of-the-moment and jet-set celebrity. Nena had class
and all the rest of it. She was described in *Harper's Bazaar*
as:
". . . an avid concert and ballet goer; she also likes art
films and photographing 'nature and animals'; but when
it comes to writing, she doesn't. Nena would rather pick
up the phone or cable to say she's arriving or departing.
Born in Mexico and raised in Peking, she became a sea-
soned traveler at a youthful age, so today it's only natural
that she spends much of her time jetting from her New
York base to various and sundry European and Asian
destinations."
Nena was pictured in *Harper's* "Suited for spring" in
"Davidow's short, cuffed-sleeve suit of coral-and-green
Italian cotton at Bonwit Teller." She could also be seen
(the back of the head only) on television sailing up the
Hudson many times a day in a Viking ship: In addition
to her other travels, she was arriving from Scandinavia
as the Eric Cigar girl—the one who announced that Eric
was here in the U.S.A. and was having more fun with
blonds.
And one more thing! Besides being a model, jet-setter,
celebrity, TV-commercial star and well-dressed woman
about the world, Nena had a mother who was a genuine
baroness.
A proper Episcopalian service was held at four in the

afternoon on December 12, at Grace Church in Millbrook. The bride was exquisitely gowned for the occasion. The church was jammed with well-wishers, but the scene was one to raise a few questions in the minds of the congregation. Leary had rich friends, yes, but he was far from solvent himself. After all, he was no longer teaching for a living. Was Nena going to pay the bills?—Nena, who had trouble writing a thank-you note. Could they afford a personal maid for Nena? And who, pray tell, would pay Bonwit's?

Tim and Nena jetted to India for an extended honeymoon, leaving the Baroness in Millbrook with Jackie, Susan, Dick Alpert and a come-and-go handful of the faithful. Not knowing they would be away until May, I visited the mansion a couple of months after the wedding, hoping to catch them at home. They were still abroad.

The estate was degenerating into complete and spooky disarray. Millbrook was beginning to look like the Cabinet of Dr. Caligari. It was a Saturday morning when I came to call. Dick had run a "special Friday session" for "a few talented guests" the night before, and friends of his from Greenwich Village were lying naked and freaked-out all around the mansion. The house was messed up beyond belief.

I went out into the kitchen to try to find Jackie and Susan, but instead, standing by the sink, which was piled shoulder-high with a heap of dirt-encrusted dishes, I found a nice-looking, blond-haired lady who could have been from *I Remember Mama,* or a TV Swedish maid.

She was not the housekeeper. She was Birgit Baroness von Schlegrugge, Nena's mother. And just staring at those dishes . . .

Sooo, anyhow, following a brief "at-home" period in Millbrook upon returning from India, Tim and Nena were separated pending divorce. Leary's spirits were not particularly dampened. He was still on the look-out:

". . . We are living in a world of expanding population in which there are more and more beautiful young girls coming off the assembly line each month. It's obvious that the sexual criteria of the past are going to be changed, and that what's demanded of creatures with our sensory and cellular repertoire is not just one affair after another with one young body after another, but the exploration of the incredible depths and varieties of your own identity with a single member of the opposite sex. This involves time and commitment to the voyage."[7]

Three years later, Tim married Rosemary. For good measure, he married her twice, once on November 11, 1967, in a sunrise ceremony at the top of a mountain in the desert near Joshua Tree, California, and then again on December 13 of the same year, in Millbrook. The latter ceremony was performed by Freaky Bill Haines, hip guru of a cult called "The Neo-American Church." This bride was less expensively attired than the last—but no less attention-commanding: Rosemary wore a simple white dress and flowers painted on her face.

Tim had found a lasting partner. There would be high times to come, plenty, all right, but not with Dick and not, somehow, without getting cleaned-up-after. No more orgies to speak of, and no more messy freak-outs, because, whether it was in a regular house with a kitchen or a teepee by a stream, the Learys' rice bowls somehow were going to get washed after every meal.

Because, as Norman Mailer says in *Prisoner of Sex,* "It all comes down to who does the dishes."

And that's exactly what Susan Edmiston now says Norman Mailer says—right here in Middle American *Woman's Day* magazine, July 1972. Yes, indeed, times have changed, and here is Susan writing for that bastion of the bourgeoisie, *Woman's Day.* My ex-editor! Between "How to Work Magic with Color in Your Home" and "Doctor, Are You Sure It's Just My Nerves?" is this advice-to-young-marrieds article by my lovely boss-lady of four years ago. Her piece is called "Happy Marriages . . ." and gives formulas for "negotiating a contract" with your husband so he will always pitch in and help with the housework. Peter, the story clearly implies, picks up after every meal no matter how busy he may be with his poet clients.

Trip

On Friday, April 26, 1968, at nine thirty in the evening, I strolled out of my little office and headed, with a handbill in my pocket, over around the corner to a combination nightclub, theater, dance hall and all-purpose joint called "The Village Gate." The handbill read, "FAREWELL PARTY, TONIGHT, TIMOTHY AND ROSEMARY LEARY, 10:00 P.M. Admission Two Dollars."

A group of the Leary faithful, led by one particular stuff-salesman, had fixed up this going-away blast to honor the couple, who were leaving next day for San Francisco. The Grateful Dead, leaders of rock, *de mortuis nil nisi bonum,* would be performing for those alive enough to hear and Allen Ginsberg was planning to chant Hari Hari for the multitude alive *and* deceased, and thus all the genuine heads and kindred spirits for miles around would gather at two bucks apiece to wish Godspeed to God and, incidentally perhaps, purchase a little stuff from the salesman and his franchisees, who would be available throughout the hall in case of need. Thus, were a profit not made at the box office directly on the feature, it would be made inside on the popcorn. Leary would get his plane fare after all . . .

On that Friday, I was feeling rather low. New York was a city full of creatures from another planet. Nobody was throwing any going-away parties for me, because I was not going anywhere.

Leary, on the other hand, seemed to be going everywhere at once. He was going up in the literary world, with two books about to be published. He was moving on with a successful marriage to Rosemary, who loved him dearly, cleaned his hash pipe and never left his side. He was leaving the police way behind—arrested, yes, but never held. Leary was still going free as a bird. And now they were going back to San Francisco to join the top of the scene and the rest of the family. Leary was going strong.

It turned out I couldn't even get inside the doors at 9:30. The crowd had fringes way over on the opposite curb. "What's going on?" "Who is it?" etc.

There was nothing for me to do but walk on by, which I did, down all the way to the Lion's Head Tavern to drown my jealousies in vodka tonics. By midnight, I had had quite a few vodka tonics.

Now, I must say that I was never what they would call a "head." I was what you might call a drinking man. When it came to literature, I liked Norman Mailer much better than Allen Ginsberg. Even more, I really liked that old alcohol-oriented Algonquin Round Table. Mankiewicz, Thurber, Benchley and Parker wouldn't have known marijuana from a monkey's ass. I wished I lived back then, matching wits with George Kaufman. That was a writers' world, not a light show.

These thoughts sulked in my brain as the vodka warmed my innards and made it all seem not quite so bad . . . By twelve, the crowd had thinned out, so I could just walk into the Gate.

It was too black to see a thing. I groped, hands in front, swaying from the vodka. I stepped on somebody's hand. Now I could vaguely see. Bodies lay zonked all over the floor. That old locker-room odor of stale locoweed hung in the dusty air like smoke from a burning ghat. Was I the only one up? Certainly I was the only one drunk— a lush among the pot-heads, serge-suited, necktied and otherwise outstanding. Somebody whispered, "Screw off, narc!"

Several strong young zombies casually lifted shoulder from pillar and moved right toward me, looking right at me.

I heard a familiar voice.

"Charlie, Charlie! My God, it's Charlie Slack."

Timothy Leary is not zonked. He's giving me a big hello.

Leary bounds gracefully over bodies and hugs me on the shoulders. Zombies turn to angels and back away from the waving arms of Leary.

"You must come to the table."

My eyes get better. Rosemary smiles sweetly, offers me wine. The Grateful Dead are looking alive and well. Room is made for me. I am glad and drunk and warm and wanted. Leary takes my hand. "You must come with us to California."

"Sure, sure," I say.

Somebody clinks her glass with mine.

"You must come with us to the hotel," says Leary.

"Sure, sure," I say.

Into my hand is firmly pressed something gummy but hard, like a nut and about the size of a marble.

"Sure, sure," I say.

2

Revolt in the Second Class

When you are suddenly high on a drug like hashish, you really feel you are going somewhere. All the sensations associated with a journey jump to mind to give you the idea of movement, of arrival, of landing at some familiar but not recently visited place. "Ah, hah," you say, "I am *there*," meaning you might be the pilot of a plane that just leveled off at thirty thousand or a high-jumping dancer at the top of his leap. At this moment of advent, all things familiar are exaggerated and all things strange are quickly familiar. *Déjà vu* is the scientific term for it. The hippy word is "wow."

"Wow," said Bob softly, looking up at Rosemary from the giant bowl of fruit on the lounge table. He was bending over, his head resting sideways on a big, expensive airline orange.

"Wow," said Rosemary, looking down at Bob. She knew exactly what he meant. They were more than just in the air together, they were *together*, members of the secret in-group, the one that really knew what "wow" meant. Wow.

Bob was eighteen or twenty, pensive, introspective or inarticulate or just young. Still waters ran deep among young hippies—but could cover pits of ignorance. Rosemary was elegant, even too elegantly dressed for flight, but her bones were showing and they were beautiful bones. Bob, Rosemary, Timothy and I were in the red-carpet lounge or whatever they called that place up front in the 727 where the seats arc around facing a short row of windows. We had picked up Bob at the Chelsea Hotel last night. He seemed to want to stay with us but he was not at all obtrusive, just sat and smiled or moved around reinforcing other people's highs with nice appreciative smiles and friendly pats. Rosemary liked him because he helped her with the bags and Leary had said he could join the flight to San Francisco if he paid his own way, which he did. "This is my son," Leary told me in the cab, patting Bob's knee. Bob liked that attention, and he became the focus of Leary's stream of wisdom—an appreciative apprentice. When we got to the airport, Leary took Bob aside by the insurance counter where no one else could hear and gave him lots of advice.

Now, on the morning flight, a half-hour after take-off, Bob, Rosemary and I were in the lounge up front. A little cocktail table touched our knees and it had a big First Class bowl of fruit on it. Bob tried to pick up an apple with his mouth and no hands but it kept slipping out. Finally, he just pretended to go to sleep with his head on top of the fruit. We all thought that was pretty funny. When we laughed, Bob looked up and said, "Wow."

Tim was back in his seat really sleeping. We all lacked sleep from the night-people's party at the hotel, but being tired just added to our highs. Everybody was smiling and together and warm. It was a smooth, relaxed, put-your-head-on-my-lap kind of high. A "hearth high," I called it, like in front of a fireplace in a cabin in the woods, wrapped up in blankets for the night—only it was the brightest daylight imaginable and we were really in a jet plane at 30,000 feet, facing a row of tiny windows onto the stratosphere. Wow.

We all loved our seats, the best on the plane. Perfect for the view when the clouds would clear. Even if it took his last dime, Leary always went first class (and now we were glad he did). It was part of his theory: "After you tune in, turn on and drop out, there will be these times now and again when you must drop *in* again, briefly—say, for travel. When that happens, always drop in at the *top*. Civilization is unbearable, but it is *less* unbearable at the top."

Not everybody in First Class was bearable. A man in a Harry Truman Hawaii shirt and sport coat with a camera around his neck came up pretending that he wanted to take pictures out of our window. We knew he was pretending because it was still too cloudy for pictures, and, anyway, there were plenty of other windows.

"Wait till we get over the plains states," he said, trying to get us to talk to him.

Rosemary made a faint smile. Her cheeks were hollow, like *Vogue* and Diana Ross.

Then the man bent over me. "I just couldn't help wondering if you were show-business people," he said.

"Not me," I said.

"But isn't that Tim O'Leary back there sleeping?" He looked from one to another of us. Bob and Rosemary searched the clouds intently, hoping the man would go away.

"Yes, that's Leary," I said with a big, nice, long-lasting smile. I answered his questions but my answers were worse than none at all. The nicer I acted, the more puzzling it was, because, well, what was an ordinary-looking person like me doing with that group? Bob, with sandals on his feet, had a white, pleated gauze shirt see-through-ing the hair on his chest. Rosemary wore an ankle-length ballroom gown of orange and purple, and Leary was back there sleeping in buckskins with a beadwork head-band askew. My business suit, the same as last night, and my square, black, shiny shoes, my short haircut—every-thing about me was oddball by comparison. He'd seen hippies before but he couldn't figure me out. Without trying, I disturbed the man as much as they did.

The clouds cleared a bit soon, and Leary awoke and came forward to teach us all how to look down from 30,000 feet. He had a theory, probably right, about the pollution being less per foot on the average when you looked down from above than when you looked across while on the ground.

". . . spectacular sight . . . eighth wonder of the world. You can see so much more from up here. This is what it means to be high . . ." etc.

And it was all true. When clouds part, transcontinental daytime jet flights become breathtaking. You can see trains and automobiles, almost see people, it is so clear. The whole country spreads out like a relief map. Geography becomes reality. Look! There is where all the food is grown, in gigantic patch-quilt squares. There is the tiny train track that carries it away. And there, if you look real close, you can see a tiny train on the track with smoke. Now, see what the wind did! Carves up the land. Water, green plant life, and last and least, man, all show their true colors from up here. Canyons open at a glance. Rivers have beginnings and ends . . .

". . . nothing like it. Wow!" said Bob.

Timothy just looked out the window, silence being the more impressive tribute.

". . . nice," said I, mostly to myself.

But the man in the sport coat, however, was *not* looking out the window. He was *not* able to appreciate the eighth wonder of the world. The man was still looking at us. His mind had been blown by us, and he was missing the view.

"Excuse me," he said to Leary. Leary couldn't pretend not to hear him, because the man's face was right up next to the back of Leary's neck. Leary was wearing his hearing aid, and the man was almost yelling right over Leary's shoulder into it.

"Excuse me, but would you mind very much if I asked you something?"

Leary looked away, smiling. He turned his hearing aid down and then he looked up at the man, smiling, but it was not a happy smile. Leary did not say, "Well, *out* with it," but that was what the smile meant.

The man was hard put to get it out. "My daughter. She would really love it if . . . I mean, if I just passed up the opportunity without . . ." The man was holding out his airline lunch menu over Leary's shoulder. He was fumbling in his sport coat for a pen. He wanted Leary's autograph.

Without ever once looking at the man, Leary complied with a scrawl. He handed back the menu over his shoulder, still looking down at the plains states. After all, he had *tried* to teach the man a lesson, but the man was not capable of learning. He was completely trapped in his role. He wasn't free to look at the world at all.

More clouds came by as we all sat back and ate fruit and drank champagne. The First Class compartment was far from full. Besides the man in the sport coat, there was a semi-hip California man in a turtleneck and suede hunting jacket covered with buttoned pockets. He had evil dark glasses. Rosemary was afraid he might be a narc. A couple of black guys in Raleigh beards with broad-brim stud's hats and Afro-print body shirts sat together in 2B and C. Way in the back, say, 6D and E, by the divider bulkhead were two doe-eyed chickie-pies, one blond and one brunette, pressed-hair starlets. They had settled down for the trip with a bottle of champagne on the armrest and one package of cigarettes and one lighter between them. They chatted softly and seriously, intent on each other. Their hands moved in studied ways. I just knew they were hookers.

Back from the john came two other sales or tourist types with sport coats. They were friends of the guy with the camera but even less cool and more mad at the world. One of them made the stewardess get him a Scotch and soda while the other studied the menu. The guy with Leary's autograph went over to talk to them. He bent down and whispered, glancing at Leary every now and then. "So what, so what," the two seemed to be saying, "we don't care if it's Tiny Tim's grandfather. They're all prob'ly faggots anyway. Let's order booze. Let's play cards." I didn't actually hear them, but I was sure that's what they said. They were trying not to be impressed by Leary, playing cards and all—but still sneaking a peak at us now and then.

Celebrity! What fun! Boo.

Traveling with the notorious Leary was a Halloween junket. Safe and anonymous, myself, I could nevertheless amaze and scare others from behind the mask of another's fame. We were blowing all the First Class minds. I put my arm around Rosemary and she didn't mind. We were all having champagne before lunch. The stewardesses were standing around Leary when they weren't pouring it out.

How to be a celebrity. A: Act like one, assume you are one, tell other people you are one, *be* one in your own mind. The world divides: Those who believe it and those who don't. B: Avoid the latter and hang around with the former. Of course, it helps if you can go around passing out a little hashish. Leary grasps one of the stewardesses' hands in both his hands as though he were going to kiss it, but just pats it instead. Then she walks away toward the center of the plane with that hand hanging down at her side but slightly cupped, as though she has palmed something. Maybe—and then again, maybe not.

Leary just knew the stewardesses were heads. The world divides in two again for Leary: Those who have tried it and those who haven't. Those who haven't also divide in two: Those who want to and those who are afraid. All the heads, those who have tried it, have an instant bond with Leary. They know exactly what he is and what he stands for. They love and respect him for being a pioneer and a saint. Wow. *I* wasn't sure they were heads. How could Leary be so sure? Leary always knew.

Rosemary saw Tim shaking hands with the stewardess and she didn't like it. Not jealousy, just that she thought that the guy with the shades might be a narc. Leary disagreed. Rosemary was still suspicious.

"We've never been so safe," Leary said to her and looked her deep in the eyes.

Bob was getting silly with the champagne and the hashish. He took the plastic headphones for the airplane stereo and stuck one end in a champagne bottle. The result looked like a hookah. If you sipped on the plastic tubing, you got champagne. We passed that around for a while, laughing and rolling our eyes at each other. We were proud of ourselves—*very* high but only quietly wild. Leary didn't think it was particularly funny. He was back looking at the plains states from the 30,000 feet, teaching us the observation lesson.

The champagne and all began to get me feeling warm and loving. When I tried to stand up, I was friendly and swaying. I went back and sat down for a minute. I took the armrest out from between some seats and lay crosswise. I hadn't gotten much sleep the night before.

It wasn't so much a dream as a hallucination.

After the food, there was more booze with dessert, and then after that there was even more if you wanted it, which everybody did.

A nice middle-aged lady came up from Tourist Class to use our john. She pushed right by the stewardesses and made a face when passing the hookers. The whole compartment was at least slightly drunk, the sourpuss salesmen, the starlets and the black cats, the Hollywood man (or narc), everybody. The Leary crowd was both high on swallowed hash and drunk. I would say that Rosemary was about the only one who didn't look wigged or freaked or both. Musical chairs: The starlets moved forward to check on Leary and the black dudes moved forward to check on the starlets. The "narc" came up too, maybe to check on Leary. The stewardesses brought out another bottle of something—maybe they thought it would put us to sleep, but it didn't, it just made the conversation louder and stronger. Even the guys in sport coats were feeling like it was a party, a strange party, but still a party and, well, why not? The starlets saw the sport coats and I guess they thought there was money there, and what the hell, don't all bills have square corners?

After all the coffee and booze, I had to go to the john, and the First class ones were full of salesmen. Before I went into the other section, I took another look at our scene. It was pretty raucous.

The Tourist section could hear our fun but was not having any of its own. Hostile eyes lasered into me as I wobbled my way down the aisle to the toilet in the tail. Every seat was taken back here, mommies with babies in their laps, grannies in straw hats and huge paper bags with string handles, soldiers on leave next to the grannies, kids under twelve who couldn't sit still, squirming up over the seat tops next to their grannies. No champagne back here, just the Manhasset Garden Club going to visit its nieces and nephews on the Coast for Easter: Disneyland reservations for families of four and six. Most had incomes ten times bigger than Leary and our crowd. This was fat, down-to-business Middle America—six abreast, coast-to-coast, wall-to-wall and sea to shining sea.

On my way back from the toilet, up next to the divider curtain, was the same surburban matron who had come up earlier to powder her nose in First Class. She was dressed in Lord and Taylor and her hair had been done for the trip. She was indignant at our unbridled sounds from First Class. As I passed her seat, she gave me a withering look. And then she followed me right up into the First Class area, where she just stood, eyes blazing, taking in all the carryings-on.

Leary smiled his winning best but she would have

none of it. Her eyes cut like Carrie Nation's ax. After thirty seconds of silence, she glared again at Leary and said, simply:

"Jitterbugs!"

It was obviously an epithet, the worst word she would permit herself. She spied candy on the cocktail table, a giant box with "727" engraved on each piece. At first I thought she was going to bean a hooker with it, but no, she just picked up the whole box and marched off into Tourist.

I couldn't believe she wanted all that candy, so I opened the curtains to see what was going on. She was passing it out back there, going down the aisle, Lady Bountiful, making sure all the children got some.

The lady had brought Leary to life. He was boundless in his praise, remarking on her dignity and poise.

"It strikes me as sad," he said, "that an obviously marvelous human being like that must remain confined to the middle class. Isn't it terrible that she was born too soon to get insights from LSD."

Quiet time for now, as the plane droned on, time for us all to sit with smiles on our faces, digging the ultimate meaning of it all, each in his own thoughts (but with all thoughts somehow related to Leary). It was time for significant glances, eye-to-eye special meanings, you and me babe, you and me buddy, deep pauses, a long and drawn-out time when, as we all are supposed to know, nothing needs to be said because our thoughts speak for themselves. During this space, I knew I was faking it, I was really an outsider, I was pretending to be in tune, not really *into* the significance of it, not like Leary, who closed his eyes and let the peace roll in. However, I gave it a good try until, at last, it was Bob who spoke:

"Timothy Leary would not exist if it weren't for the bad vibes."

"What was that?" I asked. I must really have been out of it, for not one word did I grasp.

Bob repeated, "Timothy Leary would not exist if it weren't for all these bad vibes."

"I don't get it," I said, uncovering my total squareness.

Leary opened his eyes and leaned forward with his finger pointed up to the air nozzles in a gesture of didactic definition. I was going to be taught a lesson. "What he means—*obviously*—is that there is a person called 'Tim' and then there is an image called 'Timothy Leary.' The image called 'Timothy Leary' is a product of the hostility of its detractors, just as the person called 'Tim' is a product of the love of his friends. Without love, there can be no *person*, no personality. Without hate, there can be no image. If fools didn't hate my image, then the notorious 'Timothy Leary' wouldn't exist."

Was that it? Bob's countenance gave no sign that it was. Tim closed his eyes again and leaned back. I continued to look puzzled. After several seconds, Bob spoke again.

"I mean bad vibes right *now*. Everybody is thinking about Timothy Leary. If we stop using our egos to create images, we can merge our thoughts into one pattern."

Tim leaned over and patted Bob on the arm, "You see, he has upleveled us all. You are a saint, my lad, a saint." He smiled benignly at Bob, who wanted to continue with his merging.

"If we all concentrate on one thing, all our consciousnesses will grow together and we will lose our separate identity-beings into a single giant, unconscious whole."

Leary closed his eyes again. He was merging all right.

I didn't want to be the source of any more bad vibes than necessary, so I tried to make my mind a blank, but I just couldn't. I kept thinking about how and why the middle class hated Leary and whether he was right about the hatred creating the image. I came to the conclusion that he was partly right. The other side of the coin was that Leary hated the middle class and *his* hatred also created the image. It was a two-way trip and the feeling, as they said in Levittown, was mutual.

"It's not working at all," said Bob. He looked at me to show the others that it was I who was stepping on their sand castle.

"I'm sorry," I said, "but you will all have to go ahead and merge consciousnesses without me. I can't help myself. I keep thinking about things."

"Well," said Bob with a sidelong glance at Tim and Rosemary, "we can all play his game for a while. He can tell us what he's thinking."

"No, no," I protested. "It's nothing. Nothing, really."

"Well, if it *was* nothing, then it wouldn't cause bad vibes." There was a pause, during which the inescapable logic of this was recognized by all. "Well, tell us all what you were thinking," said Bob. "It's *your* game now."

"I was thinking how Tim and the middle class don't understand each other. Trying to figure why they hate him so."

"Well, for one thing," said Tim, awake now for sure. "They think I stole their children from them. They'll never forgive me for that. Actually, they *drove* their own children away through their own stupidity, not letting them smoke pot in their rooms or make love in the car, but the parents would rather blame *me* for stealing the kids away than accept the blame for their own stupidity.

They are ready to blame me for everything—murder, rape, drug pushing, everything. They have created a myth which says, 'Timothy Leary created the hippie movement. Timothy Leary sells drugs'—something I have never done—'Timothy Leary is the cause of sex and ecstasy and joy and all the other forbidden things.' They have created a myth which is a projection of their own failure to be able to love and their own repressed wishes. They create a man of straw and then lynch him.

"But already there are signs that the mind of the middle class is being blown." Leary said this with a clear, nasal plonking tone reserved for flat-out truths of a high order and a vast importance. "First come the children. They are already turned on. Then will come the ordinary working adults, regular nine-to-five people, who will soon turn on. The professions will be next—doctor-lawyer power roles. It is impossible to remain tied to a profession during or after an LSD session. Right now the professions are the shackles of the middle class, each link forged in the power struggle for status and prestige. LSD cures the disease of professionalism. For example, I gave LSD to a group of Protestant ministers on Good Friday in an Episcopal church in Cambridge, Massachusetts. It was the first combination religious experience, freak-out and consciousness expansion ever done with Protestant ministers. What happened? Did they lose their religious values? Not on your life. What they lost was their middle-class-minister professionalism. Instead of priests, we have saints. Ministers turned into holy men. They had seen their God for the first time and they knew He was not in their temples, where the aldermen held the mortgage, but He was in their own hearts if He was anywhere.

"Half of them quit their church soon thereafter; the

other half is working to try to turn it on. Not a few of America's present heroes, the war-resisting Episcopal priests, were ordained on that Good Friday. It was the beginning of a new apostolic progression. Instead of 'laying on hands,' an empty gesture, they ingested the LSD sacrament. At that point they stopped being professional ministers and started to be saints. The professional role is the first thing to go when you blow your mind.

"The whole doctor-lawyer-preacher business is a fool's parade with medieval trappings . . . The teacher thing is perhaps the worst profession, since it is dedicated to making dull clods of children instead of loving human beings who know how to give and receive ecstatic experiences. Being a student is like being a mental patient or a social-work client. Nothing could be more degrading. So, the young turn on and drop out. Not because of Timothy Leary but because of the degrading acts they are made to perform for the satisfaction of their elders *and* because of the hopeless future they face in the loveless power struggle of professional life.

"Last to turn on will be the military and the power politicians. They will watch the rest of us having fun but will be afraid to join in themselves. They're watching right now." Rosemary slid her eyes over to the man in dark glasses. "My activities have been monitored by the secret police now for several years. They get their kicks from watching everything I do. This has become an expected part of our life, Rosemary's and mine, but I see no reason why hundreds of thousands, even millions of people shouldn't be tuning in on what we're doing. Take the FBI. At Millbrook we were watched by the FBI, but I don't care. Big Brother and the rest of the middle class like to watch us because we're having more fun than they are. *That*—if you really want to know—is the real source of hatred for the image of 'Timothy Leary.' 'Timothy Leary' is having *fun* and they aren't. I don't do anything in secret. I smoke pot, take LSD, make love to Rosemary, invent new ways of sharing our ecstasies and the whole bit—everybody knows what I *do*. And they know I am having a glorious time. Ecstatic. They also know that *their* lives are dull, lifeless, sexless, and they are *not* having fun. They are power-oriented . . . to get power you must take it away from somebody else, and that is no fun. It might be fun to rob a bank, but it is no fun to rob somebody else of his power and then use it yourself. To keep power you must see that nobody takes it away from you, and *that* is no fun. *Sharing* or giving away power is, after all, the only source of fun. If you can't share, you can't have any fun. Take old J. Edgar. J. Edgar was tapping our phone at Millbrook, but that was OK. It was the best thing that could ever happen to that poor old fellow."

Bob listened carefully to Leary's words.

"You were right, Bob, that the anger and fear of those who never tried LSD has created the image. Take the hippie movement. The hippie movement doesn't really exist except in *Time* and *Life*. Only the media believe in hippies. If LSD is going to be used, it should be used as we use it, a religious sacrament, an act of love, a road to God. When you turn on,"—here he looked directly at Bob—"you must never do so just to be a naughty boy, getting high for kicks. You must recognize that you're a spiritual voyager furthering the most ancient of mankind's noble quests."

"And to lose the sense of self, merging it into a larger whole," said Bob.

"Exactly what I have been saying," said Leary, flat out and without pause; then he went on, "and what would your roommates at Yale think about *that?*"

Bob merely smiled.

"Bob, here, is a Yale drop-out," Leary said, looking at me. Turning back to Bob, Leary became mock-serious, mock-pompous, a parody (easily done) of a Yale guidance counselor or Dean Somebody-or-other expressing "concerns."

"I am becoming very *concerned* about the spiritual and moral status of our universities. Especially Yale. Charlie, you remember Michael Kahn, don't you?"

"Yes, he was a graduate student at Harvard."

"Well, now he is at Yale. I have had good campus reports from Michael, and for a while I didn't feel that I was needed at Yale. But some alarming reports have come from Yale recently.

"I understand that some members of the Yale faculty have been putting down the sexual, spiritual and psychedelic life of the Yale undergraduate. In a recent article, a faculty member said that buses bring college girls up to New Haven, where, according to the author, unbelievably vulgar things happen. He also put down Yale students because they smoke pot.

"Well, this is exactly my point. Here is a faculty member putting down the psychedelic and moral practices of the students who pay *him* for enlightenment. This is typical of most teachers and professors: They get their kicks vicariously from young people, and at the same time they put young people down. It's a conspiracy on the part of older people to put down young people.

"Instead of criticizing Yale students for their habits, the faculty should teach undergraduates how to make ecstatic, divine love—with concepts, with women, with

LSD and with every aspect of God's energies. But of course they don't, because they don't know how to themselves. They only can imagine what the young people are doing, the fun they are having. Thus, their jealousy drives them into a rage.

"And then, because I agree with the young people, because I, too, have had LSD and know what the young are talking about, the power elite picks on me. They create an image called 'Timothy Leary' and beat it to death in a power orgy. It's the closest thing to kicks they get.

"Of course, it's more than just university faculty members. Legislators, your President and your Defense Department are for the most part impotent old men who are riding on youth. They don't want you young people to be free. Laws are made by old people who don't want young people to do exactly those things young people were meant to do—to make love, turn on, and have a good time.

"Every Yale undergraduate should do what Bob here has done. He should look at each professor very carefully and ask himself the searching question: Is this professor interested in liberation—liberating me from the evil power forces of American society and the domination of Yale University—or is this professor getting vicarious kicks out of my youth and beauty—and then putting me down because he is old and ugly and doesn't have it?

"I wanted to go to Yale and debate the faculty on this, but they wouldn't let me.

"Bob, of course, saw completely through all this Yale business. He has dropped out. Yale is the loser. It's now seven to nothing, favor of Bob. If Yale wants to win they will have to try some new plays. Change the curriculum."

"And let's *us* change the subject," whispered Rosemary with a winning smile. You could tell she had already taken this particular lecture course, and although she didn't mind Leary's little speech, she didn't particularly want to stay for the question period. She whisked out pictures of the teepee scene at Millbrook. Emitting ooos and aaahs as befits perusal of the family album, we all examined closely the Millbrook Teepee Tribe. Lots of smiling people dressed in feathers—sometimes feathers only—day-glo body paint, a few non-Indian costumes, faintly vampirish, and a couple of ponies, also day-glo-painted. I wondered, but didn't ask, if the ponies had been given LSD.

I did ask about the cops and Sheriff Larry Quinlan.

"Oh, they did their little thing," said Leary.

"Their little thing," it turned out, consisted of at least two raids.

One, in July of '68, lasting nine hours and netting the Sheriff (Leary called him the Sheriff of Nottingham) about forty people, most of them charged with traffic violations. Also a two-year surveillance by unmarked patrol cars, wherein out-of-state cars were stopped routinely, especially if they contained long-hair drivers.

"Tim," I asked, "where will all this attention from the police end? They are not going to leave you alone, and you are not going to stop your thing. If you keep up like this, you'll end up in jail."

He didn't answer.

"Maybe, you think it is OK for a religious leader to go to jail," I said. "Lots of religions start in jail."

"The crucifixion is a two-thousand-year-old trip and not for me, I'll never go to jail. The jail is not built that can hold me. I am not a martyr—get that straight. I am no believer in suffering. I am a pure hedonist and I want to have a ball—get high and have fun and this conversation is getting dragged down in a morass of questions and answers." Rosemary agreed.

Leary looked me deep in the eyes for about a half-minute and then leaned over to whisper something in my ear.

"Are you having fun?" he asked.

I didn't know what to answer so I pretended to think long and hard about it. Finally I said, "Yes."

"Good," said Leary.

Then he leaned back and closed his eyes again. I figured, all things considered, I'd better do the same, what with Bob merging and all. It was typical of Tim to ask me that, though. He was mocking me, but if I took him seriously, I could get by. Anyway, I *was* having fun. I always did have fun with Leary.

Ever since the beginning? Yes, right from the start, from our old friendly beer-hall arguments in the old friendly Harvard-pre-LSD days, when alcohol was the only consciousness-expander and Leary and I used to go, after work, over to one of the old, dark saloons around Harvard Square and talk about changing the world. We were both psychologists then, working at the Harvard Psychological Clinic, teaching and doing psychotherapy. It was OK to argue about anything in those days, nothing was life and death. Actually, one was supposed to debate while drinking. It was part of the university scene, testing ideas and besting the other guy's arguments. Leary was good at this game but he always went beyond the realm of ideas—even then, when I first met him in 1959, his actions were daring.

There is a sense in which we all admire the derring-do of the person who gets away with that which we fear to try: the TV private eye, the romatic underworld hero, the comic-book superman who lets nothing stand in his way. Leary always displayed flashes of this character. Psychiatrists and psychologists, not a few of them Leary's colleagues, called him "a psychopath."

Of course, psychiatrists were always calling people bad, Greek-root names behind their backs under the guise of medical diagnosis. "Psychopath" was just one of many. It was originally a word restricted to persons who had no conscience at all, such as incurable liars and criminals who acted completely on impulse. By 1959 the term was getting vastly overused, and everyday Leary and I would see people labeled "psychopath" at the clinic where we worked.

All of us good-guy psychologists *talked* about the evil practices of psychiatric diagnosis, but as far as I know, only Leary ever *did* anything about it. He arranged, on a couple of occasions, to have the patient sit in, unbeknownst to the psychiatrists, on the session where the diagnosis was to be given. The patient was then called by Leary as an expert on himself. When the psychiatrists found out, they called Leary a psychopath too, and banned him from further meetings.

One local court psychiatrist was particularly fond of throwing the "psychopath" label around. It seemed that every poor Roxbury street kid who ever stole a hubcap had, at one time or another, gotten himself labeled "psychopathic" by this particular shrink, one of those who had banned Leary from diagnostic sessions.

Finally, I concluded that any kid who could get the Herr Doktor mad enough to diagnose him as a psychopath should wear the diagnosis proudly and in good health. Leary disagreed.

"The only kids who deserve to be called 'psychopaths'

are those who get two or three psychiatrists in a row mad at them. I mean, you might get one psychiatrist mad at you just by mistake, and that shouldn't count toward the psychopath award."

I took a slug of beer as I considered starting a psychopath club of some kind, when Leary said, seriously, "You know, I really *am* a psychopath."

"I know you are," I said. "But I am one too."

"You aren't in my league at all," said Leary.

"Yes, I am," I said. "I am just as much a psychopath as you are."

"Well," said Leary. "Let's see if you pass the test."

"I think I have enough psychiatrists mad at me to qualify," said I.

"That's kid stuff," said Leary. "Here's *my* test: How many violations of the APA [American Psychological Association] Code of Ethics have you made?"

I couldn't think of any. Leary looked satisfied. That proved it as far as he was concerned.

"Well, what about you?" I asked.

"I think I have violated them all except the ones about money."

I said nothing.

"Well, Slack, ask me one."

I thought about it and decided on the one I considered worst at the time. "OK, here's one. Have you ever had sexual relations with a patient of yours?"

Leary looked at me sheepishly. Leary *never* looked sheepish. I had scored a beer-hall debate triumph. "Have you?" he asked.

"I asked you first," said I. "But my answer is no."

"Yes, quite a bit," said Leary.

I was shocked. It was an unforgivable taboo only a *real*

psychopath would break. Of course, what I wanted to know, but didn't dare ask, was how he got away with it.

Leary really believed in doing forbidden things. For example, he had the social-science curiosity about what would actually happen if you broke this or that taboo, as opposed to the accepted version of the consequences.

Leary, even then, in 1959, was surprisingly radical, surprisingly anti–middle class. His whole career had been a kind of flight from middle-class values, relationships, people, scenes, everything. He was a psychologist at a time when that profession had not yet met with middle-class approval. Escape from the middle class is not easy: to be born in the middle class is, by and large, to live in it—or at least to remain with that label wherever your fortunes or your efforts permit you to go. Certainly, Leary tried most of the established escape routes, upper and lower. He *felt* he was class-free, but I don't think he was. He was *anti*–middle class—and that is a different thing. The middle class is awful, of course, but you are not class-free if you are constantly fighting the middle class. Head-hunting is awful, but you can't be an objective anthropologist if you are constantly fighting against head-hunting. You are a missionary, not an anthropologist.

The perfectly class-free person would be some kind of super-adaptable anthropologist who could come and go from one segment of culture to another and blend completely at all times. I had often wished that I could do that: be at home with any tribe, unflappable during any ritual, so much so that they would always welcome me as one of them or, better still, not even know that I wasn't. Most of the anthropologists I knew then had tried hard not to disturb the cultures with which they were involved, and went to great pains not to force their own values on others. But with Leary and the middle class it was instant hostility, at least resentment and at most open warfare—and complete disrespect and flaunting of alternative values. Neither Leary nor the whole hippie movement, for that matter, were ever to become the least bit culture-free. Instead, they were to become, in their own words, a "counter-culture."

Leary was a prime mover of the hippie movement, there is no doubt about that. Leary always did want to start a social movement. He had a theory about hybrids and "hybrid vigor" borrowed from genetics. The idea was that the offspring of odd unions was bound to have a survival value, not just in biology but in music, literature, art—everything.

"Make hybrids," he said once (in pre-LSD days), "and you make revolutions." He meant by that bringing together social classes who otherwise would not meet. We all believed that the lower class was the source of new experience. Most fads and styles began in the lower class and then jumped to the upper (this union was a kind of hybrid) till finally the middle class got squeezed into line. Lipstick was a clear example: The first to use it in modern times were the prostitutes, next the debutantes; finally the middle-class mother could no longer keep her daughter from the formerly sinful practice and gave up trying.

"Make hybrids," said Leary, "and you make music and love."

"Like tail fins," I said. "They started with hot rods, jumped to Cadillacs and now—Fords and Plymouths."

Leary was annoyed with my commercial corruption of his theory. "I was thinking of philosophy—the academy

and the street, Sartre and Genêt, Higgins and Eliza, Bee-
thoven hearing the peasant dance."

We agreed, however, that the academy was inbred.
"They're talking about people who *aren't here*. Courses
on criminology with no criminals, courses on poverty
with no poor, psychosis without psychotics—music without Mingus (everybody's jazz favorite then).

"If you could only find a good excuse for bringing
certain isolated groups and individuals together and
removing their established biases," said Tim, "you could
cure most of the psychological ills of this lousy class-
bound culture of ours."

We had our last beer-hall debate at graduation time,
1960. Leary ate his first Mexican mushroom the summer
I left Harvard. My appointment as assistant professor at
Harvard ran out then, and I went to work as an industrial
consultant. I lived in the South for a year and then moved
to Montclair, New Jersey. I traveled a lot on airplanes,
and one weekday afternoon, by chance, a year and a half
later, I met Leary on a rickety old Eastern prop-jet shuttle from Washington to New York. Leary bounded
aboard at National Airport, recognized me, and plopped
down. Even though I traveled a lot, I didn't know that
you could pay for the shuttle tickets by check. When the
cart came by, he whipped out his checkbook with
aplomb.

"How is Harvard?" I asked, but Leary didn't want to
talk about that.

"How is the White Hand?" I asked. The White Hand
was a barroom society of do-gooders, consisting of
Leary, me and a few grad students. We specialized in
trying to rehabilitate jailbirds. Leary didn't want to talk
about that either.

"What's going on?" I asked.

He didn't say what it was right away. He was trying to figure out how to break the news to me. He had been down to Washington, he said, to see the "pure food and drug people." These, he said, "were wonderful people" who would not "stand in the way" because they were so "human and wonderful."

"Stand in the way of what?"

"There is no use in trying to *talk* about it," said Leary, who kept on talking about it anyway—without saying what *it* was. He laughed and told me he was throwing a scene. "Come with me and I'll show you. Leonard and Peggy will be there. Marvin and Sheila too. Aldous Huxley and Johara, a dancer"—he licked his lips and rolled his eyes—"very exotic." Tim went on making hybrids as he dropped names, obviously enjoying the hybrid mix he had created. About half were famous people: jazz musicians, writers, artists, at least one big-name actor, a young lady reputed to be the "richest girl in the world." It was a dazzling list, far cry from the days when we were happy to get a college dean for sherry. The other half were just the opposite—as in "how the *other half* lives": a couple of ex-inhabitants of a well-known Massachusetts prison for young men, one person just out of a public mental hospital, several garden-variety beatniks and a smattering of student types. These could have been the beneficiaries of the old White Hand.

"Some party," I exclaimed.

"But it's not a party, or, I should say, not *just* a party. It's an experiment, we're all research subjects."

"Studying what?"

"Visual perception, *non* visual perception, how the mind works."

"That's a big order!"

"Yes, but we have the microscope. It's LSD. Don't you want to try it?"

I had read about LSD. It was discussed in psychiatric circles. Animals and medical students were given it in experimental sessions to mimic mental illness.

"Doesn't LSD make you psychotic, crazy?"

"Only if you take it in a mental hospital. If you take it where we're going, it will make you a great scientist. It all depends on the set and the setting, where you take it and what you want out of life, your hopes and fears, your readiness to experience the *full meaning*. You'll see. We're going to the Bronx."

Well, we went to Bronx*ville*, which was hardly the Bronx I was used to. There seemed to be a lot of lawn. One could see the Hudson through the trees. The big old house was the kind advertised in *Town and Country* along with the yachts. Tim let us in without ringing and deposited me in a kind of large sun room decorated with antiques and cushions.

"Introduce yourself," he said. "I've got to change my clothes. Here. Don't drop this." He handed me a jar about four inches high. The contents were syrupy and colorless. There was a plastic stick along with the jar, held to the side by a piece of Scotch tape. Altogether, it looked not unlike a child's soap-bubble kit.

The hostess entered, looking very pretty, early thirty-ish, dressed in pajamas-for-dinner. Her ears were bandaged. I started to introduce myself, but she seemed not to want to know. "I see you have it," she said.

"This, oh, yes." I started to hand her the jar.

She drew back. "Don't drop it, for God's sake! I don't suppose you'd like a drink."

"As a matter of fact, that's exactly what I would like. You see, I've just gotten off the plane and . . ."

"If you insist," she said, pointing limply toward the bar. "I personally can't stand to mix alcohol with it." "It," of course, was in the jar.

"Don't look at my ears," she said. "When they are ready, I'll show them to my friends."

I didn't look. Tim entered, wearing a pullover sweater and loose slacks. He was leading what looked, at first, to be a blind man, very old. "Aldous Huxley, Charlie Slack." The man was not blind. "I see you're the one who has it," he said.

Soon everybody was staring at my jar, which I was trying to hold in a manner both casual and reliable, but the drink in my other hand gave me away.

"Ahem," said one tall black fellow. "Why don't you put it over here on the table while you do your drinking?"

I gave it to Leary as soon as I could.

People from both strains of the hybrid began streaming into the room. Nobody else was drinking, and nobody else even had a necktie on. There were about a half-dozen teenagers there. Several men were dressed in Kung Fu bathrobes. Everybody talked to everybody without mentioning names. Many were celebrities who didn't need names mentioned.

When I finished my drink, I noticed a circle of people bending their heads around Leary. They were not in conversation. He broke away from that group and came to ours.

"Who's next? Charlie, now, let's see your tongue," he said, like a family doctor. I extended my tongue and he wiped the plastic stick on it. I was surprised. "OK, shut the door," he said, tapping me under the chin. Half an hour later, I hadn't the foggiest idea where I was or what I was doing. I wasn't even sure *who* I was. I'd start to say something and then fail to recall the beginning of the sentence. The colors were beautiful. The designs, fantastic combinations of extremes, were things I hadn't known existed. I got frightened and thought I was going to die. I saw something I was sure was God. I had never known before exactly what God was like, but now I knew. It was the event of a lifetime or, perhaps, thereafter, of deathtime. God, *my* God, was something so simple and so obviously *there* and *with* me that I knew at once that I was as important in God's world as He was in mine. The trouble was that during the trip I kept forgetting that I had seen something I was sure was God. I even forgot that I had told myself that I had seen Him. Then God would come again and I would *know* that He was real and that I would never forget Him ever again. He would see to it that I would remember it all. But, anyhow, I forgot.

The people seemed like puppets. I kept having the feeling that I was arriving somewhere. I was a little sick to my stomach but it went away. Sometimes I would take a step and it would feel like long rubbery stilts, more like roller skating or walking on the moon or under water.

A trip to the john was like going to the ends of the Earth. I stood there and became at once the soft rain falling and the Mississippi flowing and the origin of all life springing from the flow I was making—and missing the bowl—oops, and trying to get down to Earth and still missing the bowl and worrying about the hostess and *still* missing the bowl, finally getting it all straight with the supreme aim of a marksman with perfect pitch and yaw. I had to get out of there before I drowned.

Outside, every time I closed my eyes, I had visions of vast impossible designs. Horrendous hybrid designs as though the mind were a family of funny rug-makers weaving tapestries around my eyeballs. They were tapestries you could swim in if you tried. Which I did. Which I did. Which I did. Woof, warp, kick. Woof, warp, kick. Many times, Tim would come up and tell me, "Everything's just fine," or ask me if it wasn't all wonderful.

"Yes, yes," I would say. "Anything for old Tim. So *glad* you came with me, buddy. Are you sure I'm not going to die?"

"We've all died many times before."

I had the strong impression (now I'm not so sure) that Tim hadn't taken any that night. That way he could make certain that we would all be safe. He alone was our thin thread of contact with the Bronx. "Your face, Tim, it's so funny, in a . . . reassuring way. Thank God you came with me, Tim. Without you, I might die or just . . . anything."

Blending into things was a cherished activity but it was slightly, not decidedly, dangerous. Those precious boundaries might be lost forever. When I sank into a chair, I really sank, I nearly drowned again, and I was certain that if I did I would never ever be salvaged. It was blending, bending and border-rending. A folding into the whipped cream of cloudpillows and becoming one with the droplets.

And then I turned on the lamp. When I looked into the light bulb on the end table, I nearly burned my eyes out. Oh, sun!

Tim was standing in the center of the group. Everybody seemed to be watching him.

"Mike and Pat are wonderful," said Tim, pointing to

the young men from prison. "They are so intelligent."
Everybody agreed that Mike and Pat were geniuses. "No
more of that rough stuff, right?" Mike and Pat nodded
enthusiastically. "OK," said Tim, "everybody back to his
own ecstasy."

"Right you are, Tim, right you are."

No. 2 on the *Downbeat* poll, and I looked at an abstract
painting in the hall for a long, long time. He didn't know
who *he* was except when he went to get his overcoat, a
new camel's-hair that felt very smooth. We were all together, Tim said, all sharing this same wonderful trip to
the insides of our brain cells. We all belonged to the
same family and we would remember our trip forever.

"Like being in jail together," said Mike and Pat.

"Like being in the war together," said I. "A . . . soft
war." Everybody thought that was terribly funny.

"Like going to school together," said the richest girl
in the world. All the rich people in the room thought that
was profound.

By morning, it had worn off a lot. I was standing in the
foggy dawn, looking out over the front lawn at all the
sports cars.

"Are you straight?" asked my host, the owner of the
house. He was a big-band leader and instrumentalist and
had been playing high notes in Manhattan while we
tripped out in his home.

"I think so," said I. "I've got to get to work . . . say
good-bye to Tim."

Leary came bounding out of the house and down the
lawn to us. He looked me close in the eyes.

"How's it going?"

"Well, Tim, I got to admit that was really *something.*"

"Some teenage fad, huh?" he said, waving back at a

few young faces in the French doors. "Say, Charlie, why don't you come and join us, live with the group. We do this every night. It's going to be a revolution, Charlie. Get with it."

"I don't think the top of my head could take it, Tim. Anyhow, I've got to get back to work."

"Back to the grind, eh? While we go on a picnic. LSD in the woods! What do you think about that?"

I couldn't think of anything to say.

"Well, some other time, eh?"

"OK, Tim, let me get over this one and then some other time."

"Charlie, Charlie, you'll never get out of the middle class." Leary was still shaking his head in disgust as my cab drove off.

Back at the office, I briefly explained what had happened, using a quiet tone where possible. When I got to the part about God and the light bulb, however, the office crew gently suggested that I take the rest of the day off and keep the whole thing to myself.

If I only could! LSD may not create addicts but it does make proselytizers. I began to corner people at cocktail parties for extended evangelical discussions about "substances that give internal light." I called friends and relatives long distance trying to sort out what had happened to me and to get somebody to share my incredible experiences. I seemed determined to convince the world that I had grasped some remarkable truth—without stating exactly what the truth was.

The effects lasted longer than I knew. I thought I was down in one or two weeks, but I was really still talking funny, some of the time, after six months. Eventually the evangelism which had spread a net of familiarity over the universe gave way to a mild conviction that I might know one or two things nobody else did. Finally even that stopped. Bad trips were being reported. An artist friend of mine took some acid. It was a terrible thing. He ran amok through his New York studio, tore off all his clothes, abraded his body against the walls and jumped screaming, naked, into the night from a third-story window. Lucky for him, he landed on a parked car, and the roof caved in just enough to save his life. It took several days just to clean the blood off his paintings. The Spanish press called him "Superhombre."

It was the first bad trip I ever heard of . . . but not the last. Over six years had passed since that first plane ride and the evening after. Six years is a long time at the fast pace of the sixties. Everything had changed: people, clothes, attitudes. In one way or another, Leary had been responsible for many of these changes. He and his hippie hybrid *had* blown people's minds. From an obscure experimental drug administered only in controlled research to spiders and medical students, LSD had become a social movement, an art style, a religious belief, a revolutionary political philosophy and a way of life for thousands. We were all participating in the cultural and artistic (and criminal) aspects of the revolution—its music, dance, and media aspects—if not in its entire life style. Nobody was immune to the influence of the drug revolution. To hell with the Establishment, *all* Establishments, Timothy Leary was going to do exactly as he pleased, and one of the things he pleased was to tell anybody who would listen to do exactly as *they* pleased, laws or no laws, power structure or no power structure.

Were they paying attention? Well, at that moment, I

would say over a hundred were. At least that many hippies waited at the airport to see us get off the plane. This was San Francisco, man, the *top* of the drug scene in the spring of 1968.

3

Shindigs and Shades

Tim's and Rosemary's bags were definitely delayed at the airport. Bob and I didn't have any bags at all, but we waited for an hour for the Learys to get theirs. Rosemary was up in arms about it, complaining to the attendant in a loud and sure voice, "Everywhere we go, we are searched. It is illegal for you to do this to us. Are we to have no privacy?" She was beautiful when indignant, stamping her foot at the man. He looked chagrined, but I don't think he had anything to do with it. It could have been just an error.

However, Rosemary had made no error about the man in the shades. He was hanging suspiciously around the baggage-claim area long after the rest of the bags had been returned to the others. He was watching Leary and leaning up against a post—at least, I was sure he was watching, though his eyes were hidden behind the evil shades.

Meanwhile, the Leary crew celebrated arrival. Jackie and Susan, Tim's children, had come to help. Susan was pretty, with a fine plump figure, and Jackie was healthy and handsome in high, wide, black Prince Valiant bangs. Ed the Clown, a Brillo-haired friend and live-in retainer, brought a borrowed car. Ed the Clown had rosy cheeks and a short fringe of gray-red halo fuzz around his moon face. For some reason, the tip of Ed the Clown's nose was always redder even than his cheeks, which were redder than Jackie's, which were plenty red. Ed the Clown had little to say. His eyes, often vague, would come to life and focus sharply on some key detail—the time of day, a claim check, a parking meter—ignored by Timothy in the excitement of arrival. At first I thought Ed the Clown's brain had been destroyed by LSD or STP, because when I said, "Hello," he said, "Um, yes," and when I said, "How'yer doin', Ed?" he just smiled vacantly. However, next thing I knew, he was functioning well, better organized than Leary around where we were actually going and how we would get there. I kept revising my opinion of Ed the Clown. A cheese-head, yes, but fine cheddar or Swiss. There was clay on his boots, pricker-seeds clung to his plaid hunting jacket and his corduroy pants were worn smooth in the seat. He could have been a country-bum day-hand or a professor who was building a cabin in the woods. Turned out, he was both.

Leary made a great show of getting organized—"Now we must plan. What do we all want to do next? What is the group's idea? Give me inputs," etc.—but when the bags failed to come, he quickly abandoned all plans in order to talk to the assembled crowd of students and hippies. It was mid-year time, and the students were headed to and from school, vacations and other individual pursuits. Thus, you couldn't exactly say that the crowd had come just to greet Leary. Nonetheless, it was an impressive reception as the beards, beads, and bell-bottoms gathered around to hear a few words from the master.

Leary sat on a baggage cart, ass-low and knees-high. He could have stood up on it so we would all hear what he had to say. Instead, he disappeared in the middle of the throng and whispered a few words of wisdom to those close up. Leary often spoke too softly for easy group-listening; a hush would then fall over the crowd, and his presence would carry an air of importance.

"Ask him what he plans to do in California," shouted a voice from the edge of the crowd.

"What about the revolution?" shouted another.

"When will the earthquake come?"

"Where can I get some righteous acid?"

"What's he saying?"

No answers. The *point* was that you had to get *close* to Timothy Leary to know what he was rapping about. Leary was not an impromptu public speaker. At last, all but the few who could hear gave up and went back to their student-fare stand-by lines or whatever. When he saw the crowd actually melting, Tim raised his voice a bit:

". . . and I am going to start my own *country*," he repeated for the benefit of those who remained. "First we shall buy some land, hopefully a lot of land. There is no reason why we can't purchase the land rather than take it by other means. Thus, we can render unto Caesar and keep him happy. I am going to interest an investor in the purchase of large amounts of land to the south. After we buy our land, we will set up our own government, declare ourselves independent of the U.S.A. and set up our own country with our own laws or lack thereof, as the case may be. Our laws will stress complete freedom of the mind and body: freedom to ingest any substance which will lead toward spiritual enlightenment or interpersonal understanding, freedom of the mind, in-

ternal freedom, freedom to love, freedom to live in anyway you wish with any person you wish at any time you
wish in any way agreeable to you both. There will probably be Indians on the land we buy, but, if not, we will
invite them to come. We always get along with Indians,
they obviously know about peyote and are in tune with
our minds and our ends and means. Once we have our
nation going, we will make treaties with the blacks and
Chicanos and send ambassadors to sympathetic nations,
such as Algeria. Finally, we will deal with the United
States of America—but on an equal-nation basis, nation
to nation, *not* on a person-to-nation basis, as is now the
case. No longer will we be *subjects* of the U.S.A. Instead,
we will be separate negotiating parties, gaining our free-
doms from a position of strength.

"There are some that believe that a revolution will
come. I say there will be no revolution. The only way to
handle the United States is through a treaty."

While Leary went on, the man in the shades sidled up
to me, and took me completely by surprise with these
words:

"Are you on or off here in the Bay Area?"

It was the most cool-busting, wham-downing thing.
Ohmygod, I've been caught. One minute I'm thinking
about starting my own country and the next thing . . . All
I could do was stammer, "Uh, we are just waiting."

"I *mean,*" said he, "are you going to be *here* in San
Francisco? They never inform us. They don't think we
care who they send."

"Oh, I see," I said, "You think I . . . I mean you think
I work for . . . for . . ."

The fellow took off the shades and glared. "You people are getting worse each day," he said. "There's no

communication at all. No cooperation at all. You never inform us about *anything.*" He turned on his heel and strode across the floor and out the door.

I stood watching him go.

"I think he thought *I* was a narc," I said to Rosemary.

Rosemary also stared after the man. "We've got to get you some suitable clothes" was her thought on the subject.

Leary again made a show of arrangements and plans. "Now, where do we go next? Who is going to drive? Let's get organized," etc.

I thought I should rent a car, since Ed the Clown had told me he had to return the borrowed one. All Leary's plan-making would mean little without a car, and I knew Leary was broke.

When I suggested the car, Leary had too much pride to show he was pleased.

"Well," he said, "if that's what *you really want* to do, obviously you should go ahead and do it," as though it were just some whim of mine.

After renting the car, we went to a unisex boutique and bought me a hippie shirt, white and pleated, with sleeves like lamb-chop papers. I was too tall for any pants in the store. Beatle boots my size were also out of the question. Some beads were located, however, and a belt with a buckle as big as a door-knocker. The result was half-and-half: From the sidewalk to the crotch, I was Brooks-Brothers, Ivy League narc, but from the crotch to the crown, I was an imitation Berkeley flower child . . . thirty-eight years old.

Leary would not go into the boutique with me but stood outside, creating his own scene. He didn't care what clothes I wore, because, whether I tried to look hip or not, my oddball squareness made for an interesting contrast. The idea in San Francisco was to create an interest, a scene of contrasts, a scene which raised (unanswered) questions in people's minds: "What *are* they doing?" "Why *are* they dressed that way?" "Who *are* they anyhow?" etc. Only the squarest of squares would dare actually voice the questions, but the questions would still pop into every mind except, of course, the very hippest.

On the street and from in the shop, Leary was recognized and greeted as an object of wonder and delight. Hip Frisco understood Leary. It was his home and these were his people on the street. Leary didn't get treated this well in Boston or even New York, didn't belong in those places the way he belonged here. Boston and New York kicked him out but, so far, the Bay Area was giving him a warm reception.

Next, the group split up and we dropped Rosemary, Bob and the kids wherever it was they wanted to go. Leary had no driver's license, so he got in back and Ed the Clown and I got up front in the new, fat-ass Ford from Avis, with Ed the Clown driving. Leary took some time to adjust his image to being driven around in this big car and then quietly began to issue directions to visit a few of his close and important friends.

Thus it was that we hopped over to pop in on the staff of *The Phoenix,* a semi-famous San Francisco underground newspaper. While Ed the Clown parked the car, Leary was warmly greeted by the editor-printer, who slapped palms all around and offered us seats on some piles of old inky rags and rolls of newsprint adorning the floor. After we were all squatting down on the worn old boards, a joint or two was quickly passed around.

When Ed the Clown came in and told them I was

renting the car, they asked me where I came from. The editor then started to rap away at me with pride and anger. He was proud of his newspaper and mad at New Yorkers, who he felt, perhaps rightly, were ripping off his Frisco original. I protested that I had nothing to do with New York underground newspapers and that imitation was a form of flattery but, far from satisfying him, my New Yorker's shrug of dis-identification bothered him almost as much as the alleged rip-off.

"After all, we San Francisco freaks take *responsibility* for all the freaky things doing down here in the Bay Area as a mere matter of *communal pride, group mind* and *responsible attitude.* So why don't New Yorkers do the same?" I explained that New York was a bigger place than San Francisco, but he didn't want to hear that.

"You people have copied practically every issue of *The Phoenix* in some way. I mean, you have tried to take our ideas but mostly you don't make it. For example, see this two-color cover here on the new issue? What do you think this cover was printed on? Go on, just tell me what kind of a flatbed or roto press did this quality of work?"

I didn't know the answer, so I just said it was a nice cover. It was a montage of blue and yellow phallic symbols.

"You bet your wing-wang it is a nice cover *and,* what's more, it was done on nothing but our old Gestetner here."

With that line, he pointed to the darkest corner of the room, where, in the middle of a mound of rags and crumpled sheets of paper, sat a piece of junk sculpture. Wait a minute, no, it was not a piece of junk sculpture, it was a toboggan sled with tits and a small whiskey still on top. No, no, *that* wasn't it, stupid! Up close you could easily see that it was actually a big mimeograph machine. The machine was framed by blotches, ceiling and floor —comic-book BLAM marks, a pie-throwing target with blue-black pies.

"This old mother here," said our host with a paternal pat on the tits, "this fine old *wonder* of a mother here can do things you New Yorkers wouldn't dream of trying with a mimeograph machine. Look at this three-color job here." He fished through a stack of back issues and came up with a full page of a blue woman on an intricate black-and-white background. The woman had yellow and green op-art circles emanating from her vulva like ripples in a pool. The green color was formed when the yellow circles crossed the blue vulva.

"And take *this* jobby here," he added, fishing for another issue. This one showed a man and a girl and a horse. "See that man's penis, there. Well, if this good old Gestetner here didn't have near-perfect registration, these colors wouldn't be lined up the way they are and this poor bugger would be making it with the horse instead of with the broad." I had to admit that it was a pretty tricky job of alignment.

"Yes siree, I wouldn't give any of your fancy New York presses for old mother Betsy here. Looky *here* at what the mother wonder did to this rendition. *This* one we purposefully put *outa* whack to increase the artistic effect."

It was clearly an orgy, but the blue and yellow were so far apart that you couldn't tell exactly what was going on.

"Improved the original art a hundred times over," said the fellow. "Twice as many people making it with twice as many *other* people. Some blue and some yellow. Get the effect?"

When I didn't get it right away, he seemed disappointed. "Well, when you're stoned, *then* it really comes to life. Yeah, old mother Betsy here. Rich New York bastards wouldn't understand."

Next, another member of the staff came in, carrying what first looked to be a missing piece of old Betsy but was really a good-sized water pipe made out of glass and rubber tubing, old ink funnels and cans and things. The pipe bowl, made of a glass funnel, had a piece of wire mesh across it about an inch square, and sitting on it was a pile of hashish shavings, like somebody had emptied the pencil sharpener. It was the biggest pile of hash shavings I had ever seen. Amid mumblings about how much better San Francisco hashish was than New York stuff, etc., they all proceeded to get spaced on the shavings.

I took a look at the yellow and blue orgy scene and was absolutely ready to admit that there *were* twice as many people making it as I had first thought. Also, they appeared to be actually moving. Then it didn't matter anymore whether they were moving or not.

Dusk fell, and still nobody moved. Leary was out of this world on the rags, looking at the ceiling, and the rest of the newspaper staff was equally tuned in to the infinite.

I was thinking: How do they ever get *The Phoenix* out if they turn on every afternoon like this? At least, I *thought* I was thinking, but I must have been talking without knowing it, because the Gestetner-master suddenly jumped to his feet and shouted at me.

"I'll show you how, you Eastern esthete, you! You New York snobs with your fancy, rotary, four-color, bleed-printing, photo-cell, auto-aligning presses. I'll show you how *The Phoenix* gets put out, stoned or unstoned."

With this, he grabbed a can of ink and began pouring through the refillhole in the tits. He slapped stencils on and off, trying to find the one he wanted and get it fixed right. There was much hand-winding, cranking and phift-phift sounds. There was also much ripping and wadding of sheets and throwing of wads onto the floor, which was already knee-deep in wads. Lastly, he reared back at arm's length, finger outstretched, threw the *on* button and then ran from the room.

The room light dimmed to a flicker for a tense second or two while whines and puffs of smoke emanated from the Gestetner; then more whines, and slowly a piece of paper emerged, and then another and then, faster, another. Soon, papers were streaming out of the machine at a real clip, bing, bing, bing. I reached over to see a copy of what was being printed, but when I picked up the sheet I couldn't read it. I thought I was going blind from the hashish, but when I wiped my eyes, I realized it was the ink.

Thick blue ink stuck all over my eyes. I grabbed a rag and wiped my eyes, only to see a shower of ink streaming from the Gestetner, which was not only printing *The Phoenix* but everything else in the room, including me. I looked to Leary for help, but he was gone. So was the assistant editor. So was the editor, who had started the thing to begin with. So was Ed the Clown. Only I remained, in my new hippie clothes, slowly turning blue in the flight of *The Phoenix.*

Ed the Clown rescued me in the Ford. We put newsprint down to protect the car seats, and for the next three hours I worked to get cleaned up. I ran my shirt through a washing machine two times and scrubbed my face and hands with Boraxo. I did the best I could, but I was starting to bleed while still rather blue in the face.

Ed drove me over to rejoin Leary at a party at Michael Bowen's house. It was cocktail hour but, of course, no cocktails were served. Michael Bowen was, according to Leary, "The leader of the Haight-Ashbury freak society and a famous hippie in his own right." Now, Leary was opposed to such words as "hippie" and "freak" when *I* used them, and he certainly would never have used the terms when talking to his hippie and freak friends. However, he would say to me "So-and-so is a beautiful hippie girl" or "X is a leader of freak politics" when interpreting something or acting as a guide.

Michael Bowen's house was a wooden two-family job, of which the Bowens had at least the first floor and the basement, and maybe more. I asked Leary what Michael Bowen did to pay the rent and be a freak social leader.

"Ah, um, he hustles" was all Leary would say.

We were greeted in the kitchen by a black-haired lady known as "Michael's Woman," who told me my face was dirty but otherwise was charming. She looked to be in her early thirties, like Rosemary, and about her height. The two ladies obviously got along. They compared notes on hip food and hip fashion and traded beliefs and opinions. Michael's Woman was cooking some kind of brown pilaf, which we all sampled. The women seemed to think it was delicious. The way they talked, rice and rice alone, brown, "macrobiotic" and flavored with ginger and rose petals, was going to be the *carte du jour* in hip San Francisco.

Now, Leary—at least the *old* Leary—had a well-developed taste for food. I cornered him quickly and began to complain:

"Rosemary and Michael's Woman are planning meals for the week, old man, and I gather that flesh is a sin."

"You and I can sneak out for a steak later," he whispered.

Leary didn't approve of fad diets, but he didn't want to make an issue at the time. He explained that the real idea behind the macrobiotic thing was to make your shit smell nice. I allowed as how that might be OK if you were planning to keep it around for a while, and he agreed that that was about the only value to the whole fad. I also couldn't help but remark that some folks in Haight-Ashbury seemed to be living in theirs, which would make the macro diet rather a necessity. Once again, Leary agreed with me.

"The bottom of the scene is looking bad," he said simply, and then later he repeated that remark with a shake of the head and added, "There is too much speed and horse at the bottom of the scene."

The bottom of the scene was not in evidence at Michael's salon, however. Instead, we were treated to the cream of San Francisco's freak community in the spring of 1968—than which there has probably never been a more colorful group of people assembled on Earth, a riot of hair and hide, cloth and skin. Everything that could be done to skin to conceal it and expose it had been. Some hair had been pruned, clipped, cultivated and sculpted. Other hair was matted and overgrown, bundled and tied in sheaves and shimmies; forests and thickets of hair, mountains and streams of hair (and they that dwell within). Feet were bare, booted, besandled and bound in strap and leather. Dresses and shirts were remnants and raiments, ragbag and regal satin.

It was a gathering of extras from DeMille, a bawdy house from the Gold Rush, an amateur production of Dante's *Inferno*. Black magic was a fad, and several witches and warlocks glared fearsomely from acid-etched eyes that had seen Satan and would never be the same. The beautiful hippie girls of whom Leary spoke were there, with pre-pubertal Frisco-fog cheeks of rose.

Robin Hood was there, at least a half-dozen Jesus Christs, Venus and Adonis, Mickey Mouse, an Indian tribe or two, a cave man and dinosaur, Tarzan and Cheeta, and Man Mountain Dean. Madonnas nursed infants at breasts of snow and cherry, while fathers in beards and buckskins smoked corncob pipes and drank wine from skins. There was rice and wine and brown rice and white wine and *very* dark brown rice and red wine and everywhere incense and pot and hashish and twigs and stems and seeds popping in giant cornucopias of marijuana like I was told that black whores in Haiti will roll for you under the voodoo moon if you want.

And me? Well, I merged, man. I got to where I belonged in this scene. After all, I was a freak myself, in my own way. I could blow a mind or two. I was white magic. I told Leary that I was white magic and he agreed.

"Don't worry about it," he said. "You have plenty of magic going for you. You will survive just fine. White magic is the very best kind."

"I am white magic," I told Lady MacBeth.

"Beautiful," she said. "What's your sign?"

"Capricorn," I said.

"My, God! And you have ink on your face, too."

"Yes," I said. "Ink is a good sign."

"Beautiful," she said. "Have some vitamin C." She gave me a pill. I popped it in.

"Beautiful," she said.

"Beautiful," I said.

"Beautiful," she said.

"Beautiful," I said. But MacBeth came up. "You have ink on your face," he said.

"Any suggestions?" I asked.

"Try ink *remover*," he said.

Rotten vibes, the jerk! I slid away from the MacBeths and into the meditation room.

—which may need explaining. Sometime after the San Francisco earthquake, when Michael's house was built, all middle-class architects believed that middle-class life required a separate middle-class room for dining. This room was to contain a table and on the table was to be placed a roast of beef. The Age of Aquarius, however, consumed only brown rice and vitamin C—and these on the floor and on the run. Thus, the table was removed from the dining room—or rather, the legs were sawed off of the table and it was placed at one end of the room to form an altar. In this way, the dining room was phased out and the meditation room was phased in. The meditation room was a place to go and hunker down into the lotus position after becoming absolutely stoned on the brown rice, and other things, going down in the kitchen. I hope it is now perfectly clear that the meditation room was as much a necessity in the Age of Aquarius as the dining room was during the Plastic Age. In 1968, a happy hippie home could not be without a meditation room.

Michael's Meditation Room had simple reed mats on the floor, no cushions, a few inspirational wall hangings in Hindi and Japanese and, on the floor at one end, a small altar, whose flickering candles revealed the full incarnation of sweet-sweet Lord, Blessed Vishnu, loving-devotion Krishna.

Also on the floor, sitting cross-legged in silence, if not devotion, was a group of three or four well-dressed

freaks and, standing, one nice middle-aged little fellow
in workman's clothes and a worn beret. As I joined this
group, the nice little man went out to get a chair to sit
on. He made an odd picture in the meditation room—an
ordinary man sitting on an ordinary chair.

We all soon fell silent, breathing the incensed air and
hardly moving at all except to pass from left to right and
then right to left the ever-circulating bundle of hemp,
until finally they had had enough even of that small motion and became as rigid as the tiny toy god himself
behind the candles.

I heard nothing but the molecules in my ear and the
blood in my temples, until a loud voice—the god's?—
suddenly filled the room:

"I am the Cosmic Messenger," said the voice, not coming from a god but from the little man in the seedy beret
sitting stiffly on the only chair. He told us again of his
astral origin and proceeded to take an enormous deep
breath before launching into this rare pot-monologue,
or "rap."

"Many people know me as Allen Noonan. However,
my name as well as my whole life changed suddenly on
August fourth, nineteen forty-seven, while I was working
as a commercial artist in Monterey. At four twenty-five in
the afternoon, painting a sign reading 'Eat Here,' I was
struck by a bolt of white, blinding lightning. I was up on
a ladder at the time, painting this sign as a part of my
duties as a commercial artist, when the bolt of white
blinding light reached me and knocked me off my perch.
The affect of this blow was that my personality was split
in half. First there was my earthly half, my regular or
mundane half, as it were, this half being the one called
'Allen Noonan.' The other half, a completely new self,

was my *astral* self. This self was brought by the beam of white light into a flying saucer which was hovering in the stratosphere just north of Cannery Point in Monterey.

"Once inside the flying saucer, I was informed by its occupants that it was an astral taxi which had come to pick me up and take me to another planet where Higher Extraterrestrial Beings would explain the meaning of it all. The crew of the saucer were human-looking, much like you and me, but perfect specimens and dressed in uniforms of gold and silver shining cloth.

"It did not take long for my astral taxi to arrive at this other planet, where I was led off the saucer and into a hall in one of the important buildings of that planet. Once inside, I was interviewed by several of the Higher Extraterrestrial Beings, who told me that they were the same as angels in the Bible. These Higher Extraterrestrial Beings, known to you as angels in the Bible, next asked me in the form of my astral self if I would like to be the Messiah of Mankind. As Messiah or Messenger of Mankind, it would be my duty and responsibility to bring the true vision of the New World Order to the planet Earth. The New World Order would then replace the Old World Order with all its negative hang-ups. The New World Order is nothing but positive and is an Order in which we all will share equally in the resource of the world as One Family, actually to be called 'The One World Family of the Messiah's New World Crusade.'

"Well, as to becoming the Messiah, myself, I had to think about that for a while. I just couldn't say 'yes' to becoming the Messiah right off. After all, what about Socrates? What about Jesus? I knew that Socrates was forced to poison himself and Jesus was crucified, and I worried about the possibilities of something like that happening to me.

"Anyway, I thought about it and thought about it, and finally I realized that I would have to rid myself of such negative fantasies, which I did. Next time that the Higher Extraterrestrial Beings came around, I thought only positive thoughts and told them, 'Sure.'

" 'However,' I said to them. 'How will it be that you will communicate with me on Earth?' They said that they would do it through the servo-guidance of my hand as I wrote. Now that I am back on Earth, they have been guiding my hand as I write the Plan. So that is what I have been doing ever since. I have been writing 'The Plan for Absolute Freedom, Security and Abundance to *All* People as One Family.'

"And so I now say to you all: *Out with the Old, in with the New.* It is sheer nonsense to proclaim anything less than absolute freedom, security and abundance for every person on this planet as one family. Absolute freedom, security and abundance now for everyone must, then, be the *vision of the people's revolution.* There are no shortages of anything except the will and understanding to make things right. We shall have not a government made by men but a government made by the Universe which is now being written in our hearts."

The words of the Holy Messenger Allen rapped right into the pit of my stomach. I was listening to a dope-head talk about being appointed Messiah by the Saucer People. But what the hell was I *really* doing here? I, *me*, Charlie Slack, remember? This was an insane asylum. These people were all nuts. They were out of their minds and I was going along with their insanity and being a part of it all, *condoning* this madness, lending my ear to a goof spout off and nearly believing it.

Lemmeoutahere.

With difficulty, I stood to leave, bent over and looked

Allen Noonan square in the eye. "That little speech," said I in a quiet voice surprised to hear itself so clearly, "was the craziest thing I ever heard in my whole life."

"You have spots on your face," said Mr. Noonan.

In the kitchen, Leary was holding forth with Michael Bowen while their ladies chatted charmingly about vitamin C and brown rice. Leary told Michael:

"There is simply *not* going to be a revolution in the United States. Everybody is wrong about that. The blacks are wrong, the Weathermen are wrong, the radical students are wrong."

"A lot of groups are storing up guns and things," said Michael.

"A lot of people are doing a lot of things," said Leary, "all of them wrong. Violence is no solution. The army of the pigs is too powerful. If you try to burn the pigs, they will wipe you out in no time. The pigs will win every time.

"What *is* going to happen is this: Lyndon B. Johnson is going to resign. How do I know this? Well, I know his type. LBJ is a western, ball-buster, crooked sheriff type. The big idea is to steal from everybody and then retire with the loot you stole. That's all the presidency means to LBJ and so I am sure that he won't run. Kennedy is going to be our next president, and *he* will end the war."

These prophetic pronunciamentos sounded only slightly less idiotic to me than those of the Holy Messenger in the dining room and I said so. "What makes you think you know the future?"

Leary and Bowen laughed in unison. "Oh, Slack, you've had your mind blown by *Allen Noonan!* You had better take a sip of wine or something to clear your head."

"Why not take a short walk outside," suggested Michael with mock solicitude, "sometimes that'll do the trick. Or, if you want, go upstairs and lie down."

I picked the former options, drank some wine and went for a walk around the Haight in the fog.

This walk did not have the intended effect. First off, I stumbled over a boy sleeping on the sidewalk. I kicked him pretty hard (without meaning to), but all he did was look at me and smile.

I walked through the park until the depression crept up on me and I didn't want to walk. I tried to find a bench but there wasn't one, so I just squatted under a big tree. I squatted on the ground and looked at the other people squatting on the ground. Again it came on me that I had become more than an observer of this scene. I was stoned—and I was *on the ground like the rest.*

At this thought, I arose and strode quickly out of the park, putting an extra spring to my step; I *marched* out of there so nobody would think I *belonged.*

But then marching also seemed insane. So when I got to thinking I was really trapped, I got depressed again and just shuffled.

All of these different kinds of walking had taken perhaps twenty minutes when a voice from a doorway said my name.

Out of the doorway and the body-strewn fog, under the mercury-vapor streetlamp, I could see D. It was D. all right, but she was terribly thin and pale, not as beautiful as I had remembered. A scarecrow lady with a face from Boston. I thought, D., my God, D., what on Earth has happened to you? You look terrible? Are you ill?

But I only said, "Hello, D. Great to see you. What a surprise."

She said, "Charlie Slack," again.

She smiled, and the warmth of it was still there. D., looking now not so bad after all. Kinda cute. She wore a thin white shirt with sleeves like fading morning glories and white pants.

"D., you are beautiful. You are a beautiful lady."

"Oh, I'm too thin," she said.

"That's OK. You look good to me." When I said she looked good, she did look good. Her health improved.

"How are things," I said.

"Oh, fine. Things are fine."

I took her arm and we walked under the foggy, color-corrected mercury vapors, two Boston ghosts in a foreign body-ground.

"How is the baby?"

"Oh, fine. The baby's fine."

Her elbow was cold under the thin sleeves. She moved it when she walked if she wanted to. It was a conscious thing.

"Fun to walk with you, D. Are you chilly?"

"No."

"Well, even so, I'll take you into this party that's going on."

"Fine," she said.

She went as I led her by the arm, and her toes pointed out a little when she walked, like a dancer's. Her mother had actually been a chorus girl. D. had told me that once.

D. and I had a brief time together in the very early sixties. We met under drug circumstances. Sandoz Pharmaceutical had just come out with a new hallucinogenic drug called "DMT." Leary asked me if I, as a psychologist, would want to try it out. The effects lasted for only an hour because it was injected. I agreed to have it shot into me. Zonk!

The real reason I volunteered for the drug was that I was looking for an escape. I had a middle-class life in New Jersey that wasn't working out. I found the escape, but not so much in the drug as in D. She was married and her marriage wasn't working out. She had also had DMT. About the only other thing we had in common was that one trip, but that was enough. For an hour or two, anyway.

We had shared both the drug and our fears of it then. DMT was a real dragon. It breathed fire and shot sparks over the whole world. After we had it all talked out together, we made love. It was simple. First you talk over all your bad dreams. You tell her yours and she listens; then you make love. Then she tells you hers and you listen; and then you make love again.

I needed her then more than she needed me. Unlike me, she had had lots of drug experiences. She explained things. But now I got the idea that she needed somebody. At least, you look like you need somebody, D. Do you need me?

"The party is at Michael Bowen's house. Tim is there."

"Oh" was all she said.

The party had burned to an ash. People hunched crosslegged on the floor, enjoying individualized visions.

Some soft music played from somewhere; D. and I swayed to it, nice to be together after so many months and years, really fine to be touching again. My god, D., but you are skinny. Your behind has shrunk to the spine, honey, and your collarbones show there like tent poles. Enough of rice husks and jasmine tea, baby. Daddy's got to take you out on the Diner's Club Card and get you some mashed potatoes and gravy and, sacred or not, a slice of cow.

"Are you hungry at all, D.?"

"Let's not move, I like it here."

"Whatever you want."

A woman screamed and broke our reverie. She screamed again, and D. recognized her and went over. When I got there, the woman was still screaming and pointing to another woman in a dark cape, who rushed out the door carrying a box.

"That's a witch. *There.* It's a witch," she yelled at D.

"Witches can't hurt you," I said.

"Did you *see* what she had in that box?" she asked D.

"What was it?"

The woman put her face in her hands and sat on the edge of a hall table. "She just came in, just like that. She came in with a shoe box and told me she wanted to show something. She took the top off and it was . . . a . . . skull, a tiny skull."

D. tried to reassure her. "Could it have been from a monkey or some small animal?"

"Oh, do you think so? Do you think it could have?"

She looked to us for reassurance, but we had not seen inside the box. We couldn't help not knowing, so she broke into tears again. "Oh, no, no, it *was* real. It was on *cotton.* It was a tiny baby's skull."

We all looked at each other. Nothing could be done about it. What a terrible thing. D. and I held each other close.

Then the drugs I had smoked took hold again. The whole business became a cave of bats, a witches' den, a bristling black-magic realm of shadows and shamen.

D. and I sat in the meditation room and tried to pull together. Allen Noonan was gone, but now I wished he were still here. He, at least, was a harmless, positive spirit. The whole room had now been taken over by devil-bats—well, I knew they were really hippies but they looked like devil-bats—perched from the floor-up in an upside-down devil-cave.

Skull-faced, lean witch-doctor hippies and fat-fog freak-monster hippies slowly crowded in on D. and me. I pressed her hand and she pressed back. We sat there side by side as dark spirits gathered around us, she humming softly and I a brave front, nothing more.

I heard her humming and so did they, the freaks in that room. Across from us a white teenaged devil-freak sat in the lotus position and rolled his stomach gently. Then his ugly white face broke into a smile from ear to ear. He just held that grimace without letup. And of his two front teeth, one was gone and the other was solid gold with a diamond set in it.

4

California Separates
from the Mainland

D. and I left the party before the demons actually ate us up, and we went to her apartment. It was a three-floor walk-up in the Haight, which D. shared with one girlfriend and countless roaches. D. was not working, just surviving along and covering her half of the rent with money scrounged now and then from her father, who was alive and rich to the south in Whittier. D. had lost none of her ability to sooth one's drug-blown mind and exchange fearful fantasies for real passions. It seemed I hadn't been so indulged since . . . well, since the last time I saw D.

"I'm sure glad we could touch base again," I said.

"There must be a better word for it than that," she said.

"It's a perfectly good word, honey. It means *basics* to me, fundamentals."

"You should touch me more," she said.

And I would have, too, but the girlfriend came in and pulled on the ceiling chain, sending the room's thousand occupants, including D. and me, scurrying to hide our nakedness from the sudden light. There were two rooms with no door between, and I had to get dressed as best I could behind a bead fringe.

I offered to go out and buy food for the three of us, but they didn't want me to. Instead, D. in her bathrobe began to make coffee. This was quite an operation, involving dumping out the old grounds and rinsing out the pot. Then she had to clear off the top of the stove, which was covered with pans and spoons and stuff. D. set the water on the stove in a pan and lit the gas, using expensive long wooden matches from a special "decorator" box. Meanwhile, the girlfriend was telling me about D., explaining D. to me as though there were certain things I really should know if we were going to make it together.

D.'s husband, from whom she hadn't bothered to get divorced, lived in Oakland and worked as a psychotherapist at a clinic there. He possessed their only child, a daughter about six years old. D.'s girlfriend said that D. wanted that child back in the worst way but didn't know what she could do about it for now.

D. got interested in hearing us talk about her and forgot the boiling water, so I finished making the coffee. D. lit incense and a candle and turned off the ceiling light. That made three of us around the candle, and, of course, a million eyes in the dark watching our every move. D.'s face was lovely in the candlelight, like early Myrna Loy, inscrutable and perfect. The girlfriend was not as pretty as D. and was rather domineering, coming on always with what *she* thought D. was thinking and why D. was this or that.

Here's another thing about D.: She had a way of moving her arms and body. When she walked or sat or did things like light the stove, she posed herself sideways like frieze paintings or Balinese shadow puppets. When she stood she would turn her hands out a little as though she might be joined in a ring dance. It was graceful, and although it was intentional, it was not affected. I loved to watch D. move when she washed a dish or lit a candle.

We finished the coffee and the girlfriend stopped talking and the three of us just sat there looking at the candle and at each other. I kept watching D., wondering if she was happy having me there, whether she wanted us to go on with our affair.

For now, however, it was time for me to leave. I said good-bye and kissed the girlfriend on the forehead. I had to take a cab to Leary's house in Berkeley, and D. came out with me until I got one. I promised to call her next day. We kissed and said good-bye.

When I handed Leary's address paper to the cab driver.

Indeed, the taxi ride cost a small fortune; *tick-slap, tick-slap* went the meter across the Bay Bridge. Something would have to be done so that I could get my rented car back at night to date D. It seemed like an hour before we came through downtown Berkeley and started pulling up, up into the beautiful hills around there. I had always thought Leary would live in a nice house, but I wasn't prepared for just how nice it was. It was low in front but big and roomy and, come morning, there was going to be some nice view.

On the way in, I checked on the rented car. It was there in the garage and the key was left in the ignition. The fee covered insurance, so I left the key where it was.

I let myself into the house, feeling annoyed about the taxi fare and not having access to the car. But I couldn't stay mad, because Leary had left me a long note telling me which room was mine and informing me of eggs in the refrigerator in case I was hungry. He said he hoped I had "had fun" at Michael's party and that Michael had "appreciated Charlie Slack." This was a Leary touch. He had gone out of his way to write me a note when someone said a nice thing about me. What's more, I thought, I wouldn't be surprised if Leary had prompted Michael to make the remark in the first place. Leary would do something like that if he thought I might be in need of reinforcement. Leary could be thoughtful.

He was also a good host, willing to share anything he had. Blankets were piled on the mattress of the bed, and I was given my own towel. There were even some sheets, as I recall, making it the top of the scene indeed. My room was up on the second floor toward the front but higher than the back of the house. I would have a view of the hills come morning. I fell to sleep thinking about rescuing D. from the roaches and getting her up here in a bed with sheets.

The bedroom had a row of high windows facing east as well as a big, low picture-window facing west, so the morning sun streamed into my room and woke me up. I enjoyed lying there. I felt fine, just fine. One surprising thing about all that dope was how it caused no hangover. Now, today, in this lovely house at this lovely hour, it was morning sunshine all the way.

The bathroom had a shower with hot water. There was a good razor on the sink, with an old-style soap brush. Up in the top of the mirrored cabinet I found fresh blades. I whipped up suds with bath soap and shaved myself with no battlescars while still wet and steamy. Then I dried myself off in the cold, dry bedroom and got dressed, shivering. I was chilly but had never felt better.

Downstairs was one large living-dining room, and the west end of it was nothing but glass and screen doors opening on a view that wouldn't quit. Rolling, hazy hills and then, later in the day, perhaps, the bay. The fog, low-lying and thick like a rolled napkin, was not something you regretted but was a landmark itself, something to write home about, like the bay or the bridge. It moved gently here and there among the hills and rills, folding and unfolding itself. Soon it would burn off in the sun.

It was hard to turn my back on these delights, but I was starving. I couldn't stand the thought that somebody else might get there first and eat the eggs that Tim had mentioned in his note. I decided I would cook them up and bring them out on the sun deck to eat with the view.

I went into the kitchen and was generally surveying overall food possibilities when I suspected I was being watched.

Bob was standing in the kitchen doorway as I banged around the implementae.

"Eggs?" I asked, trying to be nice.

Pause.

"In the fridg," he said in a low voice.

"I *know* where they are," I said. "I mean, do you want any? I'll cook some for you, if you do."

"No" was the curt reply. His head hung to one side. It hung so far that it would have fallen off were it not supported by the chip resting prominently on his shoulder.

"Why not?" I asked, the joy still in my voice.

Pause.

"I already ate," he said at last.

"Well, eat again," I said. By God, I wasn't going to let some post-pubertal problem child spoil my first morn in

Berkeley. I worked away with pan and fork, melting grease, breaking eggs, and what not as Bob just stood there watching me. I did not look up.

Whatever was bugging him, my cooking actions seemed to make it worse. What a change. He was OK day before yesterday.

I hummed a song, took the eggs off the gas fire and was about to put them on the plate when he spoke:

"There *is* going to be a revolution."

Pause.

"Today?" I asked without looking up.

"Ah hah!" he shouted. "You think you're funny, don't you? 'Over my dead body,' you say. And I say, 'Yes, over your dead body and the dead body of every other pig businessman.' "

"I can see you're upset about this," I said, "but I really don't get why it is *my* problem."

"Of course you don't, of course you don't. But you'll soon see whose problem it is."

"Look," I said, "it's a wonderful day. I've come all the way out here to California to visit friends of mine and I'm not a businessman or a pig—except, right now, I just want to eat like one. So if you will let me through the door, I will go out in the big room and eat and then, afterwards, we can have our revolution. OK?"

He lifted up a knife, which he looked at, and then looked back at me, and then at it again, trying to figure whether he was going to scare me with it and how far to go. He was still blocking the door, and he wasn't going to let me through. So I figured I had better give in.

I said, "You win," like I meant it. Then I put the frying pan down in the sink, hoping he would put the knife down. I tried to look like I had surrendered.

"I apologize. What can I do now?"

He didn't quite put down the knife, but instead began to clean his fingernails with it, like in some old James Dean movie. Then he reached into his hip pocket and pulled out a folded piece of paper. The paper was worn and sweat-soaked, and it stuck together as he opened it. First he scrutinized the paper himself, rereading beloved words, then he handed it to me.

"Read this," he said.

I figured I had better, even though my eggs, dammit, were getting ice-cold.

WE WANT IT NOW

by A White Brother

We want the end to all private property
    and we want it now
We want libertarian communism
    and we want it now
We want an end to the draft
    and we want it now
We want an end to the war
    and we want it now
Oppressed peoples want self-defense
    and they want it now
Oppressed peoples want complete self-determination
    and they want it now
IF WE NEED GUNS TO GET WHAT WE WANT,
THEN WE WILL GET GUNS
    GUNS NOW!
As for the pigs,
We will drive them out of their homes. We will drive
    their obscene automobiles away.
We will fuck their daughters and rip off the weird

coverings of their robot culture.
We will get what we want and what oppressed
    peoples want and we will get it now
    and we will get it BY ANY
    MEANS
    NECESSARY, MOTHERFUCKER!
Free all the men in jails everywhere
Free our brothers trapped in the military
Free our minds with LSD
Free Bobby Seale, The White Panther Central
    Committee
Free The Buffalo 9, the Ann Arbor Resistance
Free Jerry Rubin, Abbie Hoffman, Tom Hayden
Free Huey P. Newton
Free the Presidio 24
Free the New York Black Panther 21
Free all others of our brothers and sisters held on
    any bullshit crime by the REAL criminals, The
    U.S.
    Government
We Won't Wait
We Want It Now
We Want Blood
BLOOD OFF THE PIG.

I read it all the way through, honestly I did, and then
I looked up at him and figured he might not believe that
I had spent enough time on each single word, so I sat
down and read it through a second time. When I looked
up, Leary was standing between us. First, he took Bob
aside and spoke a few words to him out of my earshot.
Then he came back and got me and took me alone out
of the kitchen.

"OK," he said. "What's the problem?"

"I give up, Tim, what *is* the problem? Did his daddy cut his allowance?"

"Well, *that* kind of attitude is not going to help."

"Exactly what kind of attitude am I supposed to have? I haven't done one thing to that guy. I just came down to get breakfast and he starts in on me, accusing me of delaying his revolution. I only wanted to delay it till after I ate. I don't understand any of this. He seemed like such a nice, easy-going kid."

"Well, it's very complicated," said Tim. "There is a thing involving his mother, there is a thing involving school *and* there is a thing involving someone he admires. Right now, he blames you."

"That's pretty obvious. I mean, that he blames me. The rest is unclear."

"He thinks you, and people like you, are responsible for corrupting my views. Last night he heard me say that I didn't think there was going to be a revolution. He blames you for making me an anti-revolutionary." Slack corrupts Leary. Man bites dog.

"Bob is disappointed," Leary continued, "that I predict there will be no revolution. Actually, I am not anti-revolution. I am not *opposed* to a revolution. I just don't happen to think that there is going to be one. I am non-revolutionary. 'Aim to live,' that's my motto. I think we must achieve freedom of the nervous system before we try anything else. But Bob doesn't understand that. He thinks I should hang around more with the student revolutionaries and less with corrupting influences, like . . . Charles Slack. He's afraid you will transmit your power drives to me."

"So I represent the forces of piggery on this scene," I said. "It's Leary's movie and Slack is the bad guy."

The door of the house slammed shut. This noise drew
Leary and me to a front window. Out of it we could see
Bob driving off in the car.

"He certainly has no qualms about using my Avis
power drives!"

"To his way of thinking, that is OK."

"You mean, *he* steals the car so *you* won't be corrupted
by using it, huh?"

"He just hasn't got to know you yet, Slack. And you
don't really know *yourself.* I told him you were a generous
and non-power-oriented person. You'll get along eventually."

"In the meantime, I need that car, Tim. Do you realize
what it's going to cost me to date D. without a car?"

Leary smiled at the thought of blossoming romance.
"Well, we don't want to interfere with *that*"; then he
added, "Don't worry about the car. Jackie will get it back
for you."

"Oh, I'm not really worried, Tim. I guess I'm just
hungry."

The eggs! I ran to the kitchen to get my eggs, but the
entire pan had been emptied into the sink.

"This is the last straw, man," I said to Leary. "So help
me, I'll *murder* the little bastard."

"Now, now, keep cool." Leary smiled his winning best.
"Don't worry about food. Rosemary is planning to fix us
all a special breakfast anyway. Here, come out on the sun
deck with me. I want to show you something."

Tim drew me over to the railing, where the hot sun
soaked into the back of my neck. He put his arm around
my shoulders and told me I needed to get in tune with
my body.

"You must come more to your senses, focus on sensory energies, resurrect your body and improve your social graces. Yoga is one way. It will help your relationships with the younger generation and . . . "

"Tim, I don't give a shit about relationships with . . . "

". . . I know, I *know*, but do as I say, anyhow. It will be good for you. You need to learn how to move, how to sit, how to relax and experience each organ of your body. Your body is off-center. You *think* your center is here [he pointed to my head] and here [he pointed to my stomach], when actually it's *here*." He pointed to a spot near his prostate.

"You need to lose your mind *into* your body. Then you won't give off all those bad vibes to yourself and others." He smiled at me with his eyes squinting, much pleased at himself in the glow of the sun for having solved my problem.

"It carries through everything you do," he said. "For example, let me see you sit down. Here." He pointed to a reed mat on the sun deck.

I did as he asked and sat on the mat, squatting, and then putting out first one leg and then the other. I rested back on my elbows. My shoes looked enormous from down there.

"You see," he said, a doctor whose diagnosis had just been confirmed. "You *see*, you sit as though you *wished you had a chair*."

"I do, I do," I said.

"Well, as you can see, Rosemary and I have rid ourselves of almost all chairs. Firewood! Now, here is the way to sit." Leary just dropped himself perfectly into a lotus position, his willowy frame folding just so. It was amazing how each little segment of Timothy Leary seemed to know where it belonged on that sun deck.

"Now, as one talks, one gestures, *so.*" Leary twisted his rubbery torso from left to right and back again, and as he moved his elbows rested alternately lightly above his knees and the tips of his fingers plonked properly into emphasis.

"You see, *thus,* and *so,* and then *thus,* again, and *so* it goes. The *spine* is the secret and then the *shoulders,* suspended from above, and then the *gesture* begins at the center of the body, here where the seed is stored, and then rolls *out* to the tips of the fingers. You try it."

I tried. Believe me, I tried. But mostly I failed. However, I did think of one little idea that helped, although it was not the kind of thing I could tell Leary. I imagined I had a yo-yo on the tip of my finger and was throwing it *out* with each *thus* and *so.* Then I would catch it *back* again as I moved from side to side. That yo-yo thing was the best thing I did. At least, after I got the yo-yo idea, Rosemary came out and passed OK judgment and Leary let me stand up for a while.

Rosemary said breakfast was ready. Hope sprang eternal, but Leary wouldn't think of letting us eat until we had stood on our heads.

First, he showed me how by doing a perfect headstand himself, and holding it for about five minutes. He placed his hands behind his neck, and only the elbows and top of his head touched the sun deck. To get his feet up, he just *rolled* them up there. It was like one of those party favors that you blow and it unrolls. After the five minutes were up, he simply rolled down again.

"You try it," he said.

I tried and failed.

"Try against the wall," said Leary.

I did, and still failed.

"See how the elbows and head form a perfect tripod support? Place that tripod correctly in front of you and all is well."

Leary knelt as if praying to the sun, then placed the tripod perfectly in front of him and showed me once again.

I tried and failed again. "Somehow, I seem to need more than a perfect tripod support."

"Get Ed," said Leary.

Ed the Clown came out.

"How would you analyze the problem, Ed?" asked Leary.

Ed looked thoughtfully at me and Leary.

"I think we ought to give him one grain of mind-destroying STP to loosen up the antagonistic muscles."

"Surely not before breakfast," I said.

"That's the best time," said Ed the Clown.

"Absolutely not," I said and this time I was inspired to *really* try. Ed the Clown braced my legs a bit and I made it up. I was unsure how I was going to get down, though, and stayed up longer than I had planned. The perfect tripod began to hurt. I was in tune with my organs, all right. I could feel the underground streams of my head swelling as with melting glaciers of spring. In the caverns of my sinuses, post-nasal drips were dripping—dripping *up*. Stalactites were shrinking in there and stalagmites were growing. Also, somewhere around my center of gravity, molten lava was bubbling.

"I think I am going to sneeze," I said.

"Impossible," said Leary. "It is physically impossible for a human being to sneeze in that position. I can prove . . ."

That moment, as if written in the stars, occurred an

event long-presaged by hippie folk-lore. Lava broke through the San Andreas Fault, splitting it asunder so the western half of the State of California could slide into the Pacific Ocean.

"*Gesundheit,*" called Rosemary from the kitchen.

The earthquake left me spreadeagled on the sun deck, tripod vanished.

"I thought you said I wouldn't sneeze!"

Leary, shaking his head vigorously: "You must have exceptionally bad sinuses, Slack. My advice to you is to smoke more pot."

"In other words, Leary's theory is still correct, I am merely the exception."

Leary didn't bother to answer. Ed the Clown was doubled over with laughter. "Slack is the only person ever to sneeze from a yoga headstand."

"Some consolation," said I.

"Breakfast is ready," said Tim, to change the subject and restore proper harmonies.

A platter of small brownish-white cartwheels sat on the kitchen countertop.

"Oh, man, pancakes," I said.

"Rice cakes," said Rosemary instantly. Her lovely eyebrows lowered to show that she knew what was good for one for breakfast.

"Oh, OK." I couldn't risk another argument, but neither could I hide my disappointment.

Rosemary took a pot of boiling water off the stove with a pot-holder.

"And marvelous piping-hot green tea." She poured the hot water from the stove into an earthenware teapot, letting the aroma fume upwards, eyes closed, breathing deep.

I sulked. Marvelous, green tea.

"Do you want sugar in yours, Charlie?" said Rosemary, paying no heed to my subliminal grouch.

Anything . . . Rosemary passed me a bowl of dried mud. "It's unrefined sugar," she explained, lifting her noble nose proudly from the tea fumes.

So, this was breakfast. I hacked away at the sugar with the side of my spoon until I had loosened a chunk. I was pretty sloppy with the hacking. Then, from on high, I dropped the chunk into my tea. It went *plunk* and sprayed some droplets around.

Leary surveyed my eating habits with concern.

"Slack, you need help in every aspect of life. You are obviously the victim of an alcoholic, plastic and chrome-steel existence. You need to get away from all that and to tune in to yourself. When I say 'tune in,' I mean take the energies you have stored up and harness them to express your true intent. You are not basically a violent, drunken man but you do project some of that image. You are not meant to spend every day with a hangover from a night before, a night before spent without love because of some stupid restricting social conventions. Inside every fat Englishman is a thin Hindu trying to get out. Let him out, Charles.

"I believe in changes. You need to make a change. You must alter the way you dress, the way you look, the place where you live and the habits you form. Only then can your acts become sanctified. All actions should be a part of a sacred sequence—eating, loving, working. Slack, since you've been here, you have made some improvements, you have begun to become less of a robot. Why not go all the way?

"Much of what you do is wrong—not because you have

the wrong intentions but because you just haven't learned right from wrong yet. For example, the way you take drugs. You think of getting high as if it were like going to a cocktail party and getting drunk. You can't be blamed for this, exactly. Booze is the national sacrament of the U.S.A. and you are just participating in the booze ritual, like the other good little Americans. But alcohol is a downer. It narrows consciousness and makes you a sloppy, messy person in your thoughts and actions. The psychedelic drugs, *properly taken* with the proper attitude on your part, will have the opposite effect. They will bring you into levels of reality which aren't structured because your mind can't structure them. Thus, they free you up so that the thin little Hindu can get out and express himself.

"Take sex, for example," Leary continued. "How is your sex life?"

"I like sex."

"I didn't ask you if you liked it. I asked you how your *sex life was.* I was inquiring about your *life*, your sex *life*, a certain segment of your total existence. Do you see the difference?"

"Yes," I said. "Tell me more." I was thinking about D. Could there be a total existence?

Tim leaned back on the kitchen stool and carefully began to explain the birds and the bees, hippie-style, otherwise known as Tantra:

"There are two kinds of sex, the hot, Norman Mailer, bam-bam, alcoholic sex, which is . . .

"Sounds good to me . . ."

". . . a rape of the soul. *Slack*, I am trying to help you with your problem. If you are not going to pay attention to me, I can't do anything for you. Please be serious."

"OK." I hung my head.

". . . *a rape of the soul*. And then there is *cool sex*, drug sex. The kind Norman O. Brown writes about in Freudian terms. This is sometimes called 'Maithuna,' sometimes 'Tantric' sex. The Tibetans call it 'Yab Yum.' The idea is to mobilize your energy and hers so that two of you become one.

"Now, the more you do sex in the old, alcoholic, guilt-ridden Puritan-release way, the more you perpetuate all your sexual hang-ups. Also, you tend to perpetuate all those awkward and hostile body-language signs which stem from the basically angry approach to sex—that of bam-bam, orgasm, get-it-over-with, relief-and-release sex. After the orgasm, anxiety and guilt return and the cycle is repeated. If the orgasm was not completely satisfying, which it never really is, then you have all the more hostility to use up in the next go-round . . . and, thus, round and round it goes.

"In the Tantric sex, the man does not bam-bam the woman, in fact the man does not move. He does not try to bring on the orgasm. He is not in control and does not assume any aggressive-dominant position."

I was really interested, but Leary suddenly stopped talking. He left the kitchen and went upstairs, leaving me and Rosemary awkwardly avoiding each other's vibes. At least, I was awkwardly avoiding Rosemary's vibes. I couldn't tell exactly what she was doing. Leary was still gone when she spoke.

"You know, Charlie, I think it is good for Tim that you are here."

"What do you mean?"

"Well, you come from his past. You're a part of the old days. He can't get into that world again, and yet"—her eyes were warm—"he still is a professor, isn't he?"

Leary returned before I could think of anything proper to say. He looked Rosemary in the eyes. His eyes told her he loved her. Rosemary was telling him with her eyes that any kind of sex would do, any kind at all. He was her teacher, her professor. He kept looking at Rosemary, but handed me a copy of the San Francisco *Oracle*. It was folded to an article titled "Yoga, Sex, and the Magic Mushroom," by Thad and Rita Ashby. "Read this for homework. I will discuss it with you when you've finished." His eyes were still glued to Rosemary's as I took the folded paper from his hand and strolled out onto the sun deck, where Ed-the-Clown was resting flat on his back in the warmth. Before delving into the article, I took another peek at the kitchen. Tim and Rosemary were gone.

YOGA, SEX, AND THE MAGIC MUSHROOM

. . . Ordinarily the woman sits astride the man, facing him upright, her legs not in lotus but wrapped around his waist; the man puts his hands on her back; she hangs her hands over his shoulders. She is always the active partner. In Tantra the man becomes receptive, letting her call the tune. Whether or not his erection continues isn't important; in this position, it can't slip out.

After an hour or two of this long sweet communion (the actual duration depends on how high you are: the higher you are the less time it takes), you begin to create somehow the feeling of a third presence. This presence is made up of the two separate selves overlapping, melting down and "bleshing." When this bleshing occurs, a field is created—it pours out your pores like shoots of light opening our way "whence the imprisoned splendor escapes."

MAN INTO WOMAN

The purpose is to inhibit man's compulsion for rapid motion. Mate on lap, he can't move too violently . . . slowing a man down, eliminating his pillaging, looting motion, allows him enough time, enough eternity to experience a woman, really experience her . . .

When at last the field of electro-magnetism is whining-whining round both of you, you feel her blood flowing in your veins; scratch her back, and feel your fingernails on your own back; look into her eyes, your two eyes together create a third eye, a third presence whose eyes shine forth another color. If your eyes are blue and hers green you will look into aqua eyes—right? But then yellow eyes appear! Another presence, a new person has come into being.

How do you know when you have done it right? The communion should last at least two hours. Felt in blood and bones: we are one . . .

COOL SEX

. . . Women who practice Tantra regularly begin to look literally like flowers. The sheen of their silken skins glows with Eros. Innocence and vulnerability shine from their great soft warm dilated eyes. The communion usually inspires women with great self-confidence, for Tantra is a form of worship. Every woman is God's bridge, Sakti! Sakta! . . .

HALOES OF ECSTASY

Delaying the orgasm needn't apply to women. Women are not as genitally organized. Their orgasms do not dissipate the divine fire but diffuse it. They're more innocent, like children. Women feel just as sexy dancing or having their hair stroked. Like cats they are more tactily unusual. A man is encouraged in our Puritan/Playboy culture to concentrate his sensitivity and his feeling in his cock. Maithuna (with Moksha mushroom medicine) rediffuses man's genital energy. The entire body feels lit up in ultra-purple infra-orange haloes of ecstasy. A crown of lights shimmers round the head, and jewels of fire radiate an electric orgasm from the brain.

SERPENT POWER

This is a Western description of Kundalini, as it is called in Tantra yoga. Kundalini means serpent power; a "sleeping snake" lies tightly coiled around your sphincters. A Western counterpart is the vagus nerve which wanders all around—that's why it's vagus, same word as vagrant . . .

In the Kundalini yoga metaphor, the various sites of the endocrine system are seen as ahakras, power centers, lotus flowers. By relaxing and opening the secret sphincters, your glands which have been under-secreting now secrete abundantly. Emotionally this is experienced as a superabundance of vital power, suddenly surging warmly up your spine and out your skull. Then sky-rockets open with a sigh, and in the sky, roses-roses falling.

THE GODS APPEAR

When Tantra is successful between two people, it can then become public worship—Maithuna and then Buddhaness of the yoni, worshipped on the altar of God. To begin all this is really quite simple. The first step, get a mate, turn on by your favorite method, and begin with the Maithuna Yab Yum position described above. After a couple of hours of that you're ready to do anything, make music, dance like a god, do Tantra with a group of fellow-gods. But, whatever you do, there won't be any sense of anxiety about it. You're not trying to establish your identity. You fully exist in the Now. You are fully alive. You are One with your mate. Ready to become One with everyone and everything and every wonder of Existence. You are ecstatically aware, groking!

GROUP MAN

A group can begin to practice Tantra in a dark room listening to music, sitting in a circle, touching one another, hand to hand. Such a group, Tim Leary says, will generate a group field. A group-field is the phase before group-consciousness, the new creature, the new presence just now coming into being. At first you experience it as a tingle in the fingers, as a humming note from mind to mind, as a circuit, then as a power surge of energy, then as new consciousness: a great intra-mind capable of multi-dimensional ecstasy.

Thou art God and so is *everyone else!*[8]

I read the paper intently and so slowly that I got red from the sun. Ed the Clown had fallen asleep on his belly, and the back of his brown neck was browner still. It was almost noon. I wanted to talk to D., who didn't have a phone.

Were they telling the truth, Thad and Rita Ashby? Their prose was pretty ripe but it was, in its own juicy way, sweet and sure. It sounded true, didn't it? Nobody could write that way if it hadn't really happened to them.

I felt then that I hadn't been quite so intrigued since I was a little kid looking for my Origins in books and magazines, hoping to find a picture that would come out and show the real thing. I found such a book once.

Now I had the same awe for Thad and Rita Ashby. Well, I had a lot to learn about sex. I was just a child, wasn't I? Nothing but a baby who finds a book in Daddy's library and there are pictures of penises and vaginas and people doing it to each other—regular people. The awe of knowing that they do it and that someday you can do it too.

And as I search the pictures for answers, as I glue my eyes to pages that glimmer of past beginnings and future pleasures, somewhere, off in the upper rooms of the house, two grown-up people are doing it for real. No, they can't be. Yes they are. No, they *can't* be, not in the morning. D., we must try this one.

I spent the rest of the morning talking to Ed the Clown and helping him do chores around the place. One of the wooden supports under the sun deck was loose. Ed and I fixed it, my holding the wooden pillar or piece of telephone pole or whatever it was and Ed the Clown banging away at the nails with a hammer. On the backswing Ed the Clown would wobble uncoordinatedly, so that I thought at first he would miss the whole pole, let alone the nail, but his foreswing was, amazingly, fairly true, and although the hammer came close, it never actually connected with the flesh.

"How many times have you taken LSD, STP, DMT and drugs like that, Ed?" I asked him.

"Not sure. Not counted, but"—here he smiled at me and nodded several times—"a lot."

Before he said "a lot," I could see his computer totaling up the approximate number. He didn't give me the number, although he may have known it. It could have been thousands. Ed the Clown knew more than he could say at any given time. He spoke only in short phrases punctuated by smiles, blinks, tics and little gestures. Also, his head would nod and his expression change so that spaces meant more than words.

"Do you like doing chores around the place, Ed?"

"Mmmm." He shrugged, smiled, wiggled his ears, smiled again and cleared his throat. "Um"—smile—"to be done."

I began to finish Ed the Clown's speeches for him. "So you just do these things because they need doing."

"Mmm"—smile, frown, shrug, blink—"oh, I, mm, pretty much like."

Slam! went the hammer, missing my finger.

"Working," said I.

Nod, slam, blink. "But"—smile, hunch, scratch, clink—"but the best thing is . . ."—pause, put down hammer, rub hands, look to heaven, smile, blink, rub neck—"you know. Wow . . ."

"Getting high, right, Ed?" I asked.

"Um"—blink, swing, wipe forehead, blink, nod—"yeah."

For a couple of hours, Ed the Clown and I worked around the place together. He swung his hammer and ticked away and I asked (and answered) questions.

Ed had been married.

"Girl from the East, Ed?"

Shake, shrug, frown . . .

"Ah, from the West, then?"

Smile, chortle, heave of beams. "Um."

Ed was married to an American Indian girl. He had a Master's Degree in applied anthropology from USC. He started taking peyote in the early fifties, went native in the late fifties, discovered LSD through Ken Kesey in the early sixties and now lived off and on, moment-to-moment, high-to-high, doing odd jobs around and sponging off people like Leary. Every day, Ed the Clown would get stoned, a regular day-to-day high on hash and grass. Then, about once a week or so, he would take a major mental trip on the latest well-established big-time mind-bender, LSD, STP, etc.

About the specifics of getting high, Ed the Clown was more than usually articulate. Full sentences would emerge, seven, eight, even ten words long.

"We can get stoned now," he told me about noon or twelve thirty. "I have some beautiful STP." Smile, chortle, superciliosity, eyes aglow. "This is absolutely marvelous stuff." Ed the Clown reached into the breast pocket of his plaid shirt and felt around the bottom of the pocket among the laundry fuzz and sweaty sawdust and stuff. After a while he found what he wanted down there and, with a sure pincer of thumb and forefinger, he withdrew a white pea into the sunlight and rolled it like a jewel, blinking at it audibly and lovingly. Dropping the pea to the palm of the left hand, he flicked it carefully with the index fingernail of the right. He was looking for flaws in the exterior of the pea. None could be found.

Ed chortled and cooed, looked up at me and then down at the pea and then back at me. He pointed to the pill and back and forth at himself and me.

". . . um, I *could* split it with my knife," he said.

"What for?" I said, not catching on.

Ed just looked at me until I did catch on.

". . . good stuff. Lasts twenty-four hours." Smile, tic, etc.

"Oh, Ed, I don't think so. Not right now. I mean, it's very nice of you to invite me to share your, your . . . a, pill with you, but not before lunch, thanks. Thanks, I really mean it, Ed, thanks."

"Well, um, later then." Chortle, smile, eyebrows up. "After lunch."

"Well, we'll see, Ed."

It was not to be that day. Instead, Leary bounded onto the porch, bursting with post-coital vigor and detailed plans for the afternoon. He searched us each deep in the eyes for a few seconds to reestablish his relationship to the world of men. The phone rang and Leary answered, knowing who it was, Jackie. Apparently, Jackie and a friend had rallied in pursuit of Bob and had found him and the car. They were on their way home now. Leary outlined precise details about where we were going, whom we should see and when.

"First we shall visit the Swami "Bethdaub Djinna" and pay our respects to that noble Hindu. This will largely be for Charlie's benefit, since he needs spiritual awakening and the Swami is the one to give it. Next we shall see the Diggers in order to support our local street theater and have some entertainment in the afternoon. Dinner on

Fisherman's Wharf will be followed by dancing and rendezvousing at the Palladium Ball Room. Owsley will be there. Rosemary is calling Michael's Woman and she is getting in touch with D. Charlie will be united with D. in the late afternoon. We will meet her at the wharf. Romance will bloom. All transportation is provided by Jackie and friends. All funds are provided by the management. All is taken care of. All is well. We are off on the afternoon's journey."

5

Cures and Curiosities

Swami "Bethdaub Djinna" had established his temple in a second-floor walk-up on Fell Street, near Panhandle. Below the temple to one side was a laundromat, to the other an army-navy store. We rang and the door opened a crack while a small brown hand in a black sleeve unhooked the chain. The little Swami then stuck his brown cherub-face through the door to check us out. Recognizing Leary, he opened the door and quietly but ceremoniously let us enter.

We all smiled and bowed but did not speak. The Swami then turned sharply and padded away to the back of the flat. He was dressed, from the neck down, in a dusty black cassock that covered his feet and dragged on the floor. Leary and I removed our shoes to go into the shrine.

The shrine proper was the living room of the flat; it had two doors, a kitchen door now strung with beads and a hall door, through which we entered, bowing to honor the gods inside. Two walls of the shrine had tiers of shallow steps halfway to the ceiling. Statues were balanced on the steps along with paper flowers, candles, joss sticks, money pots and other trappings of the cult.

The place smelled of sweet dung-incense, floor wax, carpet dust and pot. Leary fell quickly to his knees to pay homage to each tinsel god in some obscure but no doubt completely appropriate way. I skidded around a bit in my socks but finally got to the floor, to kneel and watch.

Whirligig lights were flashing dervishly around behind the little gods so that they cast gliding shadows on walls and ceiling. The Swami put a record on in the back room and the shrine filled up with jingo-jango, half-tone, off-beat Hindi musik. It was loud, and it slithered and jonked all the while we prayed on the floor. After a full album, my legs squeaked from kneeling but Leary, true to form, kept up unstinting devotions.

His adorations consumed a half-hour, and then we were in for a surprise. We were beset by a young man who entered the room by leaping at us through the bead curtain. He was a half-naked white man with soft, blond hair reaching down a shirtless spine to some beltless blue jeans. Barefoot, his toenails were painted the color of his jeans. At first I thought he had stubbed them, but that was not so. He kept prancing and it became clear that his toes were undamaged and that blue polish had been neatly applied to each toenail. He wiggled and frugged in front of us, never looking at our eyes but clearly playing to us just the same. He was especially proud of his toe job, making sure, all the while, that his feet were flashed before our eyes.

Leary did not look up from his prayers, but nothing would stop the blond man from trying to get Leary's attention once he had mine. For example, the man stuck his wiggling fanny down almost on Leary's pressed hands, and was obviously bent on destroying any devotion and force attention to his own frenetic routines. At the same time, he never acknowledged our stares by even a glance of his own. As if the fanny wiggle were not enough to break up our reverie, he spun around several times on his blue toes, then stood, legs apart, blocking the altar, and began to undo his bluejeans. He did not finish the task, however, but darted coyly behind the bead curtain like a striptease lady.

I glared at Leary for some explanation, but he could only shrug. Curious to know whether the man was lurking in back, Leary got up and peeked through the bead curtain. The man was gone. Thinking that that was the end of the floor show, Tim again dropped to the floor to finish his prayers. I felt too creaky and sore to continue kneeling any longer, so I stood up and leaned against the back wall, waiting.

Well, we had not seen the last of the blue-toed fly. In no time, pants zipped up now, he was back again, and with a new diversion. This time he carried a large doll. It was a regular Raggedy Ann, red-smiled and yarn-haired, and the man thought he was the mother. He held the doll in his arms, cooing, kissing and petting. Then he slapped the doll, hard, with an open hand. Next, he socked it with his fist, grabbed it by one leg and swung it around in a big circle, banging its head on the floor and ceiling. At last, he held the doll out in both hands at arm's length, kissed it again and lectured to it in a loud, stagey voice.

"You can't get away with this, I tell you." His voice was thin and artificial with juicy sibilants. "I simply will not let you destroy the world as we know it.

"You think you have the power, you *think* you can blow us all up anytime you want to. You think your finger is on the red button. Well, you have another thought coming. You may have the power over nuclear power, but I have the power over *you*. I do, I do, I do."

With that, he flung the doll at the wall.

"*See*, you just *lie* there. You can't even get up and walk around under your own steam. How can you even imagine that you can destroy the world. You may *think* you can push the red button but you can't do it, you *can't*. Your arms aren't strong enough to push *any* button. See!"

He jumped over, grabbed the doll up off the floor, lectured it some more on nuclear irresponsibility and heaved it against the wall again.

"You can't kill us. You can't *kill us*. You are dead, yourself . . . I mean, I think you are dead. Oh, are you dead, my doll? Are you dead?"

He held the doll out, face forward, toward me and looked me in the eye for the first time.

"Is my doll dead? She *is*, isn't she?" He obviously wanted me to take the doll, but, instead, I turned my back and started for the hall door, so he winged the doll at me and bonked me on the head, with such force that I reeled about the room and bumped my forehead on the door frame. Actually, my head was hit pretty hard.

I nearly collapsed in the hallway, but the Swami was waiting there and he was able to steady me. He led me back into the kitchen and bid me sit down. The bump was bad and my knees were weak but I made it to a chair at a table they had back there. My head went down on my arm and I closed my eyes. I was quite dizzy. I could hear the Swami's voice and the blood in my temples.

"Excuse, please, the behavior of the boy. He is now inhabited by a particularly devilish devil. If only he would pray, all might be well but he insists on dancing, which only disturbs the devil within him." Leary must have come into the kitchen because the Swami said, "May I examine the head of your friend?" Tim said, "Yes," and they both began to feel the bump, asking does it hurt, which it did. After considerably pushing and feeling, they concluded no concussion was evident, and the Swami decided to back up his diagnosis with treatment recommendations.

"I believe that a vasoconstrictor is indicated," said the Swami in all seriousness.

"Yes, indeed," said Leary, "and I am sure that you have just the proper vasoconstrictor back in the temple medicine chest."

"Well," said the Swami, "now and then my friends *do* give me a little of this and a little of that and I put it away in the secret compartment of a special box I have in the bathroom. You must understand, I only use it for certain emergencies. And, of course, morning prayer."

"Of course, of course," said Leary. "Now, quickly, get the stash."

"Then, if you will excuse me," said the Swami. I pulled my head up to see him bowing off backward down the hall, saying, "Please do not leave."

I had no desire to move.

Several minutes passed before I heard the padding of the Swami again, and then some scuffling and shuffling, scratching, sucking and packing, followed by stuffing and puffing. My head was lifted gently and the stem of a pipe stuck between my teeth.

"Draw deep," said a voice so close to my ear that I couldn't tell whose it was. I was in no condition to resist, so I did as I was told—oh, three or four times—but in ten minutes I knew I had made a mistake.

Too late. First the pain became intense. My head

throbbed. Then, suddenly, all pain was gone and I could feel myself being lifted by my shoulders, buoyed up on a wave of good feelings and surging strength until, at last, again, I arrived in that first-time familiar land, the wonderful domain of dope.

Because, of course, then, simply, I was there.

The now, the immediate world. High. Being into it, at it, by it, with it, inside it. The room was brighter, the walls more wallish, the air airier. I stood to get a better view, swayed but felt absolutely sure of myself. Sure. I always knew I was tall but this was amazing. I had grown like Alice. What's-his-name, who wrote *Alice,* knew about toadstools. Many feet below, sitting curled up at a table, were two smallish caterpillars puffing on a hookah; one was brown and smiling and the other white and self-occupied. The surrounding room had grown to enormous proportions. A cathedral. I moved down the aisle and the walls receded even farther. My feet and the floor underneath were yards away. From the nave, a booming voice.

"Betta-hay"

Betta-hay? Betta-hay? What did *that* mean?

I tried to speak but could not move my tongue. I wanted badly to talk, to ask, "What do you mean, Voice, by 'betta-hay'?" but all I could make my mouth do was "Whaa . . ." I was disappointed to discover it was nothing but a long, drawn-out whoosh sound.

At the idea that I might never speak, I was frozen with panic. I sat down quickly, thinking I would try, calmly as I could, to start over from the beginning—I mean the getting up, walking around and then, when all prepared, calmly, give speech a try. After all, I had been able to stand and walk, if not talk.

As soon as I sat again, the whole surround seemed to

collapse about me as though the room were a balloon that had burst with the vacuum sucking the walls toward my head. I was even a bit afraid that the walls would hit my head, but I knew that that was impossible architecturally. I thought, then, to myself, that, although I was having certain perceptual distortions and could not speak, yet at least I knew that I was having these distortions and problems. That knowledge gave me strength: *cogito ergo sum*. Somehow, I was still in command since there was, somewhere, an I who knew who he was and what he could and could not do. The wires of my TV set were crossed. Temporarily, we hope.

As the room collapsed, so did the sounds. Instead of a booming, cavernous voice from some giant echo-chamber, a small funny voice spoke into my ear.

"Better, eh?" it whispered. "You feel better, eh?"

I tried to say yes but could not, of course, get the words out. All I could do was to stare at the brown face, which now had turned orange-brown and had four eyes. The lips were moving but no words were coming out of the orange mouth. I could not tell if he couldn't speak or I couldn't hear. I mean, I knew that I couldn't speak, and perhaps he had been affected the same way. On the other hand, his voice had grown smaller; that must have been due to my hearing's becoming distorted. If so, then perhaps my hearing had dwindled away.

I decided that there was one way to test this vital issue of whether I could hear. I would go into the temple and try to listen to the music.

No sooner had I stood again than I felt again the grandiosity of my height, the dominance, the power of my position. I, alone among those in the room, had seen fit to stand. I alone was truly high. I stood there for a moment in the doorway, watching the tiny figures at the table, knowing that they were not where *I* was, knowing that *I* had managed to rise above them. They were trapped by the confines of their table and their chairs. I alone was free to move in gliding fashion from room to room, even into the temple.

I relived the first steps of sea creatures onto land. I became the first bird to fly, the first primate to stand, *Homo erectus.* And all I had to do was walk through the halls of this old second-story apartment. Nothing to it. Could I communicate this technique to others? Not without words. Without words I was nothing. A nobody. And yet . . .

Since I had been chosen by the powers of the drug to stand so tall, could it also be that I had been chosen for some special task which required height but not words? Was I so foolish as to think I could fly? I would not, definitely not, try to jump out of a window. On the other hand, I *knew,* I mean I really understood *exactly* how somebody *could* think that they would be able to fly and might try to do it. The understanding flooded my entire being. Many other things were clear, too.

I understood how religions began. They began with someone like me getting stoned. I understood all marvels and miracles in history. I knew how all tricks were done, how Moses got the Ten Commandments and how Buddha got, well . . . whatever. I knew why all the special people were considered special, what divided the common herd from those who walked tall, the superior beings who quietly ruled. Men of few words, who did not need to talk. I also understood the special healing arts and the visions of the mystics of the past. I knew the truth of being one with God, one with His Power. I had within me at that time a power. I knew I did. It seemed quite reasonable.

You see, I was both detached and attached to the world. I was both in the world and out of it. The vast power of my mind, leashed until this moment behind the reality principle of everyday dealings and doings, was now free-floating to do whatever *I* wanted it to do. I could use the power of my mind and brain to change myself in any way *I* saw fit. I could also use the power to alter the world or to help others. The power that had been freed from being attached to the mundane details of living was now under a higher control, that of my conscious will.

For example, as I merely stood there, I could make my mind (and my mind's eye) leave my body and move, disembodied, about the room. I had read about this phenomenon but now, for the first time, I experienced it. By lifting my soul, yes, my soul, out of my body and moving it over to one corner of the room, I was able to get a new perspective on myself. I could actually see *me,* standing there as though I were somebody else looking at me. I could make out details of my face. I could see that I did not have my glasses on. I lifted my hand and saw the far-away person who was I lift his far-away hand as though he were a puppet.

If I could do this trick, and it was absolutely clear that I *could* do it, then I could do about anything. A phrase kept running through my head: "by the power vested in me, by the power vested in me."

All the superman myths of the ages were recreated for real in me. The thought was so obvious in its truth that I was quite overwhelmed. The power surged. In particular, I knew that, as a psychologist, I had the ability, now, for the moment, to change human nature—mine and

others. I could probably instantly heal anybody who was
psychologically sick. Or, to put it another way, I could
take those who, unlike me, were still impaled by what
they believed to be the physical realities of this world,
tables, chairs, pains in the head, aches in bones and the
like, and raise them into a new orbit, a new level of being,
or, to use a trite phrase, *a higher plane of existence.* That
plane was, for now, most real to me, most impressively
real. I could touch the plane with my forefinger any time
I wanted to.

But what good was all this power if I didn't use it? I
must be careful—but I must also be courageous. I must
begin to use my new strengths. I must find someone to
heal.

It occurred to me that, rather than search too far and
wide, I should practice my new abilities on those who
were fortunate enough to be around. Strange, isn't it,
that so often those who received the largess of cha-
risma were merely those who, through no particular
effort of their own, happened to be around at the time
that God chose a healer and gave him the quiet gift of
cure?

Was not the young man with the doll such a subject?
Yes, and he would be the first person to receive the
benefits of my healing gift. I walked into the hall and with
no difficulty spoke aloud to God.

"God, I am simply going to cure that man in there. Is
this all right with you?"

The answer didn't come right away, but after a minute
I heard a voice (at first it didn't sound like God's voice
but, then, how was I to know what God's voice was like?
Anyhow, it was a strange voice and perhaps, by affecting
this strange voice, God was trying to convey some extra
meanings to me.) saying, "Put a shirt on."

Now that was a strange thing for God to say. I already had a shirt on. The voice came again.

"Put the green shirt on."

And again,

"Put the new green shirt on."

If this was part of the secret of the cure, it was all right by me. Stranger things had been the hinges on which hung other miracles.

I entered the shrine to find my young subject. He was there, sitting lotus-position on the reed floor-mats facing away from the altar—his torso now covered with a smartly pressed green shirt.

"Ah," I said to him in a surprisingly clear and resonant voice, "I see that you have your shirt on. That's progress."

He just glared.

I decided to approach with complete honesty.

"I would like to try to help you with your problems," I said.

"You came with the 'great' Dr. Leary," he said. "Are you a psychiatrist, too?"

"Actually, we are psychologists. However, I have recently been granted a new power as an alienist or exorciser. I have been looking for someone to try it out on. I am quite sure I can help you. May I have permission to try?"

"You psychiatrists are all alike," he said.

"What do you mean?"

"You psychiatrists think other poeple need help when they don't."

Obviously, I had been successful so far. Instead of dancing around doing a striptease, the man was at least sitting here with his shirt on, calmly talking to me in an understandable, if not exactly rational, fashion.

"Well, I certainly do not want to force help upon you if you don't want it. However, nearly everybody can stand a little help now and then, even the strongest of us."

"You think I am insane."

"Quite frankly, I think you *were* acting strangely."

"You don't like my dancing?"

"Not in the temple, no. The Swami said he thought you should pray."

"My dancing *is* prayer. See that god there, and that one over there. You know what they are doing? They are dancing, that's what. Some gods sit but others dance. I like to dance. What do I care if psychiatrists don't like my dancing. You probably don't like my singing either. So what."

"What have you done with your doll?"

"I have put her to bed. She needs her rest. She has a lot to do in the morning, many grave responsibilities. She is the President of the United States, you know."

"I thought Mr. Johnson was the President," said I.

"Just like a psychiatrist to think that," he said. "Johnson is just a figurehead. That doll is the real President. I elected her and I know. Wait till she decides to eliminate the human world with a single press of the Boom Button. Then you'll know who is President. Johnson will die like the rest of us but Raggedy Ann, the Commander-in-Chief, *she* can't die. Just put the stuffing back in and she lives again. She will still be president then and you will be dead."

"What ever made you think a doll was President?"

"I elected her President, that's what."

"Did anybody else vote for her?"

"How should I know? Look, you have *your* idea of

who's President, I have *my* idea. What's wrong with having different ideas?''

"But a doll is not even alive."

"So what. Now look, I will *try* to explain something to you. Being as you are a psychiatrist, you probably won't be able to understand *but*"—he was most exasperated—"for example, have you ever actually *seen* this human person, Johnson? I mean for *real?* No, of course not. But you believe he is President because of the television and radio. Well, that's all it is, really, just a TV show. The government is nothing but a TV show. What has Johnson ever done with you? Nothing. Well, I happen to have my own show. I take it along with me wherever I go. Dancing, singing, news and sports. I don't like the *other* TV. I only like my *own* TV."

"Are you a performer?" I asked.

"What do you think I am saying?"

"I mean, are you employed in show business?"

"Well, I *tried* to get into show business, TV shows and things, but they didn't like my kind of act. *Some* liked it, I mean, but others didn't. They said I was inspired but not commercial. Well, the hell with them! Now I have my own show and I turn it on when ever I want. But the *point* I'm making is *this:* you are the one who needs help. You just believe what you watch on TV. You believe in Johnson and Lucy. You just sit there and watch it and don't *do* anything. I make my own TV. I elect a President I can touch. I don't need help, you do!"   .

I thought to myself that I would just let him try to help me. Maybe that would do the trick.

"In what way do I need help?" I asked.

"Well, for one thing, you are bound by media-made images of reality and you do not see the truth. Take

Johnson-as-President or the war in Vietnam. You do believe that there is a war in Vietnam, don't you?"

"Yes."

"I *thought* so," he said with a clap of the hands. "Well,
now let me ask you this. Have you ever *been* to Vietnam?
Have you actually ever really *seen* the war there in the rice
paddies? Have you ever, to your genuine knowledge,
ever, ever killed anyone, say, men or women or children
or soldiers *in* that war? Has a bullet or another such
piece of metal ever broken through your flesh and entered your body to cause pain and dire wounds? Have
you ever lost an arm or a foot or an eye or an ear in that
war?"

He paused then, and I could see his mind was occupied with the images he had conjured up for himself.
I didn't answer. He continued.

"You see, my friend, my fine psychiatrist friend, you
see that war doesn't really exist—except in one, no *two,*
or, perhaps, three or four places. First of all, your *mind.*
Next of all, your television set. And then, say, the newspapers and one or two other *insignificant* places. Just
channels, really, not real places at all. Not places you
have ever been to or ever seen or ever will actually see
or feel. Well, my advice to you is to do what I have done.
Turn these all off. They don't want *my* act, I don't want
theirs—sound *or* music, drama *or* news. Especially not
news. *Off you go!*"

He stopped. We were both now sitting on the reed
mats. He was leaning back on his elbows with legs
straight out in front, examining his blue toenails criti-
cally, turning his head and feet this way and that. I sat,
Leary-trained, in the lotus position.

He looked up for a moment from his toes at me and

then I knew that I was down again. Whatever they had
given me had worn off. I had slid off the manic, superman
high and was weak and suggestible. The young man had
converted me. I felt I was more in tune with his ideas
than I should be. He smiled warmly and held out his
hand. All was forgiven. I shook hands with my new friend
and teacher and he said,

"Now, I will get the doll for some practice."

Before I could figure what he meant, he rose and left
through the beads, returning with Raggedy Ann. He
held out the doll to me and stood, looking at the altar for
a moment. Then he turned with back to the altar and
said,

"Do you, Mr. Psychiatrist, take this doll, Raggedy Ann
to be your Lawful President and Commander-in-Chief,
to have and to hold, to cherish and obey, in sickness and
in health, till death you do part? Say 'I do.' "

"I do."

"OK. I now pronounce you *psychiatrist and president.*
OK, now kiss the doll."

I kissed the doll.

"Now hit the doll. That's right, smack it *hard.* Show it
who's boss. Now swing it around and around. Tell it
what you think. Go ahead, *speak to that doll.*"

"I hate you, LBJ," I said.

"Not *LBJ!* Oh, my, you don't get it. You don't get it
at all. Wait. Wait." He restrained my arm. "Look here.
Remember. LBJ is on TV. This doll is *real.* This doll is
here. So, speak to the doll. *Speak for real!*"

"I hate you, Raggedy Ann. I despise you, doll. I hate
you for all the terrible things you have done to all the
men, women and children of the world. I hate your guts,
doll, for causing death, for killing babies. For *war.* And

then I hate you for the awful things you have done here at home. For being such a big bully, for forcing people to do what you want and not considering their wants, for . . ." I was really getting the swing of it, and liking it. Suddenly, out of the corner of my eye, I saw Leary and the Swami looking at me through the beaded screen. Rather than stop what I was doing—and thereby admit that I felt strange about it—I continued to swing the doll around even harder and yell all the louder at it. In fact, I got hoarse and my voice cracked before I slowed down. Leary and the Swami were still staring. The Swami spoke.

"You see," he said to Leary. "The devil has left the boy." The boy was leaning against the wall, watching me closely to make sure that I said just the right things. "The devil has definitely left the boy. *But,* as you can see, it is now lodged in your friend, Dr. . . . Dr. . . ."

"Slack," said Leary.

"I do hope Dr. Slack will refrain from dancing," said the Swami. "If he will only pray rather than jump around so, the devil may leave him."

This remark made me peeved. What right did that man have to tell me not to dance? Couldn't I worship the way I wanted to? If dancing was not permitted in this shrine, why was the boy allowed to do it; why were there no signs saying it couldn't or shouldn't be done? To prove my point, I stepped in front of the curtain and turned my body so as to face directly toward Leary and the Swami. Then I performed a magnificant grind followed by a truly striking bump. Elvis Presley had nothing on me.

Leary, open-mouthed, turned to leave. On a whim, I wound back, took aim and pitched that old doll at his head . . .

There *may* have been a dinner on Fisherman's Wharf, as Leary had promised. As I remember it, we *might* have met D. there on the Wharf with the hawkers hawking and smells smelling, winds from China, *Berkeley Barb* newspapers, cotton candy and crabs the size of hubcaps. D. and I and Leary and a crowd of admirers of Leary, all hovering around the master to hear what he whispered. The impressions are in my memory, sensations, but not the substance of it. What did I say to D.? Who paid for the dinner? At what restaurant did we eat? I can't remember any of the plot, only the scenes.

I think I didn't really eat any crab. I think I just looked at it, thinking that it might get up any minute and begin to eat me. Godzilla versus the Crabman. I think I didn't say anything to D. I think she didn't say anything to me. Maybe we weren't even *on* Fisherman's Wharf after all. The only real proof I had was a burp in the cable car. That burp tasted exactly like the Pacific Ocean with horseradish.

Except for that burp and a clear memory of showing off on the cable car (I held on with one finger and dangled my shoulder so my arm brushed passing cars while my foot trailed cobblestones and macadam. D. pretended not to notice), except for that one whiff and the slight fear that I had made a fool of myself somewhere up Columbus Avenue in the cable car and had a torn trouser-leg to prove it and a little blood where the car bumper whipped my leg, I have no memory. I do not know exactly how I got from the temple of Swami Bethdaub Djinna at four in the afternoon through the sea change with rip and burp and so on and then up, up and into the Palladium ballroom at ten at night with D. in billowy bell-bottoms and low-down tank shirt in the strobelight and me with one bloody pants-leg. But there was no denying the Palladium! Fisherman's Wharf was a whiff, but the Palladium was a power-house, a boiler factory.

It was jammed. It was jumping. It was generously ju-iced out of its monstrous, collective, electric mind. Was this joint once waltzed in, or did the fox trot tread these boards? Never.

The Palladium was like the Pacific and frugging the music like surf. You had enough space to do your thing but that space was shared with other creatures doing their things. Some were dangerous creatures doing mys-terious things. There is a dance, my D., called the swim. The sharks are doing it and so am I.

D. and I are now engaged in the dance. I love you, D. The Palladium ballroom, the largest in the world that matters, has been turned entirely over to us for the occa-sion of our true romance. Can't you see we're in love? We came in with the great and famous T. Leary, every-body recognized him instantly, and so we were not charged admission. (Jackie told me that he never paid admission to any hip ballroom in San Francisco, ever!) So, it's all free. D. and me, dancing. I love you. Look at me. My thoughts. Look at me dance. See how I move. My frug will tell you how I love you.

A thousand couples celebrate our love, to our beat. Unison pistons. A thousand pile-drivers punctuate our love. The strobelights flash for us. The flashlights show for us. Monster light-show amoebas, blobs of red and orange, bleed for us. The Acid Rock Group of the Year wails for us, bleats for us, beats for us. Stomping at the Palladium.

The two of us will now become one. One with the

music and with the thousand other two-as-one couples, frugging, frugging. D. and me. Our love is everything.

The young musicians sing of love and death and dire wrongs. This is the song of wrongs. Frug to the sound of grievance, Lord. Frug to the noise of the boys. Dance to the Boom of Doom, Lord. Dance to kill the pain. Bump and fidget and hump, Lord. Look what they done to my brain.

This is the song of wrongs, Lord. These are the days of my death. Before I go to my pie in the sky, I'll hump and shimmy, me oh my. Frug my lover in ballroom ball, and ball my frugger in love. Bed-rock baby, gone to die. Bed. Dead. War! God, but I need you. One more time before I die. Shimmy and shake, rest in piece. They kill lovers, don't they, Lord? Yes, by God, they do. Dinga dong, song of wrongs. What have they done to my D. and me? Look what they done to my don't.

Whenever the music stopped, I took D. off to some corner or corridor and told her I loved her and wanted to be with her forever. What a beautiful person she was, the way she moved, her body, her face, her hands like Geisha fans. I could not stand to look elsewhere for more than a minute or two, but when I returned my gaze to her, I was overwhelmed, taken over, overcome.

"My God, D., I have never felt like this before. Not ever. It's the most . . . the most . . . extravagant feeling. I want to give something to you. I want to hold you in my arms forever. You are all that matters to me. I just can't help myself. How can I prove it all to you? How can I let you know how I feel?"

D. looked up at me and smiled. My words fell on her like a light shower or the notes of the music.

"You're sweet, Charlie," she said.

I did nearly all the talking.

"I'm feeling this awful urge to take you away, D. Come with me. Let's *go* somewhere. Let me hold you in my arms forever and go places with you. Let's walk into the night together, into the city. It can swallow us up. Who will know? Come on, D., into the belly of the city. The juices can eat away our bones. Come on."

We strode down the steps of the ballroom and out onto the street. A strung-out teenage hippie mother nursed her baby on the steps of the ballroom. They looked like Bombay beggars but D. was excited by them and passed pleasantries with the hippie mother. The baby cried softly when the mother pulled it from the nipple. The mother never smiled but talked to D. in low serious tones. D. talked more to her than to me. I felt gypped.

But then D. revealed herself to me as we walked. She turned her face down and away from me. When I looked under and around to see, she was crying.

"Oh, Lord," I said. "Is something the matter?"

I didn't hear what she said.

"What's wrong?" I asked again.

Annoyed either at me or at herself, she said, "Nothing," and then her mood improved and she grabbed my hand and pulled me toward the park. This time, I stopped.

"I need to know what's wrong."

"I said, '*nothing.*' It's just that sometimes I feel it, about, you know, my baby." At least I think she said "my baby." Maybe she said "my beautiful" or "my Barbara" or some other name. I really didn't hear but I didn't ask.

Instead, I kissed her there with her head bowed toward the sidewalk and then I raised her head and licked her cheeks where the tears had run, which made her laugh.

Still, she wouldn't look at me and everything was different . . . angled, slanted, delayed, deadened.

"Come *on*, honey, let me see your eyes. It can't be *that* bad. You aren't going to die."

"I *am* going to die," she said, "and I know when and how."

I thought of cancer and drugs and suicide.

"You're not going to kill yourself?"

"At least not right away," she said. "You'll think this is foolish but I happen to be one of the few people who know about their own death, when and how it will be. Two separate times I was told by two different mystical people. There is no way they could have known each other. Both said the exact same date and almost the exact same way of dying. It must be true. It couldn't *not* be true."

Her eyes now looked back and forth at mine and her mouth was set and firm. I had to let her know I believed her. If I didn't believe her now, I would lose her. Unthinkable. I wanted to ask her when and how but I was afraid.

"What's it like, knowing?" I asked instead.

She smiled at me and patted my cheek, and *that* was the real answer I wanted, so I took her hand and walked her into the park.

A jug band played in there. A light rain fell, more like mist. We danced in the street to the jug band and then skipped down the wet street to a place where the muffled sound of a strip-joint pit-band came through a brick wall. We danced to that and then, at last, to just the sound of the wet auto horns and the rain and crowd noises under the awnings and the record-shop loudspeakers. Then we went to the hill top in the park and hummed our own music and danced on the gravel walk the dance of tomorrow we die. Love death, D. Never part us, Lord. Boom, boom.

Finally, I asked her if it was supposed to be soon.

"Not too soon," she said.

Then, slowly, we made our way back to the dance hall, where, at last, in the crowd, we found Leary and the others, who, paying no attention to us, were swarming around a man dressed like an Indian squaw in a Gene Autry movie. It was Owsley, the person rumored to have manufactured tons of LSD. They all went into a back room. D. and I wanted to go too. Owsley wouldn't let me in. Leary said, "Slack is OK," but Owsley would have none of it. He stomped his little foot and refused to let me into the back room. D. says she will stay with me. We don't care about them.

Back on the dance floor, D. and I. Lovers.

In ten minutes Leary and crowd come out from the inner sanctum and all look happy. Something is going down. Something is making everybody overly happy. D. and I don't care. We are ecstatic with each other.

"D., I am definitely going to take you away with me. Let's go to Mexico or . . ."

"Mexico would be great!" says D.

"OK. I mean it. I mean it for real. I am going to call New York first thing tomorrow and get my money wired here. I'll bet you never realized that I had some money in the bank. About three thousand dollars. I'll get the money from the bank. They will wire it here. I'll get the rented car back from Jackie and you and I will head for Mexico City. The hell with everything. OK?"

"OK," says D.

That night D. and I made love to the idea of Mexico. As we lay together again, in the dark, the wild feeling flowed over me.

"I'm mad about you, D."

"Shh, don't talk so much."

"OK." So I touched her instead. I told her with my hands about travel and about going somewhere, deep into the heart. I would naturally lead the way. I would take her, all of her, into my hands and bring her up with me into the same realm I was in. I was on top of the mountain. My heart was faster than hers. My body was sweating, hers was still warm and dry. So what? I was going to climb the highest mountain in Mexico and then lift her up behind me, to be up on the top with her.

As long as I led the way she would follow. Why not?

My mind snapped then. I was higher than coming. The feeling wasn't even sexual, because instead of an orgasm, I was having some sort of ethereal concept about being in the clouds with my mind gone away from my body, floating around. I became some kind of spirit, a bird or a ghost. Time stopped. I was still aware, though. I knew I was having sex, moving hard and having an orgasm. I knew that I was really some kind of a person having sex with a girl who had a thin body and was just about to come and all and was making the right sounds and doing all the right things. I knew that there in the dark, her nips were like little rocks and her skin was blushing and everything else was going right. I *knew* about it just the way I knew about the rain outside and static on the radio. It wasn't a part of me. It was a grand idea, Mexico, mountains, static on the radio, ideas. When I came, I was thinking about static on the radio.

After coming, I found my ear pressed against her breast and her heart sounding like a drum. But the grand illusions didn't stop with the coming. I heard my heart with a different beat inside my own ear, sounding like the whoosh of a steam engine. At first I thought it was a railroad train but then I could tell it was just my heart. I couldn't hear her heart any more.

Then my whole body, especially my hands and my penis, got monstrous, not just in size but in importance; my heart like a railroad train, my hands like steam shovels and my sex parts like some kind of blimp. (In an old *Popular Mechanix,* I once saw a plan to use the Empire State Building to moor dirigibles.) My whole body was so heavy that I worried I might do some damage to D. I couldn't stand it. The feelings were getting worse. I had to get up. I stood and turned on the light, which brought reality, with roaches running around the remains of tacos on waxed paper and clothes dabbed in clumps all over the dirty floor.

Next day, all the bad stuff, death wishes and penis blimps, all seemed far away. I made Leary and Ed come and get me in my rented car. We left D. to do shopping for Mexico. I wanted to go to Western Union to wire my bank in New York for the money. With me beside him in the back seat, Leary laid out his plans while Ed the Clown drove us back to Berkeley.

"We have a few chores to do at the house and then a few calls to make," said Tim after I had sent the wire off to the bank. Tim leaned forward so Ed could hear and said, "We must pay a visit to the Diggers and some others and then, soon, Rosemary and I will have to throw a party ourselves. An exclusive one. Only Very Important Freaks will be invited."

Ed replied with an understanding slap of his hands on the wheel.

"Well, if you're trying to tell me I'm not invited to

some party, don't bother," I said hastily. "D. and I are leaving for Mexico on Thursday." (I actually invented the date of our departure at that moment.)

"Charlie, Charlie." Leary shook his head. "Don't be offended. You will be perfectly acceptable. Just don't monopolize the conversation. With your mouth shut you have a certain charm and, I will say, D. has done you a world of good. You seem like a different person."

He spoke up so Ed could hear in the front seat. "Ed, we must think of something to do to celebrate the charming bobby-sox romance between Charlie, here, and D. What do you think would be a fitting occasion?"

Ed's eyes began to blink. He speeded up and lifted both hands off the wheel several times to show that driving had become secondary to consideration of Tim's problem.

"Well, the best idea I can think of," said Ed at last, "would be for us to go back now and pick up D. Then we can all go up to Muir Woods." He spoke smoothly now, without the slightest tic or stutter. "Yes, indeed, we can all have a special picnic. What we *do* is to put some of *this*"—he patted his breast pocket—"in the iced tea and then we just all sit back and watch Muir Woods light up. That's *my* idea of how to celebrate."

"Celebrate what?" I asked. Did Ed really understand how it really was between D. and me? I didn't think so.

"Celebrate *anything*," said Ed.

"We will do that all later," said Leary. "For now, we have those chores. Rosemary is expecting us."

The chores turned out to involve raising their master bed up another foot or so onto a platform so that the surface of the mattress was at a level with the sill of the big window in Tim's and Rosemary's bedroom. Everybody but I seemed to understand without explanation that this alteration absolutely needed to be done with no questions asked.

Ed and I, mostly, with much directions and some help from Leary, made a platform out of boards and got the bed up on it. The bed, then, was too high off the floor. You would have to jump up to go to sleep. Leary was prepared for this hitch.

"Now we finish it off into an *altar* bed," he directed, "for the sacrament of sex and the sanctity of sleep."

To do this, two more boards were attached to the bottom, forming steps. It was much work—my holding the boards and Ed swinging the hammer in frightening fashion and Leary, always the boss, giving directions.

When we were finished and eating our reward of rice cakes and tea, I asked Rosemary to please tell me just why we had wanted the bed raised up to the windowsill.

Rosemary said she would be able to lie and see the view. I thought the extra foot didn't make enough difference. A pillow would have done the trick. Rosemary's explanation was so weak that Leary interrupted her with a lecture to me about it being a matter of a proper "vestal vista" and other aspects of the "sacredness of sex" and the "elevation of the act of love."

Later, while Rosemary took out the plates, Tim confessed that Rosemary had been roused by Michael Bowen's Woman having her own meditation room, whereas Rosemary's house didn't even have a decent place for an altar. Older houses, like Michael's, were hipper because they had real rooms that could be turned into things and not just split-level spaces without doors. (Ah, status. While the Learys had been back East losing money, the Bowens had been coming up in the Western world.)

Leary had devised a solution: Raise the bed (or rather, get Ed and me to do it), thereby to prove the sacredness of his love for Rosemary and give the Learys something that the Michael Bowens and their Haight-Ashbury set didn't have, namely an *altar on which to sleep.* It was a Leary solution. Who else could have combined sex, upleveling, broader vistas, sacred ritual in everyday life, keeping one-up on the Joneses and Tom Sawyer's fence? And the idea worked, too. Rosemary was happy as a clam. "Tim, you are a genius."

He winked. "And you, Slack, have improved considerably. You are sitting better."

I straightened my spine. My toes didn't go to sleep as much as they used to. Also, I was thinner.

"How do you feel?" he asked.

"Great!" I said.

"Good," he said. I was not quite telling the truth. I didn't feel great so much as giddy. I was far from delirious, but not so far from vertigo.

"Then you are ready for your next lesson?"

"I guess so."

"Then we will now visit local thespians, our famed San Francisco Street Theater, the Diggers."

Once again we sped across Bay Bridge with Ed at the wheel and Leary in high spirits at the prospect of visiting another oddball scene. Each span of the bridge was familiar now. 101/80. We spent huge amounts of time racing from one part of town to another. The point of it all slipped me for a minute.

"What are we doing, Tim?" I asked. "Why are we going around town like this?"

"Keeping on top," he said.

"You mean your position at the top of the scene?"

"Slack, this is my world. This is my scene. I made it and it made me. It is the way I want it. It isn't my only world. I have one in the East, another in Southern California with the Indians, and I have others, but I like to move from one scene to another. You swim in the ocean, lie on the sand and then dive into a freshwater lake. Do you understand?"

"No. Oh, well, I guess so."

"Look at it this way: You ask, what have we been doing since we arrived? I say, first we paid our respects to our neighbors and friends, then we went to a social gathering. We went to church. We spent a few hours enhancing the value of our property. We, or at least you, have been going to class. Now we are going to support our local theater. We have been doing what any responsible member of a community does. Only it's *my* community and we are doing it my way. Do you understand when I explain it in those terms?"

"Yes, I do."

"I love this world. It is one of the worlds I love. I have everything I need here. It's all very together. I have beauty, laughter, art, companionship, sex, style, *gorgeous chicks around every turn.*" (Tires squeaked as we eyed a paradigmatic sample on the corner.) "And most important of all, I have spirituality. After all, I am a religious leader and I must behave like one."

"I'll bet you are on personal terms with every stoned, kooky religious nut in town."

"Every one," said Leary.

"And so, forth you go," I said, "God or guru, to check up on the competition."

"I have no competition. They're my flock."

OK, Timothy Leary, you win. You have it made. You are famous where you want to be, and infamous too. And, by comparison, what do I have? Almost nothing. Only D., and I found *her* through Leary and she thinks she is going to die.

We were stuck in traffic. Ed rolled up the windows so the fumes couldn't get in. The car hushed inside. I asked Tim a serious question.

"What is the Leary secret of getting to be famous, not famous exactly, I mean having your own way, things as you want, and being desired and admired in the middle of it? Everybody you think counts knows *who* you are and wants you to know them. How does that work? How did you do it?"

"Charlie, Charlie, these are exactly the wrong questions to be asking at this point."

"But I knew you 'when' and I have always been your buddy, sort of. You owe me an explanation. It is an unusual world and my old buddy Leary is at the center of it. I have a right to know how you got there."

The traffic started and Ed took off. Leary's head joggled with the new movement. He just stared at the back of Ed's neck till we got up speed; then he snapped around to me and looked me in the eyes.

"This is for Charlie Slack," he said, thinking out loud and laughing. "Yes, yes, here are the terms you will understand."

"Tell me," I begged him.

"OK," he said, "Faust."

"You're joking," I said when it sank in.

"No," he replied, "but it often begins as a joke."

"You mean you . . . you don't mean it. You didn't."

"Yes, I did," he said. "Didn't I, Ed?"

"He sure did," said Ed in a steady voice.

"Oh, my God," I said.

"But that's exactly what I said, too, at the time."

We had parked and were just sitting in the car. It was time to go to the show.

6

Upside Down

One sip of the Diggers' sweet raspberry tea and I was hearing echoes. Not that I wanted to get high or to do anything more to myself. Not even that I knew for sure that there was anything *in* the Diggers' tea except raspberry syrup and oolong. It *could* have been just a conditioned reaction, like Pavlov's dog salivating to the bell. I was at the point where I would freak out just by climbing a second-floor walk-up, peering through a bead curtain and smelling green tea.

In any case, it was a decidedly altered state of consciousness involving magnification and duplication of many sights and sounds. Some objects seemed larger than life. The teacups, for instance, became like plant pots. People were heroic in proportion and the sounds of their speech seemed conveyed to my ears through the *Hall Of The Mountain King.* The echoes, annoying at first, became phenomenally interesting when the Diggers started rapping and soliloquizing.

When the echoes hit me, Leary and I were lotusitting on the floor beside the Diggers' double deckers. These beds were draped with curtains so you couldn't see into them. The whole pad was draped in curtains—like the tents of Ali Baba or backstage at a little theater. After each act, for instance, saying hello or serving raspberry tea, the Diggers and their women would appear and disappear through these curtains. You couldn't tell how many there were. They could be playing more than one part.

If I give the impression that the Diggers were putting on a play for us, that is not so. Nothing was formally staged. With the Diggers, there was to be no distinction between life and drama, no proscenium to shut off their public from their art.

"We here before you are the direct artistic descendants of the traveling street players of England. Everybody *knows* that," echoed one tall Digger with jingle bells sewn on his puttees and boots. "What many people *don't* know is that street theater is not our real bag. Our real bag is communism. True spiritual communism, zim, zim."

"Ah, yes," says Leary from the floor, looking up at the tall Digger, "tell us about that, at, at."

"If you so wish, ish, ish," says the Digger, handing his giant cloak to his giant woman so as to free his monstrous arms for gesturing. The big Digger then shoots his cuffs, which are large as paper towels. Above the cuffs, he was ruffled sleeves and huge leather doublet and bells sewn here and there. Every little movement has a measure all its own, own, own.

The Digger clasps his hands as if to hold a hoe or an ax, raises them and brings them down sharply in strenuous strokes. This is the illustration. Another Digger, just as tall, then stands and recites this accompanying chorus.

"The first Diggers were English egalitarians who cultivated common lands to protest against private property. We also, who you now see before you, are protesting against private ownership, not particularly of farm lands but now, today, of city common lands as well. Private ownership of space is immoral. This is what we stand for."

"Tell us how it all began," says Leary.

"OK, eh, eh," says the big Digger. "The name 'Diggers' was *first* given to a group led by a Mr. G. Win Stanley and his pal Mr. W. Everard in sixteen hundred forty-nine in Surrey, England. They had been taxed out of their farms by Bad King Charles the First, and believed that, now he was dead—which he was—their land should be restored to them or at least the new government should give *some* land to the poor to cultivate as farms. The group was called 'Diggers' because they believed in digging right *in* to the land. Anybody could dig anywhere for food he needed for himself or his woman or children. They were also called 'True Levelers,' because they practiced *true* communism with no ownership of any property. They were wonderful people. We are just like them. We have nothing but the sincerest thoughts about communal property and leveling."

"Fascinating," says Leary. The giant Digger smiles a piano keyboard through his lips. He jounces heels against the floorboards a couple of times and the whole house shakes with thunder and bells, ells, ells.

"Yes, isn't it!" say the other Diggers, almost in unison. A Digger woman comes among us again to fill our teacups. She wears a high-waisted silk dress and a nanny's cap. She smells like sweet powder. Unusual.

The big Digger goes on, "*Thus,* to continue the work of G., for Gerrard, Win Stanley and his courageous crew, we, the Diggers of California, the new Diggers of Haight

Ashbury, we cultivate the public lands for our food for thought. We go into the streets and into the parks of the city and do our own digging, metaphorically speaking. We demonstrate true communism in every act, complete sharing of the wealth and complete leveling of all individuals to the common good." There arises a chorus of Diggers: "*Smooth out all differences, ez, ez.*"

"Now, exactly like the Diggers of old, we, too, are harassed by legal actions and by the enemies of our level-headed communism. The original Diggers ran smack dab into the Commonwealth government, who sent soldiers and police to drive them off the common lands which should have been assigned for use by all for food. Now, today, we find the same type of action taken by the evil forces who hold private property, represented by the City of San Francisco and especially the local precinct here. When we Diggers go onto the streets to perform our street theater, we also run into opposition from those who feel that the park belongs to the police instead of to the people for the common good. In the end, the sincerest thoughts shall prevail and we, who have nothing but sincere thoughts for the common good, will release all the land for all the people.

"But neither we nor the Diggers of old ever used force. We have always abjured force. All we do is to take over land for common use. When force is used against us, we practice our own brand of passive resistance. This brand was developed by G. Win Stanley long before Mahatma Gandi and Martin Luther King."

Another Digger joins in: "We dig in. That's what we do. Don't we, comrads, ads, ads?"

"Yes," yells the chorus of Diggers and their women behind the curtains, "Yes, ess, ess," and, as if on cue, five or six appear from nowhere and take bows. All the time they jockey their legs up and down to echo and boom, the finish of Part One. As the lead Digger bows and jangles, I clap as hard as I can and Leary bangs the floor with his fist.

"Right on, Diggers, right on, on, on."

For the second act, the Diggers' cast of thousands all enter and hunch down around us, pressing back the curtains to make room. Are we to be the performers, Leary and I? The Diggers look at us. Leary tells them how happy he is to be there, how wonderful it is to absorb their communal spirit and drink their tea. He says Slack feels the same way.

"Thank you all for everything," I say, emphatically.

"You are welcome, anytime," says the Digger. "All this space in here, everything we have"—and at this cue the other Diggers look and gesture around the pad at the curtains and at each other—"all this belongs as much to you as it does to us. We are poor men and women and we possess but one genuine possession. That possession is our grand idea of communal living and leveling, nothing but sincerest thoughts. *And,* of course, we, like our ancestors, Mr. Win Stanley and his cohorts, also write pamphlets. Our pamphlets are quite popular through the world. Digger thought is catching on all over the place. In nearly every major city in the world, common people are digging *in.*"

"I should like to see a pamphlet," I say, but not Leary. He is shaking his head.

The Digger does not move. "Well, the pamphlets have been so popular that they are out of print. It's the old story, I'm afraid. No money!"

"How are Digger films and plays going along?" asks Leary, I think to change the subject.

"Same old story *there*, as well," says this other Digger with a sad expression. "It would be fair to say that the camera is ready but the film is missing. No money to buy film."

"Wrong, brother," shouts still another Digger from the back of the pack, "the camera is now gone too. Went yesterday to the pawnshop."

"But does that mean that Illegal Films is now dead?" asks Leary. To me he explains that Illegal Films was the production company. "You were making an epic. What was it called again?"

"*Level Heads,*" answer several Diggers in unison.

"Yes, *Level Heads,*" said Leary. "The story of a tiny revolution that changed the world. A small communal group takes over one small square yard of public park land to grow food and the repercussions cause the downfall of the entire Complex Society. They mail a tomato to the mayor and he eats it by mistake, thus unwittingly becoming a Digger himself. Earthshaking."

"It *will* be earthshaking, when we get the money to finish it."

"How much do you need?" I ask, with another glance at Leary, who does not look at me but just glares at the floor.

"Well," says the head Digger quickly, "I cannot say right off because I, of course, do not really know the *exact* amount—not being in charge of such things personally. Um, tell us, Digger Smith, how much does the Illegal Films project require at this stage of production?"

Digger Smith thinks for a reasonable pause, not too short and not too long to lose the thrust. While thinking, Digger Smith peers from the corner of his eye at my torn pants leg, which doesn't seem to go with my Florsheim wingtips. "I think, brother, that fifty dollars will get us going again. Now, Mary Lou, you are the star of *Level Heads,* don't you think fifty would get us going?"

Mary Lou's cheeks are the color of raspberry syrup. She can star in my movie any day. Her voice is rich and throaty. "Well, fifty would at least buy enough film to shoot the revolution. It's only black and white and we can get surplus stock from GAO." Mary Lou also eyes me up and down, coming to, perhaps, a slightly different conclusion from Brother Smith. "But what about getting the camera out of hock?" asks Mary Lou. "How much will it cost to get the camera out of hock?"

Before the price gets any higher, I think, I had better see how much funds I actually do have. "I don't think I *have* fifty dollars," I say, reaching for my pocket.

In my wallet is a return airline ticket with smudged red carbon ink and exactly five dollars in green ones. The Diggers as a whole show instant scorn, a new side of their nature, unexpected and unpleasant.

"Oh, hell, man, cut the *crap.* You'll *need* that," says Brother Smith with a snarl, "to get home on the *bus.*"

A thought shoots through my mind: Where are Ed and the car?

"Yes, *mister,* we think you had better keep your *change,*" says Mary Lou, grabbing at our teacups, planning to remove both them and her lovely cheeks from our now unworthy presence.

I looked at Leary, he looked at me. I guessed this was the end of the show.

When I went to put my wallet back in my pocket, I felt a strange bump in my other rear pocket—something I hadn't noticed. It was a thick bump. So, after I put my wallet away, I reached down into the other pocket and pulled out two items I didn't know were in there: a brown bank envelope and a black plastic folder-book the same size as the envelope.

The Diggers, who only moments before had turned away in unified disdain, now drifted back. Even Mary Lou paused with the teacups to see these two objects, which, I swear, were also foreign to my understanding at that moment.

I opened the black folder-book first. It came readily unsnapped, to display, in full glory, countless repetitions of that strikingly familiar portrait of the blue countenance of Mr. A. P. Gianinni, founder of the Bank of America. Quite quickly, I was sane. One thousand in travelers' checks. Merely a cool thousand, and in the brown envelope? A mere two thousand in bills: forty fifties. So, I *had* been to the telegraph office and to the bank. Now it came back to mind: the Chinese-American clerk at Western Union, the waiting forever in line, all that sort of thing.

There were no echoes in the room. Some Diggers stared silently at the money in my hand, others purposefully looked the other way. All of them, I know, had nothing but the sincerest thoughts about communal property and leveling.

And who was going to be leveled?

I felt a slap *down* on my back, hard, and a light slap *up* on the back of my hands and the brown envelope, at least, was gone. I stood like a bolt. The money was gone, but so was Leary. He had rolled himself into one of the curtains. The big Digger, who had been eyeing the money, was as surprised as I to find the potential common property vanished. The Diggers didn't have the money. Leary had it. I still held the travelers' checks, though, clutched in my fist. But now the Diggers were looking at the checks.

"These are no good to you," I said as sincerely as I could. "They are not signed. They are no good. They can't be cashed." As I repeated these words slowly and sincerely, I also slowly and sincerely walked toward the curtain that I thought hid the door.

The curtain did not hide the door; it hid Leary, whose face held, for a microsecond, a look of utter disgust at my ineptitude. When the look went, so did the face and the body. I followed. He knew where the door was. Out we dashed like Keystone cops and down the steps and into the car, where Ed was sleeping at the wheel.

"My God, Slack, how *could* you be so dumb?" Leary bounced the brown envelope into my lap as Ed took off into the traffic.

"I didn't know they were thieves," I said.

"They are strung-out junkies," said Leary.

"You mean they use heroin."

"I mean they use heroin."

"But how can you be sure?"

"Every indication. Long sleeves to hide needle tracks. Sweet syrup to wet their lips. And anyhow, I can smell it. Junk smells like talcum powder."

"I gather that you strongly object to narcotics."

"Slack, I have told you several times . . ."

"Not that I remember."

". . . that I object to narcotics. My friends and I— people like the Bowens, our crowd—we do not use turn-off drugs. We do not use heroin."

"OK, OK." I was angry at his anger. "But what, then, was that stuff going down at the Palladium? What was Owsley passing out?"

"None of your business, but it was not heroin. I can tell you that."

The silence was pretty thick. Ed, up front, said nothing.

"Tim." I couldn't stand the bad feeling. "I'm sorry to cause trouble. I was a fool to flash that wad. Why didn't you tell me about them before we went in?"

"Some things can go unsaid, can't they?"

A party at the Learys' was planned for next day. All the famous freaks would come. The day after that D. and I would leave for Mexico. Life was a complete joy.

Rosemary went to the Berkeley Co-op, a supermarket, with me to buy stuff for the party—rice, nuts, strawberries, plums, black bread, honey, fresh mushrooms, ginger root, goat's-milk cheese, other kinds of cheese, celery, tomatoes and strange lettuce. People in California have better vegetables than other people. The Co-op is expensive on some things but it's worth it to get that wonderful non-profit feeling. A few of the customers are poor blacks and Chicanos, but most are hip academics and professionals. This store is one of the great classy groceries in the U.S. And across the street there is a wine shop where you can get anything you want. As everyone knows, there is nothing wrong with California wines. We bought several gallons of white wine. We bought a few other things, a table cloth and a big dish. When we left downtown Berkeley to rise up into the hills again, I had two thousand eight hundred and seventy-nine dollars in cash and checks.

The feeling-tone is smooth and light. The sky is not bright but there are no clouds. We all lie on the sun deck and read and listen to the music on the stereo. D. has joined us in the afternoon. She says she likes the way I look thinner. I fall asleep leaning against the glass doors, feeling lightheaded. I dream of D. and Mexico.

When I wake up, it is raining like hell and we do not get indoors in time. Leary starts a fire, we dry out and that is wonderful, D. is knitting something. I am reading Nobby Brown, *Love's Body*. Leary gives me something of his to read, a tract called "Start Your Own Religion." This is how it went:

> . . . Into this Garden of Eden each human being is born perfect . . .

DROP OUT. TURN ON. TUNE IN.

Drop Out—detach yourself from the external social drama which is as dehydrated and ersatz as TV.

Turn On—find a sacrament which returns you to the temple of God, your own body. Go out of your mind. Get high.

Tune In—be reborn. Drop back in to express it. Start a new sequence of behavior that reflects your vision.

But the sequence must continue. You cannot stand still.

Death. Life. Structure.

D. L. S.

D. L. S. D. L. S. D. . . .

Any action that is not a conscious expression of the drop-out-turn-on-tune-in-drop-out rhythm is the dead posturing of robot actors on the fake-prop TV studio stage set that is called American reality.

Actions which are conscious expressions of the

turn-on, tune-in, drop-out rhythm are religious . . .

HOW TO TURN ON

To turn on is to detach from the rigid addictive
focus on the fake-prop TV studio set and to refocus
on the natural energies within the body.

To turn on, you go out of your mind . . .

To turn on, you need a sacrament. A sacrament
is a visible external thing which turns the key to the
inner doors . . .

Today the sacrament is LSD. New sacraments are
coming along . . .

HOW TO TUNE IN

You cannot stay turned on all the time . . . After
the revelation it is necessary to drop back in, return
to the fake-prop TV studio and initiate small
changes which reflect the glory and the meaning of
the turn-on. You change the way you move, the way
you dress, and you change your corner of the TV-
studio society. You begin to look like a happy saint.
Your home slowly becomes a shrine. Slowly, gently,
you start seed transformations around you. Psychedelic art. Psychedelic style. Psychedelic music.
Psychedelic dance.

Suddenly you discover you have dropped out.

HOW TO DROP OUT

Drop out means exactly that.

Most of the activity of most Americans goes into

robot performances on the TV-studio stage. Fake. Unnatural. Automatic.

Drop out means detach yourself from every TV drama which is not in the rhythm of the turn-on, tune-in, drop-out cycle.

Quit school. Quit your job. Don't vote. Avoid all politics. Do not waste conscious thinking on TV-studio games . . .

To postpone the drop-out is to cop out.

. . . Dropping out is the hardest yoga of all.

TO DROP OUT YOU MUST FORM YOUR OWN RELIGION

The drop-out, turn-on, tune-in rhythm is most naturally done in small groups of family members, lovers, and seed friends.

The directors of the TV studio do not want you to live a religious life. They will apply every pressure (including prison) to keep you in their game.

Your own mind, which has been corrupted and neurologically damaged by years of education in fake-prop TV-studio games, will also keep you trapped in the game.

A group liberation cult is required.

You must form that most ancient and sacred of human structures—the clan. A clan or cult is a small group of human beings organized around a religious goal . . .

You must start your own religion. You are God— but only you can discover and nurture your divinity. No one can start your religion for you.

. . . For thousands of years the greatest artists, poets, philosophers, and lovers have used con-

sciousness-expanding substances to turn on, tune
in, drop out. As part of the search for the meaning
of life. As tools to reach new levels of awareness. To
see beyond the immediate social game. For revelation. For light in the darkness of the long voyage.

Every great burst of activity has grown out of a
psychedelic turn-on. The visionary then rushes back
to tune in, to pass on the message. A new art form.
A new mode of expression. He turns others on. A
cult is formed. A new TV stage set is designed, one
that is closer to the family-clan-tribal cell structure
of our species.

Do you wish to use marijuana and LSD to get
beyond the TV scenario? To enhance creativity? As
catalysts to deepen wisdom?

If so, you will be helped by making explicit the
religious nature of your psychedelic activities. To
give meaning to your own script, to clarify relationships with others, and to cope with the present legal
set-up, you will do well to start your own religion.

HOW TO START YOUR OWN RELIGION

First, decide with whom you will make the voyage
of discovery . . .

Next, sit down with your spiritual companions
and put on a page the plan for your trip . . .

Develop your own rituals and costumes. Robes or
grey flannel suits, amulets or taboos. You will eventually find yourself engaged in a series of sacred
moments which feel right to you.

Step by step
  all your actions

will take on a Sacra
mental meaning. Inevit
ably you will create a ritual
sequence for each sense organ
and for each of the basic energy ex
changes—eating, bathing, mating, etc. . . .

Spell out on paper explicit plan$ for handling
financial interaction$. Money i$ a completely irra-
tional focu$ for mo$t We$terner$. A$ $oon a$ your
clan member$ detach them$elve$ emotionally from
money, you will discover how easy it is to survive
economically . . .

Sexuality is the downfall of most religious cults.
Clarity and honesty are necessary. Karmic acci-
dental differences exist in people's sexual make-
up . . .

Your mode of sexual union is the key to your
religion. You cannot escape this. The way you ball
(or avoid balling) is your central sacramental activity. The sexual proclivity of the clan must be explicit and inflexible . . .

. . . You will find it absolutely necessary to leave
the city. Urban living is spiritually suicidal. The cities of America are about to crumble as did Rome
and Babylon. Go to the land. Go to the sea.

. . . Use psychedelic sacraments only in desig-
nated shrines and only with members of a psychedelic religion. If you are going to be naughty and
smoke pot in the washroom of one of Caesar's stage
sets, why that's all right—but be clear; you waive
your religious rights. Do what you will, but be conscious and don't mix up your naughty game with
your religious game . . .

In all of these activities there is no hostility, no competition, no conflict with Caesar. Love and humor are the means. The ends will follow.[9]

Is Leary right? Will the hippies conquer the world? Will money go out of style? Will people live in clans and tribes? Will everybody drop out? Will the middle class smoke pot? Will the whole world turn on? In the tract, Leary concludes:

> . . . This revolution has just begun. For every turned-on person today I predict that there will be two or three next year. And I'm not at all embarrassed about making this prophecy because for the last six years . . . I have been making predictions about the growth of the new race, and have always been too conservative. Let no one be concerned about the growth and the use of psychedelic chemicals. Trust your young people . . . Trust your creative minority. The fact of the matter is that those of us who use LSD wish society well. In our way we are doing what seems best and right to make this a peaceful and happy planet . . . Trust the evolutionary process. It's all going to work out all right.[10]

Sleep, with D. knitting.

Wake to buzz in the head and timeless evening. In the fire are dragons and in the dragons are emeralds. Rich stones of the Orient in the bellies of lizards with round ruby eyes. The mouth of the dragon is opening and closing as I breathe. It spits pearls of blue flame. D. is still knitting. Love.

We are joined by a couple of guests of Leary's. A leopard and his girl, who is a golden-skinned gypsy mother who nurses her baby all the time and never speaks. The black cat is into something beautiful with his body. He moves like Hindu magic, his thumb and forefinger always mark a perfect eye of the peacock. It is the slow-motion Krishna. My sweet Lord.

And, then, bursting like fireworks, is the incredibly beautiful scene, D. knitting, the fire creating pearls, the black god entranced on the floor, the tiny hippie mother over by the fire with the tiny baby and everything, all of these wonders, wrapped in the glow of the emerald ambient light of the mind dragon. The shine of Shiva. O, strange gods, and mysteries of sight. This moment will show forever.

"Tim." I crawled over to Leary, sitting with his back propped against the wall and legs outstretched, surveying the wonders his house possessed at this particular instant eternity. "Tim, I know this religious jazz is just an excuse to get high, isn't it?"

"Of course," he said, "it's the only excuse that's worthy of the scene."

I agreed.

Then, later still, when the black cat had withdrawn with the little white mother of his tiny black kitten, I reached for D.'s hand and drew her up the stairs with me through the black of the hall and into the star-lit bedroom. There, among the shadows of stars on pale sheets turning icy damp, I closed the gap between us, forever. Or, at least, that's what I thought.

But my thinking wasn't too good. Only my sense of beauty was working. I was not in my right mind. The time was mine alone, not hers, and, even knowing she was awake, I fell asleep and dreamed of bats.

"Charlie," she called softly to me at some small hour,

waking me from my hang perch, upside down. "Charlie, I want to tell you something."

"Yes."

"I don't want to go."

"Oh, fine. That's fine. Go where?"

"I don't want to go to Mexico."

"OK, then we won't go to Mexico."

"But I mean I don't want to go with you."

"With me?"

"Charlie, wake up and listen to me."

"OK."

"I'm getting my daughter."

I was trying to understand but my head was not on straight. I still had wings.

"I need her and I am going to get her. He can't keep her away from me. Not with all the lawyers in San Francisco. Do you know about custody law? Well, they hardly *ever* give custody to the father unless, of course, he proves that the mother is completely, completely unfit. Well, he proved it. He just proved it, I mean to the judge, he proved it but he didn't prove it to her. Not yet. So, I'm going to get my baby."

"OK. OK. Is there anything I can do to help?"

"You're in no condition to help."

"Come back soon, let me know, you know I need you, honey."

There was no answer. I heard her dress quickly, moving quietly about the room, then I fell stoned asleep, again into my cave.

In the morning it dawned on me that she was gone. There was not a trace of her in the room. She had taken the car keys and all the money except the travelers' checks.

Downstairs, during morning tea and rice cakes, everybody asked about D., everybody but Ed. He didn't say anything. Maybe he knew. I didn't want Leary or any of them to know that she had taken the money. She really had needed to borrow the money for her daughter and would return it to me. If Leary was to find out about the money, it might needlessly cheapen his opinion of her. She would return. She *had* to. When I saw her again, I could find out what was wrong and fix it. Also, Leary would, if he knew, undoubtably think me even more of a fool than now. She had just gone on an errand and would return any minute.

Leary was busy arranging to get the "group radar" operating to announce the party. It was to be a going-away party for me and D. Many important people were coming, artists, poets, freaks, hippies, actors, musicians and hip intellectuals. No liquor was to be served, just the light wine Rosemary and I had bought.

"The host never provides psychedelic refreshments to people like this," said Leary. "The truly hip people of this world provide their own highs. That is but one of the major differences between the cocktail party and the modern gathering such as you shall see today."

My heart fell every time somebody mentioned D. Rosemary asked me when D. was going to get back and would she help in the kitchen. I said "soon" and "yes." The phone rang with partygoers asking time and place details. Leary explained that the party was to celebrate a "romance and a trip" by two friends of his. It was just awful. Next time the phone rang, I walked away so as not to hear him talk. I just knew she would never call. And she didn't. Each minute etched my humiliation deeper. Finally, I asked Ed what he knew. He slept on the living-room floor near the front door and might have gotten to talk to her before she left.

Before he came around to the point, he blinked and blundered. "Why should you care?" he volunteered. "Get high and forget it all. There are"—pause, pause—"more fish in the sea."

"But what did she say?" I asked again.

"Well, actually, she said she was leaving you."

"But did she say *when* she was coming back?"

"She didn't say she *was* coming back."

I was whispering hoarsely. "But did she say *why?*"

"Do you really want to know or wouldn't you just rather forget about it?"

"I want to know why."

"Well"—an interminable pause was accompanied by every tic in the repertoire—"she said it had something to do with your being too much. 'Coming on too strong,' I think she said. Also, she said you were getting into too much drugs and she didn't want her daughter to be around you. That must have been just an excuse, though. She sounded pretty square about it. You must have done something to turn her off."

I couldn't answer. The house was filling with people, famous people with famous love lives, some of them. Richard Brautigan, the poet, smiled at me and handed me his trademark—an envelope filled with vegetable seeds. The Michael Bowens bowed and said hello. Susan and Jackie were there with friends. Folks gathered in groups to talk about political matters, their harassments by the Establishment, their plans to embarrass Amerika, their arrests. People cooed softly about their hippie homes, their hippie children. Food and wine were put out. Music played. A fine rain came. I went to Leary, nearly in tears.

"I think she isn't coming back," I said.

"Oh?"

"Talk to Ed about it," I said.

"I will."

He did.

Leary came back and said he was sorry but that life would have to go on as usual.

The party went on but I couldn't. I climbed up and lay down but that made it worse. Back on the steps, I looked down at the group. I caught Ed's eye, and he came over to the stair side. I sat on the steps and he stood on the floor. I placed my finger on his shirt pocket and whispered in his ear, "OK, Ed, now let's split that pea."

It took an hour of anticipation before I knew what this one was going to be like. It was going to be like turning to wax and stone and becoming a tree or a bat. Waxy flexibilities. I could place myself in some posture and remain there forever—or until one of us gave out, the drug or me. Nothing else except some detachment and sparks in the antagonistic muscles. I watched the party. However, there was to be more. The influences piled up and up until I was granite. There were to be some involuntary movements (well, my oh my), interesting rolling motions of the hands and graceful but uncontrollable movements of the arms. So I was going to be made to do things, was I? I was made to sit slowly into a lotus and my stomach began to roll and my shoulders heaved to the rhythm of a distant drummer. I had not written this script!

Slowly and gracefully, I was lifted by strings until my arms and hands pointed to the rafters. The moves were not mine. I was not to see what I wished. My eyes were forced to search for a place where I could . . . could . . . *suspend* myself. I was not hurried in this task. I looked at each wall. On one wall in the dining area near the food table, I found a big nail holding up a heavy mandula and five feet away from the nail was the end of a beam. If I stood on my toes, I could just reach. I took down the mandula from the nail and then waited for the next move. The move came and I was lifted to my toes and turned around so that my back was to the wall. My right hand was raised exactly to the nail, which I clasped between my thumb and forefinger. My left hand lifted itself upward and drapped itself over the beam. The string holding my head broke and my chin fell like lead on my chest. The world turned beneath me. The party went slowly on its way to the end. Somebody brought in a big blue tank of nitrous oxide and half the guests proceeded to get gassed. The other half went home. I spent all that night as a bat in a black mass, hanging from my parody of the cross, feeling no agony, knowing that I was possessed. In the morning, I was mock-dead and mock-buried on the sun deck, and on the third day I rose again and flew back to New York on American Airlines 727, non-stop, Tourist, Kennedy.

7

Going Downhill
in New York and Beyond
in the Sensational Sixties

So that's the story of how an ordinary New York psychologist and alcoholic pop-writer became, at least for one week, a freak loony and monster madman hoist by his own petard. And let me assure you that every incredible event of the story is the truth, the whole truth, etc. Only the credible events are lies. I have fudged a little about persons and places, trivia and terrain, just to protect the innocent and save the guilty from more than their share of dues. On the other hand, I tried to represent Leary and me exactly as I knew us then, to accurately expose the charm, danger, foolishness and morbidity of the microcosm. That world seemed insane to me then most of the time, as it does now. But I was insane then myself, more so than now. We all were, I'm afraid.

When I left San Francisco in late April and returned to New York, I thought I could pick up the threads of my real, or New York, life. The prevailing view of the sixties was that one went from scene to scene with no lasting influence. There was to be no adding up of the sins. If personal integrity was in jeopardy, nobody cared. "Awareness" was the only character trait that mattered —the rest was *Boy Scout Handbook,* Miss American Pie.

So anyhow, I came back to my normal, New York routine. Trouble was, the old pieces no longer looked so normal. Routine, yes, but not sane. My San Francisco trip had been an episode of acute insanity. Now my New York life was just a chronic phase of the same disease. Having freaked out on the West Coast, I now freaked in on the East, settling into the boozy pattern with its alienation and stereotyping of relationships, and I couldn't (or wouldn't) do anything to change.

I was never concerned about myself. Nothing mattered much. I dropped a few more inhibitions (or values, depending on how you looked at it), I ate and drank more, I worried less about myself and others. I was going downhill. I didn't care.

Going downhill in New York is easy. Follow the simple directions, follow the crowds into the joints. I was not leading the trip to hell on a bandwagon, like Leary, but I was getting there just the same.

I arose late in the morning and dragged myself downtown to a dusty one-room office I had set up to write with my collaborator. (We were working on some reading materials for school children.) Then, in the afternoon, I argued on the phone with our publisher about leaving the good stuff in. It was forever a battle. At six I would head for one of about five drinking places where I was well-known and liked. Next, I would go to a restaurant and overeat. After that, my evenings began among the singles' haunts of the Upper East Side of town. Everything was done with the eyes.

You never got to know anybody, leastways not all the

way through. In fact, that was one of the things you talked about with girls—how we didn't really know each other all the way through. Talking about alienation doesn't cure it. I remember a girl I met in a singles' bar, Friday's. She was a very intelligent girl and we talked about art and philosophy and old comic books and, of course, alienation. Also, she liked swing music. I liked her views and she was really a nice person, so I said what the hell and took her to Sam's for dinner. She wasn't used to having money spent like that and she didn't act married. The married ones always had girlfriends. Cozy Cole was up at the Rainbow Grill and it was never crowded there, so I took her up and we did the Big Apple. Nothing makes you laugh and laugh at each other like doing truck on down in the Big Apple. I think she liked me. We shared opinions on everything, and she never brought up horoscopes or other cheap talk. When we ran out of opinions, we talked about immediate feelings, which was all the rage. Finally, we ran out of feelings and I started to tell her about my job at the university and a problem with a student. She stopped me, saying, "Don't feel obligated to tell me about your personal life." I changed the subject. On Monday morning, I offered to take her to where she was going but she refused. I was only supposed to meet her at Friday's. I did just that a couple of times more. We shared every thought in our heads while we were together but, as far as she was concerned, I could have been Wayne King or Bruce Wayne, and as far as *I* knew, she could have been Brenda Starr or Tillie the Toiler, and that was going to be that, forever.

Once or twice a week I would go by my magazine, which was dying, and pick up, from an editor, who kept being fired and replaced, some absurd article assignment ("Twenty Ways To Be More Loved," "Do You Have Rock-Star Quality?") destined to help shorten its life. Three times a week, I taught my course at Columbia Teachers College: fifteen nice middle-aged ladies listened carefully and worked hard to get advanced degrees to rescue themselves from the fifth-grade classroom and make them (ah, that sensational word) "authors."

And so my days were filled with assignments about which I didn't care but which I didn't reject (I was very professional), and my nights were filled with the kind of sensation that attends the opening of pornographic films. Acute is exciting but chronic is dull: how thrilling our first hour in hell—but how boring the next millennia.

My life was boring because it lacked the loving influence of responsibility to others. Irresponsibility characterized the age. Nobody cared. Leary once told me, "There is no such thing as personal responsibility," adding that it was "a contradiction in terms." I couldn't believe he meant it so I asked him, what about children. He replied, "Responsibility for children ends at birth."

In retrospect, such neglect seems as ridiculous as it was tragic, because our responsibility toward each other is one thing that can keep us from making complete asses of ourselves. So, I am now convinced that in the long run even the soberest accounts of the mad sixties will make its characters, New York and San Francisco, look foolish. Far more silly than sanctified, despite the religious experiences and the pious put-ons and pompous, hipper- and holier-than-thou attitudes. In the beginning, Allen Ginsberg had said, "Do not hide the madness," so they didn't. They let it all hang out, baby . . . and it was folly, mostly folly.

Extraordinary folly. Like the Great Cataclysm. Many intelligent, hip Californians in the late sixties became genuinely convinced that their part of the North American continent was going to detach itself from the main body. This expectation took several forms, including the San-Andreas-fault or California-sinking-into-the-Pacific prophesy. New Yorkers had different beliefs. New Yorkers believed in nuclear holocaust, nerve-gas release, massive contamination and the like. So what's with sliding into the ocean?

Hip people weren't the only holocausters. Squares had plenty of absurd, catastrophic visions: for instance, a world of brittle bones from fluoride, or one overrun by hippies. Hip and square, East and West, each had his own view of disaster.

Catastrophic beliefs and absurd behavior. Why did people *do* such things—take dangerous drugs, dress like tatterdemalions, mouth absurd slogans, print salacious tracts, quit their jobs, burn classrooms, lie in the park all day, dance in the street at night, live in filthy pads, worship strange gods, riot, and make love to everybody in sight? And in between, why was life so dull, nothing but *angst* and stupor? The job dragged on, the divorce awaited settlement, the present affair edged into the future affair, the war continued, things got worse (not definitely worse but probably worse) while one waited for the next chance to get some kicks. Why was Leary right? Why were we all dropping out, not just students and writers but housewives, businessmen and teachers?

I think the insanity of the late sixties was mainly caused by the war. But it wasn't just the war or only the war. Another reason was obviously the drugs, because they added to confusion and weakened discrimination, but the drugs didn't cause riots, revolts and revels. (By and large, the major effect of the drugs of the sixties was stupor.) "Life style" has been touted as a reason. I don't think the main reason had anything to do with life. I think the main reason had to do with death, Big Death.

Big Death is my term for a certain imminence, a feeling that there is not going to be any future, for anyone. Big Death is a nuclear bomb in the hands of an Algerian terrorist being chased through the nerve-gas dump by an Alabama sheriff. In the late sixties, Big Death meant all-out race war or revolution, nuclear holocaust, the world coming to an end, California sliding into the ocean, that kind of thing. Everybody in the sixties believed in Big Death. Some were frightened of it, some were resigned to it, some believed that it held secret knowledge for them and they were special people because of knowing how and when it would come. Even level-headed people realized that the chance for survival of the human race had dropped several points, but for them this was not a cause for an impulsively altered way of life. Most of us, however, were too unstable to place in proper perspective the probability of world's end. For us, I feel there were at least three reactions to the idea of Big Death. These I call Group Last Rites, Ignoring Small Death, and Big Wake.

COLLECTIVE PREPARATION

Hell-with-tomorrow drug taking, neck-risking life styles, apocalyptic music, chants and prayers, and insane group murders (Manson) were all examples of Group Last Rites, as was group occult spiritism, which blurs the boundary between this world and the next.

I found myself impatient with optimistic people—

didn't you? I hung around more and more with people who were down. And I don't mean poor. (Eric Hoffer says that the poor lead purposeful lives scrambling for each day's bread. They may have been skipped by the madness.) No, indeed, the carelessness of dress, disregard for sanitation, the lack of plans for bed and board by the people I knew, were not necessitated by poverty but were practiced as positive Big Death values. To be completely beat or strung-out was to give evidence that one was "aware." Aware of what? Well, mainly, I think, that the end was near.

BIG NEWS.

People differed as to the form and substance of Big Death. A few held to a kind of apocalyptic model, the blessed and the damned, that sort of thing. Others believed that the end was simply an end which would come for all. Believers became transfigured. Henny Penny, the sky is falling.

But screaming doom was only one phase of the hysteria. Some became rather cool and spaced about it. After all, they had plenty of time to adjust to the idea, take some drugs and see how the idea went down while high. Then, each day could be lived as though it were the last. How better to spend one's last hours than getting *into* the depths of a flower (knowing it might be the last flower ever to bloom) or seeking out the eyes of (doomed) passing children?

WHERE IS THY STING?

In the careless sixties, everyday, ordinary, *individual* death was small potatoes compared to Big Death. Big

Death was bigger than all the small deaths in Indochina. It made all the highway deaths seem like nothing. Death by disease, drugs, murder and the other ravages of city life were trivial beside Big Death.

Big Death was the square justification for Vietnam violence (prevent all-out nuclear war) and the hip justification for deadly drugs. Because of it, the President of the United States could order the killing of women and children and a hippie could watch his friends die of drugs and not be bothered. It would all stop soon anyhow. Everybody would get theirs if the boom went off, the big overload in the sky. Tomorrow, maybe.

BIG WAKE.

Then there were those, heavily into drugs, who felt that they were already dead. No kidding! The conviction that one has already passed through the veil is a common consequence of taking large doses of hallucinogens. Of course, to produce a lasting impression of having died and gone beyond (Big Wake Experience) requires heavy indulgence in really strong drugs. Or, now and then, a real-life experience such as a violent narrow escape can do it.

Leary had both. Before ever taking any strong hallucinogens, in 1959, he had a Big Death Experience in an apartment tunneled in rock at the foot of Calle San Miguel:

"It began in the head . . . My hair was a cap of fire . . . my face began to swell . . . In the morning I was blind —eyes shut tight by swollen tissue and caked with dried pus . . .

"By night the disease had spread to my extremities. My wrists and hands were swollen . . . I was weak and trembling. I slumped in the chair for the rest of the dark night, wrapped in a Burberry mackintosh.

"I died. I let go. Surrendered.

"I slowly let every tie to my old life slip away. My career, my ambitions, my home. My identity. The guilts. The wants."

In Leary's experience, Big Death is then followed by Big Wake.

"With a sudden snap, all the ropes of my social self were gone. I was a thirty-eight-year-old male animal with two cubs. High, completely free.

"I could feel some seed of life stirring inside and energy uncoil. When the dawn came I moved my hands. The swelling was gone. I found a pen and paper. I wrote three letters. One to my employers, telling them I was not returning to my job. A second to my insurance agent to cash in my policies. And a third long manuscript to a colleague, spelling out certain revelations about the new psychology, the limiting artifactual nature of the mind, the unfolding possibilities of mind-free consciousness, the liberating effect of the ancient rebirth process that comes only through death of the mind.

"The ordeal in Spain was the first of some four hundred death-rebirth trips I have experienced since 1958. The first step was non-chemical. Or was it?"[11]

Leary had another, earlier, Big Wake reaction after the suicide of his first wife back in the fifties. Any suicide is a dirty trick on the survivors, but a get-even suicide causes a Big Death trip. Hers was obviously such a retaliatory act: She did it on his birthday.

The reaction was not what you might think. Living each day as though it were *his* last, now, he swung himself into life in an explosive and risky fashion, hoping that the excitement would erase the memory. Instead of feeling guilty, the survivor became even more irresponsible and careless of others.

The worst had already happened. Nothing in his future, not even his own death, could compare. His became a charmed life with many narrow escapes. After all, she could have killed him, too, while she was about it, but instead she left him here for some unusual destiny.

Death held no terrors, and he could do anything at all with his life.

"High, completely free."

Such free impulses, unleashing the repressed to do anything and everything just because it is one's *own* thing stemming from one's *own* inner seeds, was the inner origin of the madness of the sixties. The outward reality causing the same madness was the variety and certainty of technological overkill. From these roots grew the full flower of what Freud and Marcuse had carefully predicted to have two parts: the sexual or life-wish component, Eros, popularly known as the "sexual revolution," and the death wish, Thanatos, *Big Death.*

Realistically, the pill and penicillin caused the sexual revolution, whereas on Death's side we had the war, the bomb, politicians, pollution and overpopulation. A dash of drugs weakened the ego still more and, voilà, the flower of the madness bloomed one night. Surprise! It pressed through the cracks in the institutional foundations, a deadly riot of the collective unconscious, furious orgy of juicy sex, paroxysms of the body politic and rips in the fundament of social control.

Most people were touched by the *meshugaas,* rich and poor, right and left. Some went loony flat out. Some slowly crescendoed in a tarantella. Some did it alone, others in hysterical tribes. The variety was endless, the magnitude extreme. By the standards of the fifties, when I was a clinical psychologist, we are all nuts today. Of course, as the pendulum swings back, we recover a bit— but never to the same level. Farewell fifties. Goodby Columbus. We can never go home again to Ozzie and Harriet. We don't even want to.

WAS ESCAPE IMPOSSIBLE?

Well, to avoid lunacy in the late sixties, one had to be resistant to group pressure, able to withstand intense confrontation from both right and left. Enormous patience with human folly was required. A sturdy belief in the hereafter coupled with a proper respect for life on this Earth was necessary in order to keep small death in mind and not overreact to Big Death. Also, one probably had to be religious (to avoid Big Sin) but without the slightest overreliance on religious organizations (which always let one down) and without falling into believing oneself to be God (the madman trap of Leary's religious trip).

One had to avoid becoming drugged or drunk, and this largely meant avoiding those who used drugs or drank too much. I think, furthermore, that to avoid prolonged contact with the madness, one had to reside somewhere away from the centers of infection, the big cities, college campuses and other "in" gathering grounds. One couldn't be in the war, of course, without being driven insane by it, nor could one work for the

industrial-military complex or the media. Most occupa-
tions were infected in one way or another, yet dropping
out was almost more risky than hanging in. One couldn't
teach without great risk of being overly influenced by
students. Or, if you were immune to influence by students, you were likely to be "confronted" by them—
causing the square, or reactionary, variety of the plague.

Lest we go too far and conclude that nobody could
escape the madness of the sixties, let me say that I
finally met one who did escape—and a New Yorker,
too. I was fortunate in meeting this sane person in
1969, the end of the decade. She saved my soul. Her
name was Eileen and she had a highly unusual background as a liberated Catholic who had been a nun.
She left her order before the order got to her; the
convent had not yet driven her mad but, rather, had
merely isolated her from the insane ambience. All
things considered, she and her ex-nun friends were
the finest people I met during the latter part of the
decade, and the most normal, by contrast to myself
and everyone else I was aware of at the time.

But my level of awareness was low. I didn't even see
her at first. She was a nun, nuns were dull. Everything
was dull, as I recall. Movies were longer and duller. I
didn't see them either. The stock market was going right
down. The magazine dimmed (along with all the stars in
it). Drugs were downers. Barbiturates and tranquilizers
were obviously flat-out dull. If you had real money,
which I didn't, or were really bad, which I wasn't, you
took cocaine, which was subtle but dull. Politics was dull.
Everything, the whole world, I mean the same world that
was supposed to have come to an end and didn't. Instead, it went on and on. Tea for two.

We mustn't forget to mention Old Multiversity. Departmental meetings and cold eggs in the cafeteria. Specific objectives in general terms. Visions of Summerhill while waiting for the bell.

Now, if I had had a better *attitude* (remember attitudes?), I could have opened my eyes and seen where I was and known what I was doing and all that. But I didn't.

And that's why I never got to know Sister Eileen when she was a nun. She had her desk in a part of the room we used for the dullest meetings. I met no one at meetings.

Especially when Earwig was running things. Earwig, acting chairman of checklists and professor of passive voice. He hated my guts. That was because I knew everything he would say before he said it. Earwig had a one-track mind, a low-gauge slow freight with whistle-stops at each point on the agenda. And what *was* the agenda? Item after item of Who Did What That Was Wrong. And who had done all the wrong things? Why, me, of course. Ho hum.

Except that at this *particular* meeting, there was this chick, Miss Eileen Newton. No, a lady professor. No, by God, a *chick*. And exactly what was she doing here, listening with her tiny ears to Earwig and the other memorandum-mouths and mugwumps? What, indeed, figuring so prominently in her pink and white mini from, say, Peck and Peck basement and her eye shadow and her knees crossed? Huh?

Miss Newton sparkled. Right from the mint and twenty-four karats. What on Earth could she learn from Earwig? He was so old and she was so new. In fact, there was just a mite bit about her that was too *new*. Her purse was new. Her shoes were new. She lit her own cigarette (Earwig's poor manners) from a fresh new pack with a brand new gold lighter and smoked with perfection—like a boarding-school girl on summer vacation fulfilling the winter's wish.

How could anybody *look* so new? Maybe she was just out of the hospital. But no, *no,* she was too healthy for that. Her skin glowed. Her hair shined, and, no kidding, it was done. *Done?* Nobody her age ever got their hair done. Earwig was leering, catching her up on his latest research. How could she stand it?

Maybe she was just off the boat from somewhere. Yes, that must have been it, a visiting student from London University, mod but not hip, a London lady, too polite to brush off Earwig, definitely not hip but definitely mod, a Petula Clark of the primary grades. Oh me, oh my. She asked Earwig for something. He didn't have it. God, he was a fumbler. She turned to me and spoke. She wanted to borrow my "pin." She had a fine voice.

But, uh oh. I heard it. "Pin" instead of "pen." That wasn't London, folks. That was *New Jersey,* Nerk, New Juersy, but only the slightest trace. She'd been away a long time but Hoboken would out. (I should know, I was burn and rays there. East Arenj, near Mablewould.)

So here she was and it didn't make sense. I mean, her jewelry was *coordinated* or something. She was well-groomed. Nobody had been well-groomed since 1965. She had taste, elegance, class, style. Nobody had those things in 1969. (Nobody from Newark, N.J., had ever had them.)

Earwig was rolling his backside in the chair, examining the staple on his agenda and making "um, um" sounds. OK, Earwig, so begin already.

He would start with some kind of apology. He always did. That way he thought *he* would be off the hook when he told us about *our* mistakes.

"I must, um, um, apologize to you all in terms of the typing on our agenda for today but my regular secretary is out sick with the hives and the replacement girl, is, um, um, I'm afraid, not up to par in terms of spelling. Thus, if you would all look down the agenda to item number five, I would appreciate it. I wouldn't want anyone to blame *me* for spelling 'function' without the first 'n.' After all, ha ha, my own book, *Structure of Function,* has the word in the title, so that I, of all people, should . . ."

She had an excellent figure, small-boned but perfect, lovely bosoms, cute legs that wouldn't quit. I looked for flaws. She just *had* to be in her thirties, even *well* into them *but,* maybe not.

I was embarrassed but I couldn't stop looking. I knew she knew. I knew she knew I knew. Did she mind? I thought she didn't mind. She slid my pen back to me along the table. Smile. She didn't mind.

Earwig droned on, ". . . although there is certainly no necessity for us to agree with Dean Dolt in terms of his rather drastic criticisms, still I feel we must all agree with him that *some* of us here in this room have been remiss, seriously remiss, in terms of effort toward adequate planning . . ."

It was just impossible. She was the only completely new, unused adult in the whole world. The rest of us had been through the wringer-cycle ten times a year with polluted rinse-water. She wasn't even damp. It was impossible because, as we all knew, *they didn't make them like that anymore.*

Earwig continued to dish it out, ". . . for example, I do not believe that we have yet received a planning report from Dr. Slack even though it was specifically mentioned at the last meeting that *all* planning reports had to be into Dean Dolt's, um, hands by the first of last month. If we can't plan for planning how can we, ha ha, um *plan . . .?*"

Perfect Person, don't feel sorry for me. This man does not hurt me with his staple-darts. I brush aside his prickles and feel only the pain of not knowing you better. Anyhow, it's time for old Earwig to begin to take it all back. That's right my sweet, before he lets us go, he says he didn't mean it.

". . . before I let you go, I just want to say that there *are* extenuating circumstances here. I don't want anybody to get the idea that I am singling any one person out for particular blame. After all, we have all been in situations where planning was difficult . . ."

See, my dear, he took it all back. Next he says, "Well, if there is no further business . . ."

"Well, if there is no further business . . ."

Now, up. Jump up. Quick. Otherwise . . . too late.

"Miss Newton." Earwig calls her name.

She speaks. "I would be willing to help Dr. Slack with the planning forms."

Blessed Fortune brings in some boats that are not steer'd.

"I shall be most grateful, Miss Newton. Thank you very much. Would this afternoon be possible? Say, three?"

"Four would be better."

"Marvelous, four it is. Where shall we meet?"

"My desk would be fine. I have all the forms there."

"Perfect. Miss Newton, just tell me where your office
is."

Earwig is stunned. "Slack, you . . . , don't you know?"
"This is my office, Dr. Slack. I use that desk over in the
corner."

"But I thought that desk was reserved for one of the
n—." I wish to draw a veil of charity across the remainder
of this scene.

For excitement, and because it seemed such a reasonable thing to do, I went to her for counseling, not just
the Earwig kind of planning but for a chance to talk about
myself. I think she felt sorry for me—she had a kind of
soft spot for bums. At one point in her career as a nun
she had managed a big food-service department for a
women's college in New Jersey. In the kitchen she employed men who were down and out, alcoholics and
drifters. To get the meals on time, she had to dry the
men out and fix their fouled-up lives. She was a real
manager and I began to rely on her more and more—
who to contact around the university, how to call editors
who weren't calling me, that kind of thing. Also I made
some reasonable plans in my life: little rational goals
slowly emerged in my conversations with her and in my
thinking afterward.

For a month or two, I continued to call her "Sister,"
thinking she was still a nun in street clothing. She let me
do it for a while but then told me she had been released
from her vows by Rome. She remained a Catholic in
good standing but was no longer a nun.

Eileen had two, count 'em, two M.A. degrees before
her doctorate, but she had never really wanted any extra

degrees. She taught high school perfectly well without extra letters and told them so. Pupils liked the pretty nun who sang and played the guitar, and she liked them. But might not a popular nun who plays the guitar also be prone to a bit of trouble with Mother Superior? I got a hint of that. And when funds were available for someone to go off to graduate school, whom would Mother Superior pick to send away to New York? Mother Superior is no fool when it comes to choosing those for higher degrees at distant universities.

So the girl with all those degrees was knowledgeable but not intellectually ambitious, smart but not scholarly. Her degrees were in active things like nutrition and administration. Which brings us to the subject of work.

I put a new value on work. I had done much hard work before but always as a means, not an end. I wrote magazine articles out of a vague desire to be appreciated. I taught students just for the money. Then, because of Eileen these motives switched. I went into the classroom to work for my students. It made a big difference, and they said so. Being appreciated, I became excited by teaching. Then I turned down an assignment from the *Village Voice* because it paid only fifty bucks. In other words, I began to write more for the money and teach more for the fun, and it made me happy.

One reason nuns like hard work is simply physical. Hours of kneeling put a burden on their knees and back. (Eileen once had water on the knee from too much praying.) Prayer is confining and solitary. Work is a chance to move, to reach out to people and to live out aspirations formed in prayer. Prayer creates the need for work.

So they are all good at it, competent, happy employees, a personnel man's dream. Their orders send them from job to job, teaching them to do everything. They learn to run the whole show without letting anyone know. They do not hoard arbitrary power. They don't worship success and are not afraid of failure. If Harvard Business School could turn out such executives, the stock market would rise forever.

Eileen and I worked together the rest of that year and then, on the last day in 1969, we went to our first party. It was New Year's Eve at the apartment of friends. That's all there were at the party, Eileen and me, George and Burrie. There was champagne and inspired cooking and we danced and sang. Eileen played the guitar. I played the piano. Just before midnight, a neighbor, Stephen Kamfer, dropped in and strummed the mandolin and sang his own songs for us. After midnight, I rode Eileen home on the subway to protect her from muggers. The sixties were over and this was the only nice party I had been to in a long time.

We decided it was best for me to leave New York. The magazine had finally breathed its last. Times were bad. Teachers College was short of funds for all but the tenured professors. If you hadn't quite made it, you didn't have it made.

Also, the city was a horror. It couldn't get worse and did. Fleshpots became sumpholes. Sin progressed to super-sin, with heroin on every corner and the whores lined up on Times Square like cupie-dolls at Coney Island. At least they were working. Nobody else could get to work: The trains didn't run, the subway stopped. You paid a hundred dollars a month to park your car in a garage but the attendant moved it out onto the street as soon as you left and sold your space to a tourist for four fifty an hour. When the cop came by to give your car a ticket, the attendant gave *him* ten dollars. The cop then turned around and gave the attendant back five to play a number. When the number never came in, the cop called the Mafia to see if the attendant was honest. The Mafia suspected the attendant was holding back so they put him in somebody's car trunk and sent around a more reliable man to the parking lot. The new attendant asked you for an extra twenty-five a month to keep the car inside this time. You didn't pay so they scratched your hood all up and slashed the seat covers, which cost three hundred to get fixed. The new attendant *was* handy to have around, however . . . if you happened to be a junkie. Also, occasionally for needy folks, he could be counted on to deliver a little cocaine.

But I didn't need New York. I wasn't hooked on the city. Because of Eileen, I didn't even smoke pot. I was refusing it at parties.

In our talks about getting away from Gotham, I came up with the theory that a few small cities might still be living in the old fifties—not yet touched by the new madness. If, by chance, something had happened to retard urban growth and a city had not yet boomed, then it had a chance. The place to go would be some underrated city, say in the Deep South, a city still wrestling with problems of the fifties. Bad as these were, they were not inexorable, like urban decay, heroin and Big Death.

Sometime in 1969, I visited Birmingham, Alabama, and it seemed to me to be such a city of the past. Not only was Birmingham living in the fifties, it was trying to live down the early sixties, when its bathrooms and busses became such a national scandal. Church bombings and cross burnings then had discouraged immigration of both whites and blacks. Atlanta grew, Birmingham shrank. When Bull Connor closed the parks, even racist corporations were afraid to open plants. By 1969, U.S. Steel, the leading employer and polluter, was on the decline and the university complex had replaced it as the biggest payroll in town. The university was booming because it had an old medical school and a new medical center serving a doctor-starved Southeast. If U.S. Steel would only hurry up and die, Birmingham could be a very healthy place to live.

The health business created a new-rich middle class where the old, poor middle class had been. M.D.s and Ph.D.s built patios and swimming pools which they sat around in the evening, talking about real estate. Their wives took the kids to school in new Ford LTDs with M.D. plates and then stopped at the beauty parlor to set their beehives. All the social distinctions that attend a richening bourgeoisie had a medical twist. There were doctor-dominated country clubs, jammed on Wednesdays, with dining rooms booked for debutante parties where boys from fine old families could meet the daughters of the doctors. There were giant interior offices (medicine is always windowless) for ranking administrators and free new automobiles for university deans with name and title on the parking space.

It was a strange academe ruled by surgeons instead of scholars. A medical school had spawned an infant university. Pathologists were vice-presidents. Dentists were deans. And at the top of the social ladder, on a rung once trod by mine-owners, now perched the President of the University, a former dentist, living in turn-of-century splendor at Woodward House, a reconstructed coal castle, with several ballrooms and umpteen baths. Fascinating.

I met one learned and articulate official down there, an

orthodontist (of course) born in Boston. He had a solid textbook to his credit and did his own illustrations. We talked about art and writing and working in the South, which was difficult, and about living there, which was easy. Academic routine was the same as North, gossip and grudges, infighting over status space and computer time. But this university was expanding, not contracting. The official admired my "candor." I liked his wit. He hinted around. The medical center might use an educational psychologist who wrote learning materials. A school of education was even on the drawing board. The university was growing. The South might rise again. What did I think?

I said I thought I might be able to find somebody for him and went back to New York to think it over and tell Eileen. I still had a few prospects in New York. I sat down and tried to list the reasons for staying up North. I came up with only one: a luncheon date with a Big Editor from a Big Publisher. It was well known that Really Big Book Deals were instigated at a Big Lunch. Over the prosciutto and the scampi they *might* come around to deciding if you were the one to be handed some really Big Assignment. Finally they let you know. This was just the way it was always done.

But *why?* If they wanted me to do a book, they could tell me over the phone. I called the editor. He wanted somebody to talk to at lunch. No book, just food and talk.

I didn't even cradle the phone, but joggled for a dial tone and called the orthodontist in Birmingham.

People always ask you how you like it down South, and I had to admit I didn't like *it* much, meaning the society that was all ass-kissing and flag-waving with too much stab-thy-neighbor for my thin blood. Still, I didn't dislike the way I was handling myself in *it*. I had lived through *it* before up North, the same gray-flannel-suit period in the suburbs, keeping up with the Joneses and trying to keep them down, and so I felt I understood *it*, how permanent *it* could seem and how transient *it* really was.

In Birmingham, I was snubbed and conned, as were all new people. I was a Ph. D., so the M.D.s wouldn't answer my memos asking what I could do for them. All "important decisions" were made at lunch. I prepared long reports and the administrators would say let's have lunch and talk about it. Then, at the last minute, they would break the date just to show rank. Finally, I said, what the hell, and gave up lunch. Eileen sent me a weight-watcher-style diet. If they wouldn't let me be a doctor, I might as well be a good patient, lose weight, quit smoking and get healthy. Also, I worked hard for little recognition.

Whenever the Southern-fried chickenshit got too deep around my ankles, I would shake it off by jogging twenty laps around the roof of the YMCA. I counted the first ten laps by cussing out the bastards, starting with the president of the university (or U.S. Steel or U.S.A., it didn't really matter) with his big houses and small soul. Then, still blowing my wrath to the wind, I would work myself down the hierarchy of brown-nose power pushers. On the last ten laps, I got my second wind and tried to love mine enemy, recalling at least one nice thing about everybody, even Nixon. If I couldn't think of anything good to say about someone, I ran penalty laps till it came to me. Luckily, Nixon went to China, or I would never have got off the roof.

Somebody, probably W. J. Cash, said you could look at the South from two angles, the rotten society or the good guys who stood up against the rotten society. Both were features of the South. Since the society wasn't asking me in, I might as well stand up against it whenever I could. I only did little things, like criticizing deans at every opportunity, never joining private clubs and always being nice to the wrong people, but it all made me feel good. I wasn't beating the system but I was beating *on* it, punching the bag to exercise the character muscles.

I missed Eileen badly. After she finished her thesis, I flew up to be with her. We went out on the town. I didn't drink too much. I looked thinner and stronger. I told her of my work and new-found strengths and asked her to visit me. She would think it over.

When I got back, I lay awake. I had made changes in myself to show Eileen. If I couldn't bring her into my life, I could go to hell again. My gains were not too firm.

8

Headlines

In March of 1970, while I was going steady with Eileen in New York, Timothy Leary was going to jail in California with two consecutive ten-year sentences for possession of a grand total of under an ounce of marijuana. It was an outrageously severe punishment for a crime which had also been committed once or twice by many millions of Americans, including me and, no doubt, you.

However, in September of 1970, when I started work in Birmingham, Leary, the invincible, showed them all up, those dirty pig fascist narc bastard philistine finks, by escaping from jail and going to Algeria, of all places, to live with Eldridge Cleaver.

And that about sums up the difference between us. I mean, he pulls the jailbreak of the century to practice absolute radical Panther political freedom and my idea of escape is to move to Birmingham, Alabama, to teach school.

In February of seventy-one, Eileen visited me. On Valentine's Day, I went over to Loveman's Department Store on Eighteenth Street and bought a diamond ring. I planned to be dignified about it but I was scared to

death she would say no, so instead I rushed in holding
out this paper bag from Loveman's, asking, "We are
going to get married, aren't we?" She said yes and in May
we were, with a three-buck Alabama license and a garden
apartment in Homewood. She did the cooking and I did
the dishes and she got a job so she could work near me.
The job didn't pay much but it was important social work
with pregnant teenagers who had been kicked out of
school. Two competent people working closely and in
love make fast friends and jealous enemies. We invited
both over to the apartment for cocktails. Some of both
came. After they went home I flopped on the bed, waiting for Eileen. I knew we were going to hate it but also
take it and get to like it. At that moment, I lost all basic
doubts about anything personal.

But now Leary was having some troubles. Eldridge
Cleaver proved to be straight-laced about drugs, while
Leary, a non-revolutionary at heart, had a hard time mak-
ing himself proclaim the shoot-'em-up line of the Pan-
thers—although he did try. Finally things came to a head.
Algeria was too small for the both of them.

The inside story of Leary's travels and troubles since
sixty-eight is unknown to me. However, I have on hand
a fair sample of the outside story as reported in the press,
a complete headline history put together by Eileen and
me from the newsclipping file of Mr. T. Walden Pond of
Massachusetts.

"T. Walden Pond" is my name for a distinguished
living gentleman from Boston who, like all distinguished
living Bostonians, is scrupulously conservative in business while surprisingly liberal in every other way. Mr.
Pond's business is professional trust management and
tax advice, which means that widows and orphans give

him their money and then, whenever they need some, it is all still there and more besides.

To Mr. Pond, a client is a sacred trust worthy of nothing less than truth in counsel and sure capital gains forever—even if you happen to become a drug freak or get arrested or go to jail. Neither Leary nor I ever had any trust funds handy for Mr. Pond to manage, but during the 1950s we had some tax problems. Mr. Pond was my find. He saved my day and I told Leary about him and that's how Leary became Mr. Pond's client, for better or for worse. After Leary lost his job and began to make more trouble than taxable income, Mr. Pond continued to consider Leary a sacred trust as long as he possibly could.

For lack of other information about his client (Tim was not one to keep ledgers), Mr. Pond began to fill up the file with newsclippings. Mrs. Pond, being both well-read and well-dressed, supplied clippings from *Women's Wear Daily* and *Vogue* while Mr. Pond added chronicles from *The New York Times* and, of course, *The Boston Globe*. The Boston papers, by the way, could be counted on to give gleeful coverage to all Leary's run-ins with the law. Harvard boy makes bad, and all that.

So anyhow, given Mr. Pond's file, you can pretty well keep track of Leary's problems step by step. Mr. Pond was kind enough to send me the clippings, and I, in turn, now pass them on to you. They begin, of course, at the beginning of the troubles, and the troubles, of course, begin with a bust.

The Boston Globe, Friday, 12/24/65: DRUG CHARGE HITS LEARY

LAREDO, Tex. (UPI)—Dr. Timothy Leary, a professor who left Harvard under a cloud because of research into hallucinatory drugs, was jailed with his two children and two other persons Thursday on charges of possessing marijuana.

Border patrol agents seized Leary, 45, his son John, 16, and daughter Susan, 18, as they crossed the border from Mexico. Arrested with them was Mrs. Rosemary Woodruff, 30, who said she was Leary's associate in a research foundation . . .

Officials said two ounces of marijuana were found in Susan's underclothing. Marijuana sweepings were found in their car, they said.

Appearing before U.S. Commissioner Jacob Hornberger, Leary's bail was set at $10,000. His children had bail set at $2,500 apiece and Mrs. Woodruff . . . at $5,000 . . . None raised it and they were sent to Webb County Jail pending grand jury action.

Leary said he would get a lawyer.

The Boston Herald, Monday, 4/18/66: LEARY SEIZED IN DRUG RAID

MILLBROOK, N.Y.—Dr. Timothy Leary, former Harvard professor arrested last month [*sic*] for transporting marijuana, was arrested Sunday at his rented estate here on charges with three others, of possessing narcotics.

A raiding party of 20 [was] led by Dutchess County Dist. Atty. John R. Heilman and Sheriff Lawrence Quinlan, armed with search warrants for the 64-room chateau. Heilman said they seized a "suspected quantity of marijuana."

They were arraigned before County Judge Raymond Baratta in Poughkeepsie and pleas of not guilty were entered for all . . .

Judge Baratta set bail at $5,000 for Leary.

. . . An avid experimenter with LSD–25 and other

hallucinatory drugs, Leary and a collaborator, Richard Alpert, were released by Harvard in 1963.

Nathan M. Pusey, the school's president, said at the time that Alpert, then 32, had broken a promise not to use undergraduates in the experiments and that Leary had absented himself from his classes without permission.

The Boston Herald, Monday, 4/18/66: INNER SPACE

[Leary] . . . said they were setting up an "international foundation for internal freedom" to explore "the inner space of man's consciousness."

Leary's experiments at Millbrook reportedly included eating morning glory seeds and doing Yoga exercises.

Leary was expelled from Mexico in June 1963 along with 19 other Americans after setting up a religio-psychological center at Acapulco, where LSD and other "consciousness expanding" experiences could be bought for $6 a treatment. The center lasted only a few months.

Leary has testified he used marijuana in research on its effects by his foundation at Millbrook and also in religious rites as a member of a Hindu sect.

The Boston Herald, 9/24/66: DR. LEARY CHARGES DROPPED (By Sidney A. Zion)

POUGHKEEPSIE, N.Y.—Narcotics charges were dropped Friday against Dr. Timothy Leary, the leading exponent of the hallucinatory drug, LSD, on the grounds that recent court decisions affecting confessions and search warrants made it "extremely unlikely" that he could have been successfully prosecuted.

Indictments against . . . others arrested with Dr. Leary in April on charges of possession of marijuana were dismissed for the same reasons. The motion to drop the cases was made by Dutchess County Dist. Atty. John R. Heilman, Jr. . . .

The mansion, used in the past for "simulated" LSD sessions, has been a storm-center of controversy in Dutchess County. As many as 150 followers of Dr. Leary would arrive each weekend to participate in workshops concerning hallucinatory drugs. But no actual drugs were taken, according to Dr. Leary.

In moving for the dismissals of the indictments, Heilman told County Judge Raymond C. Baratta that Dr. Leary had agreed to end these activities at Millbrook and "transfer them to New York City."

In an interview later, Dr. Leary said he had already put an end to "public activities" at Millbrook. He said the decision had nothing to do with the charges and were not a "quid pro quo" for the dismissals. He said, however, that he and the other defendants had agreed not to sue the county for the raid and the arrests . . .

The New York Times News Service, Monday, 5/19/69:
COURT SAYS LEARY RIGHT REFUSING POT TAX
WASHINGTON (UPI)—An eight-member Supreme Court today upset the Federal narcotics conviction of Dr. Timothy F. Leary, former Harvard psychologist known as the high priest of the LSD movement.

The 47-year-old Leary—a controversial figure because of his experiments with hallucinatory drugs—was found guilty in Laredo, Tex., of transporting illegally imported marijuana and of failing to pay a transfer tax of $100 an ounce.

The court—handing down decisions for the first time since the resignation of Abe Fortas as an associate justice —struck down a provision of the narcotics importation statute which made mere possession of marijuana sufficient of a presumption that it was illegally imported and that the possessor knew it.

The decision suggested that Leary had a valid defense when he contended that if he had paid the tax he would have been subjecting himself to self-incrimination.

The court took these other actions: Declined to interfere with a California Supreme Court ruling which threw out the conviction of a "topless" dancer and her night club manager. . . .

Sunday Herald Traveler (Boston), 8/3/69: TIMOTHY LEARY, THE PSYCHEDELIC PARTY HOPE, TRIPS INTO TOWN

Dr. Timothy Leary, high priest of LSD, tripped into Boston yesterday with the admission that he, his family and friends take LSD once a week.

Wearing an elastic tied short pony tail, plum colored see-through shirt and white, corduroy pants, the former Harvard professor was greeted by a cheering band of followers and supporters. The group, carrying hand painted signs proclaiming Leary as "St. Tim" and "Gov. Leary," couldn't have been more enthusiastic in their welcome for the guru of turned-on drugs . . .

During a press conference that could only be as serious as Dr. Leary would allow, the gubernatorial candidate fessed up that he would be "forced to be a presidential candidate in 1972" because of his "approach."

". . . I will probably end up representing the majority when you add up all the free people, the eccentrics, kooks and rugged individualists and old western frontier types."

. . . he advocated special benefits for the "unpopular

and underpaid group . . ." the police, who arrested him twice in the past week, which he considered "a little better than average."

"The police are very interested and curious and like to spend a day with me once or twice a week."

As for LSD . . . "It is my religion . . ."

Boston Globe, 1/21/70: LEARY STAYS 'COOL' WITH DRUG CONVICTION

LAREDO, Tex.—A Federal jury yesterday found Dr. Timothy Leary guilty of smuggling three ounces of marijuana from Mexico in a silver snuffbox stashed in his teen-age daughter's underwear.

Leary, high priest of the psychedelic set, "stayed loving and kept cool" and promptly called the verdict a victory of Capricorn over Venus.

National Observer, 1/27/70: TIMOTHY LEARY CONVICTED

Timothy Leary, the 49-year-old defender of LSD and marijuana use, was convicted by a Federal Court in Laredo, Texas, last week for transporting one-half ounce of marijuana from Mexico to the United States in December 1965. Leary had been convicted in 1966 for failure to pay tax on the same packet of marijuana, but the decision was reversed by the Supreme Court. Last week's conviction, which was given by a jury composed entirely of Mexican-Americans, could bring Leary a maximum sentence of 20 years in prison and a $20,000 fine. When released on $5,000 bond, the hippie-style spokesman advised American young people to "stay loving and keep cool."

Boston Globe, 1/21/70: 10 YEARS IN POT CASE IM-
POSED ON DR. LEARY

HOUSTON—A federal judge today sentenced a smiling
Dr. Timothy Leary to 10 years in prison on charges he
helped transport from Mexico to Texas three ounces of
marijuana in a silver snuffbox hidden in his teen-age
daughter's underwear.

U.S. District Judge Ben Connally ordered the high
priest of the drug set held without bond.

"He poses a threat to the community," said the judge.
"His conduct has been such that he openly advocates
violation of the law. He poses a danger to other persons."

Leary, calm and relaxed, smiled as the judge read the
sentence. The former Harvard lecturer then clutched his
wife, Rosemary, 34, and kissed her.

Leary's lawyer, Atty. Mitchell Standard of New York
City, said he would go to the 5th U.S. Circuit Court of
Appeals in New Orleans later today to try to get bond for
Leary on the prison sentence.

Leary flew to Texas during the week-end from Santa
Ana, Calif. He, his wife and 20-year-old son, John, were
convicted Feb. 19 in Santa Ana of possession of
marijuana and LSD.

Leary was convicted Mar. 11, 1966, of failing to declare customs on three ounces of marijuana brought
across the border by his 18-year-old daughter, Barbara
[*sic*], who carried the marijuana in a silver snuffbox
stuffed in her underclothes.

The United States Supreme Court overturned that
conviction and Leary was charged with importation a

short time later. Leary was convicted Jan. 20 of that
charge in Judge Connally's court in Laredo. Leary was
released on $5,000 bond.

The maximum sentence Connally could have given
Leary was 20 years in prison and a $20,000 fine. The
minimum sentence was five years in prison.

The New York Times, 3/22/70: LEARY GOES TO
PRISON ON COAST TO START TERM OF 1 TO 10
YEARS

JUDGE DENIES LSD ADVOCATE BAIL IN MARIJUANA CASE—
LAWYERS PUSH APPEAL (By Steven V. Roberts) *Special to
The New York Times*

SANTA ANA, Calif., March 21—Dr. Timothy Leary, who
helped make the world aware of three unsettling new
letters—LSD—has gone to prison for from one to 10
years here this week for possession of marijuana.

Superior Court Judge Byron McMillan, who refused
to set bail here after sentencing Leary this week,
called the former Harvard psychology professor "an
insidious menace" to society and a "pleasure-seeking,
irresponsible, Madison Avenue advocate of the free
use of drugs."

"What's wrong with wanting to be happy?" retorted
George Chula, Leary's attorney. "I thought that was the
whole basis of life."

Leary, whose wife says he is "49 going on 5,000," is
in the State Prison at Chino while his lawyers work on
appeals and raise money to finance them.

The conviction in Santa Ana, the county seat of
Orange County, came about six weeks after a Federal
District Judge in Texas had sentenced Leary to 10 years
on similar charges of possession of marijuana.

TERMS CONSECUTIVE

The two sentences are set to run consecutively. Thus Leary faces a maximum of 20 years in jail for possession of less than 1 ounce of marijuana in the two cases combined.

The Texas sentence stems from the same incident several years ago in which Leary was given 30 years in jail for importing marijuana from Mexico.

That charge was unanimously thrown out by the Supreme Court in 1968, but Leary was then retried in Texas on charges of possession and convicted again.

Michael Kennedy, another of Leary's lawyers, predicted that the current charges would also be overturned by higher courts. "That's why the judge wouldn't give us bail," the San Francisco lawyer asserted. "He really is of a mind that Tim should be punished and so he's using bail to punish him. After all, despite all the charges against him, Tim has never done any time."

... The lawyer also felt that long sentences for possession of marijuana helped to confuse young people about the effects of different drugs.

"Tim has always said that we must make a distinction between dangerous and non-dangerous drugs," Kennedy said. "If we don't we do two bad things. We create a whole new criminal class, and we deliberately confuse young people. They think that if there is no damned difference between marijuana and heroin, then why not take heroin?"

SEES HIMSELF AS SCIENTIST

Mrs. Rosemary Leary, who was sentenced to six months in the Santa Ana case but was granted bail, said in an interview that her husband, who holds a Ph. D.

from the University of California, still considers himself a scientist.

"The proper place to experiment with new substances is one's own body," she said. "You shouldn't violate someone else's body, either a patient or a guinea pig. All Tim has done in the last few years is publish the results and findings of those experiments on himself."

Leary's present concern is the increasing use of heroin among the young, his wife said. "Anyone can see the correlation between the war, smog and the use of heroin," she said. "Of course kids want to turn off. The world as conceived by their elders contains very little joy and beauty . . ."

Although he has been one of the prophets of rebellious youth, Leary is trying to close the generation gap, not expand it, his wife insisted.

"We're trying to give peace a chance," Mrs. Leary said, "and not escalate the polarization between the young and the old. We want to create a space in time in which the wisest and the sanest and most humorous of our people can get together."

———————————

Radio news report, 9/15/70:

California prison officials announced today that Dr. Timothy Leary was missing from prison on September 12. Leary, a former Harvard professor and a convict since March of this year, was interred at the California Men's Colony West in San Luis Obispo, serving a ten-year sentence for possession of marijuana. Exact details of Leary's escape from the minimum-security prison were not available but officials stated that the prisoner had apparently climbed over the fence at night.

———————————

The Weatherman Underground, 9/20/70:

Timothy Leary has escaped from San Louis Obispo and has joined us in the underground. We are free outlaws . . . we've got everything we need and the law can't touch us at all.

Radio news report, 9/20/70:

. . . when asked about the Leary escape, FBI Director J. Edgar Hoover commented that the Bureau would soon capture the escaped convict. "We'll have him in ten days," said Hoover.

Women's Wear Daily, Friday, 10/8/71: HOW TIM LEARY FLED JAIL FOR GREENER GRASS (By Peter Ainslie)

NEW YORK—"In the name of the Father and Mother and the Holy Ghost—Oh, Guards—I leave now for freedom. I pray that you will free yourself. To hold men captive is a crime against humanity and a sin against God. Oh, guards, you are criminals and sinners. Cut it loose. Be free. Amen."

With these words, left behind on a piece of paper in his prison locker, Timothy Leary took leave . . .

. . . Leary's [made his] escape over the prison wall dangling from a cable and with black paint applied to the edge of his tennis shoes so they wouldn't catch light . . . A list of 22 points Leary draws up as a plan of action begins:

"1) Wait for moonless night."

The list also indicates the escape plan was to be executed with precision timing. "Slip out side door and walk to tree—five seconds," Leary notes. "Climb tree— five seconds.

"Climb down bank and ease through outer prison compound, avoiding barracks and staying alert for fire watch. Reach highway in four minutes."

On the matter of timing, Leary remarks, "In escape, as in impregnation, the cellular intersection, the tantric union, the margin of life and death is seven seconds."

Leary is understandably obscure in dealing with certain aspects of the escape. He refers to a group instrumental in the plan by the code name, "Vandals," though later passages indicate the group is the Weatherman, and he suggests he received assistance from the Black Panthers . . .

After his break, Leary's prison clothes turned up in a gas station near Los Angeles, apparently in an effort to lead authorities on a Mexican chase. But Leary says he traveled in a series of four vehicles provided by the Vandals through a circuitous route to Salt Lake City and then Detroit, from where he boarded a TWA international flight . . .

―――――――――

Playboy, 7/71: LEARY IN LIMBO (By Donn Pearce)

. . . The planning took three months and was engineered by Bernardine Dohrn, Jeffrey Jones, Bill Ayers and Mark Rudd, tribal leaders of Weatherman and the SDS, and all of them fugitives . . .

There were 40 people involved. A fund of $30,000 was raised through contributions from dope dealers all around the country. The final nine-member escape group was commanded by a 19-year-old kid assisted by a ten-year-old. Four cars were used, all equipped with two-way radios.

. . . Suspicious of possible roadblocks, the four escape cars leapfrogged ahead of one another, radioing back when everything was clear. One car was given the job of leaving Leary's prison clothes in a gas-station rest room eight miles in the wrong direction.

He was joined by Rosemary, who had also been given a ten-year sentence but had been free under an appeal bond. Together, they were shuttled across the country, hiding out in a string of safe houses provided by the Weatherman underground. To board a plane for Paris 13 days after the escape—using false passports—Rosemary changed her appearance with glasses, make-up and a wig. Timothy cut his hair short. The center of his head was shaved to simulate baldness and the rest of his hair was dyed red. He removed his false teeth and his hearing aid, wore heavy-rimmed glasses . . . He was wearing a business suit and tie.

Boston Evening Globe, 10/21/70: LEARY JOINS PANTHERS IN ALGERIA

ALGIERS (AP)—Dr. Timothy Leary has turned up in Algeria, and the fugitive guru of the drug movement reportedly plans to take up residence and work for the Black Panther party in Algiers.

The official Algerian news agency said last night that Leary, who escaped Sept. 12 from a California prison where he was serving time for possession of marijuana, arrived "recently" with his wife, Rosemary, and had been granted political asylum.

Shortly before the Algerian statement was issued, the Yippies—the Youth International Party—announced in New York that the former Harvard lecturer was "alive and well and high in Algiers."

The Yippies held a news conference outside the Women's House of Detention in New York and released a letter signed by Leary that said: "I offer living gratitude

to my sisters and brothers in the Weatherman underground who designed and executed my release."

... Informants in Algeria said the Learys arrived Saturday and are staying with Eldridge Cleaver, fugitive minister of information of the Black Panther party, in his villa
suburb of El Biar.

Leary ... apparently scaled a chain-link fence while on
a work detail and walked away. His prison clothes were
found the next day in the rest room of a filling station
eight miles away ... In a telephone interview with a Los
Angeles radio station Friday, Leary said he would work
with the Black Panthers "in their struggle in America and
around the country and the world."

Leary said he knew "from the day I was arrested" he
would escape. He said he would return to the United
States "in two or three years, after the revolution."

Boston Evening Globe, 1/7/71: LEARY TELLS RADI-
CALS TURN TO KIDNAPPING

NEW YORK (AP)—Dr. Timothy Leary says he advised
the radical Weatherman group to escalate from bombing
ROTC buildings to kidnapping prominent entertainers
in order to free imprisoned militants.

"We're at war with the United States government," he
declared in a telephone interview from Algeria where he
fled last September after escaping from a California
prison.

He was interviewed by Alex Bennett of radio station
WMCA.

The one-time Harvard instructor who became an out-
spoken advocate of LSD said he was at work on a book
about his escape which he said was engineered by the
Weatherman.

He said he believed there should be mass action but

added, "We still feel there is a place for urban guerrillas, and my advice to the Weatherman when we left was that they should not continue just bombing the ROTC's.

"They should escalate the violence. They should start hijacking planes, they should kidnap prominent sports figures and television and Hollywood people in order to free Bobby Seale" and other militants, Leary said.

The Boston Globe, 2/20/71: LEARY URGES YOUNG: QUIT DRUGS, REVOLT

SAN FRANCISCO (UPI)—Dr. Timothy Leary says the time has passed for the young to "tune in, turn on and drop out" with psychedelic drugs.

Youthful radicals today should be following the "correct way" of the militant Weatherman and Black Panthers rather than "clowning or tripping," Leary advised in a video-taped interview shown here yesterday.

"There is a time to expand and a time to contract," he said. "This is the time to tighten up, organize."

The one-time high priest of the American drug culture recanted while standing beside Eldridge Cleaver, the Black Panther leader who put Leary under virtual house arrest last month, allegedly for taking too many LSD trips.

Both men are exiles in Algeria, while they fled from California authorities. Cleaver is wanted for a parole violation and is fugitive from an attempted murder charge. Leary escaped jail while serving time on drug charges.

Leary said he had settled his differences with the Panthers and now agreed with Cleaver that young radicals should quit drugs and take up revolution.

He said he was under "no coercion" by the Panthers and told Cleaver, "We're here voluntarily with you."

Cleaver, the Panthers' "minister of information," announced last month he had "busted" both Leary and his wife because it had "become very clear to me that there is something seriously wrong with both Dr. Leary and his wife's brains . . . I attribute this to the unaccountable number of acid trips they have taken."

The two men discussed drugs and revolution for 57 minutes in the interview taped Feb. 12 in Cleaver's apartment by Glen Angell, a 27-year-old San Francisco documentary film maker who spent five days with them. Excerpts were shown over KQED, the local public television outlet.

Boston Record American, 10/27/70: LEARY PLANS JORDAN AND SYRIA VISITS

BEIRUT (UPI)—Fugitive American LSD champion Timothy Leary plans to travel to Syria and Jordan after his stay in Lebanon, sources close to the former Harvard lecturer said Monday.

Leary spent most of the day refusing to take calls in one of the two rooms his entourage has taken at $46 a day in St. Georges Hotel on Beirut's swank waterfront.

Sources close to Leary said he wanted to study the Palestinian resistance movement and hoped to travel to Damascus and Amman. But guerrilla sources in Beirut refused to comment on the fugitive professor's clandestine arrival from Algiers or to confirm they had been in contact with him.

Leary arrived late Sunday aboard a scheduled flight from Cairo. He was accompanied by his wife, Rosemary; Jennifer Dohrn, whose sister, Bernardine, is one of the

10 most wanted persons in the United States; the national chairman of the Black Panthers in New York, Martin Kenner, and "Field Marshal" Don Cox of the Panthers' eight-man Algerian Staff.

American authorities formally notified the Lebanese police of Leary's presence in Beirut, a U.S. embassy official said.

There was no comment from police sources, but the embassy said Lebanese officials were investigating Leary's arrival.

The officials pointed out that there was no extradition treaty between the United States and Lebanon, and therefore Leary's arrest by Lebanese police would not be of any use to the United States.

Women's Wear Daily, Friday, 10/8/71 (By Peter Ainslie):
. . . an anonymous Swiss financier . . . is currently picking up Leary's tab for the residence he maintains in a chalet outside Lousanne, Switzerland, . . . [according to] New Yorkers, John and Sharon Rodney, whose publishing firm, Rodney & Rodney, is negotiating publication and hopefully film rights [for a book by Leary].

"Leary has been protected for over a year now by people who simply picked him up—maybe to some degree they were admirers—and they took care of the hospitalization of his wife and put him in Switzerland, which seemed to be the safest place, and through legal maneuvers arranged his bail from Swiss authorities," says Rodney, who recently left *Vogue,* where he was business manager.

Rodney . . . says Tim is heavily into acid now and that he has his ups and downs. . . .

EXTRADITION REMOTE

Extradition proceedings are underway but Rodney thinks the big money interests and legal knowledge available to Leary may delay the court for at least 30 days and possibly up to 6 months. "I would say that the likelihood of his being brought back to the States is reasonably remote, despite a lot of pressure," Rodney says.

Meanwhile, Rodney himself has been the object of a number of visits and phone calls from a U.S. State Department official, who claims his only interest . . . is to determine how Leary got his passport.

Boston Sunday Herald Traveler, 6/6/71: LEARY OUSTED

ZURICH, Switzerland (AP)—Swiss police sources said yesterday LSD prophet Timothy Leary and his wife were ordered to leave Switzerland on May 14 as "undesirable foreigners" after a two-week stay.

A friend of the couple in Algiers had said earlier they apparently had been kidnapped.

Their whereabouts remains unknown.

According to the friend in Algiers the Learys were seized in Zurich on May 4 after disembarking from a Swiss air jetliner while enroute to a lecture engagement in Denmark.

But the Swiss police informants said Leary and his wife came to Zurich from Algiers, where they have been granted political asylum, because Mrs. Leary needed medical treatment. They did not describe her ailment.

The sources said neither Leary, wanted as a fugitive after escaping from a California prison, nor his wife was wanted on any infraction of Swiss law.

They were told to leave after their two-week-stay period had ended, the police sources said.

The police declined to say exactly how the Learys left Switzerland—whether by air or land route. They did not say where the couple went from Switzerland.

Nowhere.
Leary never left Switzerland. He went to jail instead . . .

Boston Herald Traveler, Saturday, 8/7/71:
Dr. Timothy Leary . . . [was] release [d] . . . on $18,500 bail pending extradition to the United States to face drug charge. He spent four weeks in a Switzerland jail.

. . . and after he got out of Swiss jail he remained in Switzerland —always under the threat of expulsion, never actually being expelled.

And in late July 1972, Eileen and I decided to pay him a visit.

9

Journey to the End

My next magazine article after starting life with Eileen was a short biography of Leary for *Psychology Today*. When they first asked me to write it, I said no to them, but then I remembered Mr. Pond's clipping file and, what the hell, I said yes. Within a year, the little potboiler article had cooked up a Big Lunch, which in turn dished out a Small Advance. On August 24, 1972, Eileen and I were on the New York-Zurich 6 P.M. TWA Economy, heading for Switzerland to try to track down Leary.

The idea was to catch up with him and find out where he was hanging out, how he was hanging on. Was he the same Leary? Had prison got him down? Was his sensorium still fairly clear? Was he still lucid? Was he still insane?

Yes or no or whatever, I would study the scene, tell all, update the perspective and close the case. The idea was to do this safely—without getting loaded or busted or broke or making any other bad dreams come true. It was 1972, the high noon of Law And Order, and we (especially Eileen but don't count me out) had our nightmares about Leary and his drugs and his friends and their drugs and anybody else with drugs that might possibly become *our* drugs and the police of three nations or anybody else who might be led to conclude that some substance that really belonged to Leary or his friends or anybody else could be construed as belonging to us. God forbid, and I mean it. So, now, out over the Atlantic, with no turning back and the TWA Tourist capon refusing to enter the duodenum without a squawk, scary-wary visions pestered our prefrontal lobes. Leary got nearer and we got leerier.

It must have been a crime, of one sort or another, to visit Timothy Leary in 1972. President Richard M. Nixon certainly wouldn't have approved. President Nixon didn't approve of interviews with notorious hippies. He said so in a speech. He wanted us all to strengthen our ethical and moral fiber. Timothy Leary had limp moral fiber.

Leary just didn't fit in. Under Our President, the whole country was moving to a right rear corner of the stage. Republicans and romantic revivals—not just the Ike fifties, gang, but the Coolidge twenties, oh you kid. Normalcy, nostalgia and *No, No, Nanette.* Timothy Leary wasn't in the cast. *Hair* was out. The really big show was *Grease,* a rock-around-the-clock backslider into the numbskull fifties. Suffering Shirrells, Brenda Lee, Elvis P., Bobby Vinton and Bobby D. Would you invite Timothy Leary to beach-blanket bingo? Could he surf?

Yet, in ruminating about his significance, about half the time I would logically conclude that Leary was an important man. After all, he started the hippie movement, East Coast style, and introduced us all to LSD. He just dished out the stuff right and left to people in the early sixties, and many of them were important or stylish or creative people. The consequences for the arts were notorious and would be analyzed for many years. Music and fashion and even religion were influenced in strange ways. He would be remembered for this.

On the other hand, he didn't really do very much—except turn people on, and that only at the start of the decade. (Later they brought their own.) People who don't do much are hard to assess. All you can pin on them are their attitudes (or their antics), and these have a way of sliding out of the history books. Leary belongs to the sixties and to no other time. He was with it when other people didn't even know what *it* was. So what? That just makes him interesting but unimportant, someone to tell stories about until everybody has heard them all—Joe Frisco or Doris Duke. (Tim Leary, the Zelda Fitzgerald of the nineteen sixties, man, gave *fabulous* parties and, like, will you *ever* forget the punch?)

Of course, he writes. If you search his writing you can find things of interest and beauty. Obviously, his early books weren't written as such. He mostly just put together essays and stuff, even margin notes. (LSD can lend significance to any detail.) In other words, Dr. Leary, the former professor, took notes about his new experiences. Some of these developed into articles, others just remained notes. Then, every so often, old Professor Tim would sit down at the SCM electric portable and bang out his best beliefs and latest insights into a special kind of doctrinaire form known only to old college professors: the student handout. This is Leary at his best—writing instructional materials: how to be a saint, how to be a smuggler, how to escape from jail. Some of this could well survive, I think, as audacious examples of the medium. "Start Your Own Religion"! Good Lord, it may not quite be as profound as de Sade, but it is certainly pounded home with as much relevant detail.

So maybe Leary will go down in history as a pamphleteer or tract writer, a Tom Paine of the dark side, declaring death to the tyrant Ego and freedom for the bondaged Id and, incidentally, whispering to Junior that he is just as much a God as Jesus or Jehovah and suggesting that he take drugs to prove it. This kind of stuff is more often suppressed than forgotten.

In the long run, that is. But not now. Now is August of '72 and Leary is out of mind because the sixties, never exactly built to last, have come apart at their seams. The flower children have withered. Everybody is in jail or in the grave. Owsley is in jail, busted on a minor rap. Morrison is dead, killed himself with booze. (Turns out he was impotent, kids. Couldn't make it with chicks. How about that for your sex symbol?) Then, Joplin is dead. She took an overdose of heroin. And so on. Most of the groups are dead. The Beatles are off. Only the Rolling Stones still hang in there haunting the halls, Mick Jagger on the far, far side of thirty and new generations coming along who never heard "Satisfaction" and don't want to.

Like the kids on our plane. It was filled with American Field Service teenagers from the vast-majority Midwest of the Conservative Seventies. These kids are clean-cut and clean-living, with round muscles and pure skin that smells like Ivory soap. They boarded carrying copies of *Sports Illustrated* and *Mark Spitz Fan Mag.* They watched every move of the oxygen demo. Clean little ears tuned obediently to your captain speaking. Seatbelts fastened, kids, and backs up for the takeoff. So who's Mick Jagger?

All these beautiful, J. C. Penney kids were settling now, adjusting their little post-pubertal bottoms down into the Scotch-guard Kodel and wrapping their vitamin-enriched skin into tiny TWA blankets to watch the adult movie. This particular adult movie starred old Marlon Brando as the grubby gardener in another *Turn Of The Screw* by Henry James. Marlon's muscles sagged, and his skin had brown hickies. The dialogue turned to significant pauses. The kids wanted to sleep, anyway. They dreamed of football and 4-H prizes.

The sixties are dead. LSD is bad for the skin. Freaks, Fugs, fantasy, drugs, gone. Groups dead. Shocking image fizzle. Heads dead. Grateful Dead, dead. Dust.

The movie droned on, and so did the plane—on into the eternal half-light of that East-to-West transatlantic dusk-dawn where the sun somehow rises at night before it sets in the morning and first you wake up, stiff and moss-mouthed, before you actually go to sleep, half-dreaming of mishaps. (This is the year of High-Jacks, also low-jinks like baggage boobytraps and boogy-man mail bombs.) Only a thin steel skin keeps us all from sucking out into the clutches of the rosy-fingered stratus-vacuum.

And if the time-bombs don't get us, the Interpol will. Can anybody hang around the likes of Timothy Leary without becoming involved? If involved, arrested? If arrested, jailed? The Youth of America have (temporarily?) forgotten Leary, but not the State of California—or Texas or New York or the FBI or the CIA or Interpol or the Special White House All-American Anti-Hippie Secret Task Force. Gotcha!

Eileen can sleep anywhere—or rather, deeply rest, eyes closed but mind open. It's a trick she learned as a nun. She refused to buy the movie headphones. Now and then she wakes and worries but mostly, having been to Switzerland once before, she dreams of Lucerne, of coffee and hot milk, of Bucherer's on the Schwanenplatz.

We don't have money so Eileen doesn't buy, she just shops. Her rather definite ideas involve a maximum of shopping and a minimum of Leary. Leary is necessary, she concedes, but could he not be got over with at the beginning? We could have an interesting, yet brief, Dr.-Leary-I-Presume scene in some accessible spot, say, the Zurich train station. This would be followed in quick succession by a) a luncheon interview in a charming coffeehouse right there in the Bahnhof, b) friendly but hasty good-byes outside on the street corner, c) three leisurely weeks of glorious scenery and high-level shopping by her and me. Or, I could stay back in the pension and sort notes while she shops. Either way, if all went well and we were not arrested, then Leary and I might get together once more—say, at the airport just before flight time for one final schnapps and farewell at the good but crowded American bar overlooking the runways. In general, sightseeing is planned to avoid crowds, Leary-meetings to encounter safety in numbers.

I knew Leary would never be partial to railroad stations and airports. Secluded chalets would be safer for him, if not for us.

Leary the mountain bandit, alone in an Alpine cave, only a goat for a companion. He is smuggled cheese and wine each day by sympathetic sheperds. A compassionate Franciscan bakes him bread.

I told Eileen it was too soon to plan. First, we must see where he wants to meet us. If his plans sound dangerous, we make a counter-offer. It is his game. He may even want to avoid us, in which case we could search till doomsday. (My only knowledge of the terrain came from old Alfred Hitchcock movies.)

Leary the fugitive in the north, a Black Forest band of Merry Weathermen to do his bidding. They rescue fair Rosemary from the evil canton sheriff and seclude her in the deep wood. Leary outsmarts all biographers, completes his own wonderful memoirs by candlelight with the help of elves.

Engines drone, grind, groan. Eileen sleeps. The teenagers sleep. The stewardesses catnap. I am awake.

I see no reason to worry. The plane will land. We will call Leary's lawyer. He will give us Leary's latest phone number. We will call that number. Leary will want to see us on our terms. He will want to meet Eileen. He will be living, say with a rock group in a recording studio in Zurich, noisy but safe. In between numbers, he will tell us what exciting things have happened. He will want my book to be a success. He will give me an autographed copy of his book. Then he will offer me a joint. I will refuse the joint, saying I have to take notes. He will get angry and say I am a turncoat fink. I will call him a son of a bitch. The bass guitar player will think I am a narc and will take a swing at me. He will miss but a fight will start anyway. Eileen will be shocked and frightened. The police will come and find five hundred Swiss francs' worth of cocaine in the book binding.

In reality, Leary was more impulsive than ever. I had gotten that impression from his agent. The agent was a scholarly, sincere Leary-supporter whom I called to help set things up. He said Leary was mercurial, guided largely by astrological signs and gut feelings. The stars and the stomach. The agent did not rejoice at the idea of my going.

"Tim has been ripped off so much by interviewers. Magazines and newspapers have been awful to him. They send people like you over to spend a few days asking interview questions, which Leary abhors, and then they come home and put out something pop and clever which makes Tim sound insane, which he is not, or foolish, which he also is not."

I said I wouldn't think of asking Leary a single interview question. "I'm not a reporter, I'm a colleague."

"Yes, but aren't you still trying to exploit him, use his name and reputation in some way? Not that you're the only one."

He was exaggerating Leary's notoriety. The hero's fame meant much to him.

"Well, he asked for it," I said.

"That's just what I *mean*. You think he's fair game. You can say anything you want about him, print outrageous lies and quote things he never dreamed of saying, and, since he's a fugitive, he can't sue or even reply."

"I don't want to do that."

"That's what they all say. You should ask yourself a searching question: Why do you want to see him? If the answer is to rip him off in a book, then, please, don't go. Write about something else."

I told the agent I would think it over, which I did. In the end, though, I decided Leary had asked for it. I called back the agent and told him I thought Leary had asked for it. I got Leary's lawyer's phone number in Zurich and called his office, leaving the word that we were coming. Finally, Leary himself called from Switzerland.

SWISS OPERATOR: We have the collect call from Dr. Timothy of Berne for Dr. Slack of Alabama . . .
  (*Come, come, Dr. Timothy. Is Interpol to be fooled by semi-incognito?*)
ME: Tim!
LEARY: Charles Slack.
ME: Yes.
LEARY: Yes.
  (*Pause.*)

ME: Well, Tim, we are coming to Switzerland. We want to come. We are taking the plane. Six P.M. Friday.

LEARY: Why?

ME: To see you of course. I want to see you.

LEARY: Ah hah.

(I can't tell if this is a satirical "ah hah," or a doubting one, or he is just pleased to get attention. I say nothing.)

LEARY: Is that the only reason?

ME: Oh, well, Tim, you know that can't ever be the whole story. I have other reasons, too.

LEARY: Ah hah.

(Pause.)

LEARY: And what are the other reasons?

ME: I am writing about you and me.

LEARY: I thought so. Will I like it?

ME: Probably not. As I remember, Tim . . .

LEARY: Yes, Charles.

ME: As I remember, Tim, you never did particularly like anything I wrote. I always seemed to like your stuff more than you . . .

LEARY: Charles.

ME: Yes.

LEARY: . . . when you get to Zurich, at the airport, call this number.

(He reads the number two or three times as I copy.)

LEARY: Got it?

ME: Got it, Tim. And, Tim, one other thing.

LEARY: OK.

ME: I am married to a wonderful girl I want you to meet.

LEARY: Wonderful, Charles.

ME: And Tim.

LEARY: Yes.

ME: How are you, Tim?

LEARY: Fine, and how are *you*, Charles?

ME: Fine, and how is the family? How are Rosemary and Susan?

LEARY: Oh, she is fine. She has gone to India.

ME: Who has gone to India?

LEARY: Susan. She went with her husband.

ME: And how is Rosemary?

LEARY: Yes, they left for India.

ME: Rosemary?

LEARY: No, Charles. *Susan.* Gone to India.

ME: But what about Rosemary?

LEARY: *(No answer.)*

ME: OK. I hope they have a fine time. Give my best to Rosem . . .

LEARY: Good-bye, Charles. See you when you get here. Call the number in Zurich.

ME: Goodby, Tim.

What *about* Rosemary? Didn't he have his hearing aid hooked up right? Oh, of course, he could always have been stoned—multiplexing my call among higher internal communications. But as time went by, I must confess, I knew better.

No romance had ever had more claims made for it, ecstatic, spiritual or orgasmic. It was the shining hope of love with dope for the whole love generation of the sexual revolution. If Mom and Dad would only turn on and fuck like Tim and Rosemary, there would be less hate in the world. War would end. Tim and Rosemary, their life was a lesson to us all. And now—here endeth the lesson.

10

Getting There

Shit! Arizona. Shit. California. Shit. *Of course,* Montana. Shit. I am standing on the wood deck of a pea-sized swimming pool on the roof of the Arizona. It's a slat-wood deck with big splinters and wide gaps to lose your keys between. I am in my bathing suit, leaning against the deck rail at the deep end of the pool, which is an above-ground pool, like optometrists buy in Alabama; only this pool is on top of the Arizona (pronounced Ah-ritz-own-ah), a Swiss-movement imitation American West hotel in beautiful downtown Lugano, Switzerland. It has Z-shaped balconies and private baths and imitation Grand Rapids built-ins and, naturally, up on top, this above-the-roof swimming pool. Shit.

Lugano is a north Italian resort in south Switzerland with West German tourists and American names on the hotels. You can see some of the names from up here on the Ah-ritz-own-ah: California, New York, Montana, Nevada. It must have been quite a fad, once, naming hotels. Now, hardly any Americans come here because, although it *is* a lovely spot with a lovely lake and a sheaf of rolling mountains filled with lovely Etruscan ruins, Lugano is, let's face it, dull. No gambling, skiing, swimming or jet-set loving. No hard drinking (with Scotch at ten francs a shot) and no film festivals, porn or corn. The music on the built-in radio is pure Welk, Mantovani-Muzak, like Alabama FM. Just about the main thing to do in Lugano, besides sit on the Piazza, is ride the sightseeing boat around the *lago*. Lugano would be perfect for a convention of American dry Baptists—if they knew where it was. As it is, we have Italian plant-managers up from Milan for a quiet weekend with their secretaries, we have the same Germans who are everywhere else in Europe, we have one or two English holiday-tours that chose Lugano this year over the Isle of Man—and we have Eileen and me on top of the Arizona.

Then, somewhere out in the Etruscan ruins, amidst the sheaf of rolling mountains, we have Timothy Leary and his band of Hell's Angels of 1966. Timothy Leary and the fat-assed motorcycles and Redbeard and Robin with Baby Orion and the thin man and spooky ladies— but, of course, no Rosemary. Timothy Leary riding his giant Yamaha up the narrow roads to the house of crumbling clay. Gray-faced, lean-and-dry Leary climbing up the old stairs of the dilapidated house and lying down on the mattress in the dining room. Leary in dirty white slacks and white sneakers and white sweater with nothing under it, shivering in August, wiping his lips, fixing up, tying up, letting go and pumping shit, then lying back on the rotten old mattress waiting for Liz the Cosmic Whore. Timothy Leary pumping shit.

And the shit with whose description I now offend your eyes is not fecal. It is not the common brown and mushy stuff, smelling of hydrogen dioxide and partially decomposed garlic from last night's anchovy pizza. No indeed, this shit is pure white and soft, a present pillow on whose downy bosom pain becomes the memory of pain and worry the remnant of some lost, half-formed recollection of the remotest possibility of a dry tit. *This* shit merges with the warm blood to make a warm rush of perfect pleasure as the heart, unwitting organ, pumps the shit up to the brain and past the barriers into the little nooks and capillary crannies where all the tiny painlets and stop-sign worry-warning signals are hiding, waiting for the shit to come and turn them off—which it does, which it does. Then, I am told, life's greatest joys of bed and board, of work and love, soon surrender to the complete satisfaction of this shit.

If that's all there was to the story, it would be bad enough—shit instead of food, shit instead of sex, shit instead of love and work—but there's more still. You see, after a while, the teeny, turned-off pain things and corked-up rivulets and venules of *angst* seem to want more and more shit, yes they do, and, what's more, they want their shit right on time, by golly. Those little gnomes and gnobbits that operate all the micro-circuit panic-buttons and alarums with which we are so generously equipped by the Great Quartermaster in case of attack—all these guys start wanting more and more shit in their shit-envelopes. They want shit-of-living increases and more beneshits. But most of all, by God, they want to get shitted *on time.*

All this causes inflation and a severe alteration in the balance of shitments. As the demand for shit goes up, well, the supply better go up too because . . . if, by chance, the supply goes down as the demand goes up . . . the International Brotherhood of Nerve Endings, man, they mean business. No little wildcat strikes or occasional shit-downers for them. They're organized for sabotage, they are. Actually, what they do is, they all push their buttons at the same time. They all hold a little meeting, decide when to let her rip and then, hot-line baby, the whole damn early-warning network goes popping off together. The tornado hits the siren factory.

Now, some people say they can take it. Some actually *do* take it pretty well, hanging on for dear life with the fires of Moloch up their ass, but most give in to the demands of the Brotherhood. After all, it's nothing but shit.

(Can Leary take it?)

These thoughts are an obsession with me now. They have only come over me recently. I didn't even *think* about it when I saw him, which was yesterday. We conversed, had tea and met the boys and girls (what a crew!), but *just* tea and talk, strained interactions, filthy surroundings, little lies. The idea that he might be using heroin, junk, shit, didn't even enter my head until just three hours ago, when I came up on the roof to go swimming and dropped my key between the slats. I had been moping around before that, trying to understand what, if anything, was wrong with him, asking myself why this and why that, until, next thing you know, the thought jumped to mind like finding a face in the clouds (or *it* finding *you*) and, once found, you can't *not* see it anymore. Shit. I know it. I just know it.

But I don't *really* know it. I mean, I didn't actually *see* him shoot up. I hadn't actually come out and *asked* him. (He hadn't told me, either.) The sun sets behind the diving board and the Campari signs go on down by the lake. I *could* be misjudging him, which would be awful. As light fades, so does conviction . . .

. . . which returns with drinks before dinner. I *know* it.

I just know it. And then after *entrecôte* and wine and a dance in a rotten nightclub (we can't keep up this spending), we are lying in bed under that feather bag that keeps the Swiss warm and productive and I'm telling Eileen that maybe it's for the best. If he wants an end, he should have it. He once said that heroin users were "wrapping themselves in a cocoon." Maybe that's it, poor old guy. If he must turn out the lights, let him. Everybody's got to sleep his own sleep.

And wake up someday. He *told* me he never would. He *told* me. Next morning, I'm doing sit-ups in the chilly air and yelling to Eileen that I have always been so sure that there are two *kinds* of drug users. First there are the heads and freaks who use hallucinogens, the mildest of which is pot, and *then* there are the junkies who use opiates. These are completely different breeds of cats— the turn-oners and the turn-offers. They do *not* come in the same body. They don't even *mix*—socially or in the bloodstream. Leary is a *head*, a freak. He would *never* use junk. Leary is the head of the heads. It was so written in the book—my book and everybody else's. Leary is a freak and does not use junk.

But I know he does.

And if Leary is using junk, then I'm wrong and Anslinger is right. Commissioner Harry J. Anslinger of the Federal Bureau of Narcotics, who called marijuana a lethal drug, right! The fed narc FBI (killer-weed) cop Kiwanis mentality. Anslinger and Louria, Donald B, M.D., who writes books with chapters called "Approaching Young People" and the Junior Chamber of Commerce pamphlets. Right! One toke and you're on the way to the nut house. Right! *One thing leads to another.*

But what about all the scientific data that show pot

doesn't lead to junk any more than mother's milk leads to crime? Wrong. What about all the statistics against the cycle theory? Wrong. Leary is the only statistic needed. Leary, *the* leading example *and* exponent of the non-cycle theory. Leary *personified* that one thing did *not* lead to another. So, if Leary is using junk, then Anslinger is right, Louria and the scare comic-books are right.

IF. IF. I'm sure he is, but I certainly can't prove it yet. Maybe I don't want to.

After we had landed in Zurich, wound our way through Customs and gotten some Swiss coins, I called the number Leary had given me. A law office answered and a girl there read me another number. I called it and got Leary, who seemed in a mellow mood.

"Ah, Charles, so the mental radar is working, isn't it, orbiting you in toward the center."

"Well, we're here. What do we do?"

"You see, I have shifted the entire operation from north to south. We keep on the move. We are now south, in Ticino, the Swiss wine country. Entirely different atmosphere, very soft, very charming. Now, let's see. What would be best for you? You do not have a car, I suppose?"

"No, Tim, you didn't say anything about getting a—"

"—or motor bikes? That, of course, is the very best way to travel, bikes. You wouldn't have—"

"No, Tim, we don't have motor bikes."

"I didn't think so. Well, then, I guess you will take the train, right?"

"Right. Which train?"

"OK, so, if you must take the train, then you will have

to find out *when* the next train leaves for Lugano. Lugano is a resort town in Ticino county. Find out the next train for Lugano. Then call and tell us when to meet you."

It meant another two hours' wait at the station and then two or three hours more from Zurich to Lugano. We were dead tired and off-base from the time-zone changes, but the spectacular view would not let us sleep on the train. Inside our compartment were more eye-openers: a talkative pair of naturalized Canadians, mother and son, heading back to native Yugoslavia for a visit. The boy shucked his boots, disclosing hose unchanged since Saskatoon. The sock-it-too-me was dreadful, so we spent the ride with our noses hung over the transom, sniffing the mountains as we ogled them.

Our little train eased into Lugano right on time, the early Italian afternoon when society ceases. The sun was bright and the air soft. Everybody but us was having Campari and soda in some cool café. I piled the bags out onto the empty platform, along with the raincoats, in case of rain, and the overcoats, in case of cold, and the plastic suit-bag and the carry-on bags and Eileen's camera and my doubleknit sport coat (with passports in the pocket) that it was too hot to wear. Our eyes, bleary from the night flight and the windy train ride, could not adjust to the bright, still air. However, we were not blind, and obviously there was nobody to meet us on the platform.

I grappled around with the bags and stuff and, since we had nowhere to go, I led the way. An underpass promised to lead out, so we trudged through and up the other side. Framed in an arch of light at the top of our stone steps was a thin, handsome, white-haired man dressed in white slacks, white sneakers and a big, loose white sweater. Tennis, anyone? He tripped lightly down the stairs to us. It was Leary—or the ghost of Errol Flynn. The pants were grayish, worn yellow and used. The sweater was new. There were gray lines in his cheeks. His eyes were pale and bleached. He looked at the luggage but made no comment. He fidgeted much, wagged his shoulders and knees. He had no hearing aid. Shaking hands was not hip, so we didn't. His fingernails were dirty. I thought about giving him a pat or hug, but that didn't seem right either. He smelled like talcum powder.

"This is Eileen," I said.

"So now we have Eileen." Leary kissed her, put his hands on her shoulders and looked her up and down and finally deep into the eyes to test her soul. I guess she passed. Anyhow, he took up a bag, did the steps with grace and led us out into the sunny afternoon of the piazza.

There, on the sidewalks of the Via Maraini, stood all the good Luganese I had thought would be lounging in cafés at this hour. Instead, they were out and on their feet, the better to observe a svelte hippie mother in a silk evening gown perched on a fat motorcycle, nursing a near-naked infant at the breast. Nearby, two leather-jacketed young men with stocky builds and thick beards slouched against another, even fatter road-hog. A third easy-rider, thin as a wire, hunched on a bench next to a dark girl. He was so thin as to have no hips or legs, just folded bluejeans. The girl had a hollow face with big liquid eyes. She, too, wore an evening gown, a long black one. From under it poked a big toe and from the toe dangled a high-heeled silver pump.

Fat-assed motorcycles, spooky girls and hipless men in leather jackets—"Hell's Angels of 1966," playing Lugano for the first time. Coal-eyed cherubim sniggered behind their ice creams. Naive Etruscan peasants gaped in wonderment. And now, in ring three, entering from the tunnel, all could see the leader of the pack, the notorious American crazy-professor, Dr. Timothy Leary, dressed in white, and his two tourist friends from Alabama.

There were no introductions, of course. Instead, Leary took out a beat-up pack of Gauloises and offered them around. Eileen and I were both at that stage where we automatically said, "We've quit and so should you," but somehow you couldn't say that to Timothy Leary, so we mumblingly declined. Leary shrugged and then lit his own, puffing fast and deep.

"Well," he said, "what do you want to do? Let's make plans." He looked at me for a moment as though he really expected me to have some plans, and when I didn't, he shrugged again and repeated the question to the others: "I mean, we *do* have to decide what we are going to do, where we are going to go. We can do anything we want, anything at all, as long as we know it is what we want."

The easy-riders and their womenfolk had all moved in now for a closer look at the pile of luggage and our Lord and Taylor doubleknits. It was some kind of a confrontation but what kind I don't exactly know. As far as Eileen was concerned, it was time for names. In a clear voice, she introduced herself and waited. Mumbles. The baby's name was Orion, the father was Dennis, the mother was Robin, and I didn't get the rest.

Dennis raised his hand. "I'll tell you what," he said. "Let's put these bags in the car." He smiled at Eileen. She smiled at him. I smiled at her. He smiled at me. The crowd smiled. Dennis and I lugged bags.

An old Volvo, full of dents with rust on the creases, was parked at the curb. Most of the luggage squeezed into the trunk but, embarrassingly, a couple of bags still wouldn't fit.

"That's OK," Dennis told Eileen. "There'll be room up front."

We leaned against the car, watching from a distance while Leary continued with the planning. He stood, jiggling his knees, talking rapidly to the thin man and the others, smoking constantly. Once or twice he picked up his butt from the street for final puffs before stomping it and lighting another. At last, he came to us to announce results.

"We're going home," he said. "Who wants to ride the bikes?"

Eileen looked longingly at the Volvo. Leary shrugged again.

"I choose the bike," said the woman in silver shoes, eyeing the thin young man. "Bikes are much better than cars."

"You'll want me to drive," said Dennis. "That gearshift is sticking worse than ever."

"I'll drive," said Leary.

Behind the wheel, Leary brightened. "We have taken a town house in Carona, an ancient place on top of a mountain, San Salvadore. Once we get out of Lugano traffic and going uphill, you'll appreciate the drive. Charming hamlets hang all over the mountainside. Roads, narrow and steep. Of course, bikes are really the only way to travel."

Dennis sat up front to help with the sticky gearshift. It took both hands to get us into second and, once in, it didn't look as though we were going to get out.

"That's OK," said Leary, "second is the best gear anyway." With that, we lurch up the Via Carona with the accelerator to the floor. "Everybody drives fast in Ticino." Leary launches into a lecture about Luganese driving habits and the advantages of motorbikes on narrow mountain roads. Frequently during this symposium, he points out the window at landmarks or turns full face to us for punctuation. Dennis, up front, tries occasionally to take us out of second but fails because Leary has the engine full throttle. Once in a great while, Leary checks the road to see if it is still there, and even takes his hands out of the window to rest them on the steering wheel— but this only to avoid the most obstinate of pedestrians.

After fifteen minutes of ascending thrills, I am about to comment on how nimble the peasants are to keep out from under our wheels and all, when suddenly the lecture stops and all hell breaks loose with much honking and revving and waving of hands. A motorcycle zooms past, going twice our speed and trailing yards of black silk. I was glad to see that Baby Orion does not appear to be a passenger.

"Oh, but Orion loves to ride the bikes," replies Dennis. "Too bad that he and Robin stayed in town. They went to the bank to get us some money. We are having a big party tonight."

"Yes," says Leary. "First we go to the top of San Salvadore—and then we go *much* higher." He floors the gas again, and we are really making dust.

Resigned to second gear all the way, Dennis turns to tell us some stories about other exciting rides, including the time he drove the Volvo all night on Swiss mountain roads while stoned on five hundred micrograms of "beautiful, crystalline LSD."

We pull this way and that through town. Hubs scratch
curb and door stoops as kids jerk their toes out of the
way. Then we dive up a steep driveway into a slanty old
courtyard of sandy cobblestones, orangy-brown tile
roofs angling every which way and ancient, crumbling
façades. It's an abandoned Etruscan flea market.

"And *this,*" says Leary, bumping smack into a brown
clay wall, "is *home.*"

Pause for prayer in the back seat.

"Marvelous," say I, falling out of the Volvo.

"*Great* to be here," echoes Eileen, looking up, "and
the place is so . . . so *permanent,* isn't it?"

"Absolutely timeless," says Leary, "and now for some
more plans. What do we want to do now?"

Nobody has plans.

"Of course, the bike got here long ago," says Leary.
The fat chrome buggy sits propped near the wall. Its
riders join us. The girl is hobbling. On the exhaust pipe,
the high heel of her slipper has melted like cheese on a
griddle.

"Man, you two were burning tracks, weren't you," says
Leary. "Should we stay out or go in or have tea or what?"

"Have tea," says the girl. Others nod. We go to a
square hole in the clay over by the motorcycle.

The hole is a front door. It leads to a small room with
one big, ugly, round painting on a pedestal next to some
old stairs. We take the stairs to an upper room with one
window and nothing on the floor but two mattresses and
a few dirty pillows. There's a woman waiting up there,
dressed only in a shift. Leary shoots her a frown and she
departs. Leary and Eileen plunk down on one mattress.
I get the other. Everybody else gets floor. Eileen leans
back, tired. Leary ceremoniously fluffs some dust out of
a grimy pillow and stuffs it behind her neck. The woman

returns, wearing a long silk gown and taking orders for tea. A boy of about seven tugs her sleeve.

"I'm Liz," says she.

"It's a striking dress," says Eileen.

"Thin queue," says Liz, very British.

"I'm Davie," the boy tells Eileen.

"OK, now," says Leary, settling his legs, taking up his tea and his cigarette and leaning forward to direct the group. "Don't we all think it would be good if Slack, here, told us about himself?"

Interest was only mild but Leary went on. "Slack's orbit and mine intersect every . . . what is it now, five years? I think he should give us an idea of what he has been doing in the five years."

"Well, we're living in a university environment. We seem to like it. I am a professor of education."

"Surely there's more to it than that. 'Professor' is a title, not an activity. I used to be a professor, myself. Tell us all what you *do.*"

"Well, I teach . . . and do research and some writing. Do you want to hear about the writing?"

"Not particularly. No, Charles, what I, and the rest of us, are entitled to know is: Is Slack *involved* in anything? You must be involved in *something,* a little departmental politics or committeework? As I remember, you used to have some liberal causes, skirmishes with the establishment. Any more of those?"

"Oh sure," I said.

"Having trouble with the dean?"

"Always."

"I see." He winks at them. *He* is interviewing *me.*

"Nothing serious enough to get you suspended, I suppose."

"No."

"Or fired."

"No."

"Or famous."

"No."

"Or arrested."

"No."

"Or jailed . . ."

"Come on, Tim, why this—"

"I am *merely* getting out a few facts for the benefit of these people here, who never heard of you. How can you expect them to be interested in someone they don't know? So, tell us about yourself. We want to know what you are *into*. If you are into anything, tell us what it is. Any exciting drugs, for example? Any religious experiences? New interests?" He is edgy, fast with the questions.

"Recently, I have become active in computers," I say. "Computers have a big potential in psychology, I think."

"I'm sure they do."

Pause.

"Well, are you going to tell us about it or should we imagine it for ourselves?"

"I'll tell you."

"Yes, yes, I'm sure we would all be interested in *anything* you might be able to tell us about computers." He sighs heavily, sips tea, puffs the Gauloise and waves it at me. "So, go right ahead."

"Well," say I. "There have been many advances, especially something called 'time-sharing' . . ."

"Made by freaks," he says.

"What?"

"I say the *advances*. Made by freaks, you know. The fundamental discoveries and inventions, the *real* innovations down in basement labs. Wild youngsters quaffing LSD and making things nobody has ever seen before—like totally new *kinds* of computers. Freaks."

"Well, um, *any*way, using this time-sharing computer, my brother and I—you met my brother back at Harvard, didn't you—he and I do research . . ."

"Never met him in my life."

"Are you sure?"

"Absolutely."

"Um, well, anyway, he and I, we and some other people, we programmed this time-sharing computer to collect data from people—"

"But what does it all really *mean?*" Leary interrupts.

Dennis answers this one. "I think it's *vastly* important. I read recently where soon we will *all* have computers. The important combination is computers and electromagnetic fields. In the future, the central computer will emanate rays directly out to all the smaller computers. The brain is nothing but a computer. This means that *all* our computers will be in tune, so to speak. They will all be of one mind, guided by rays from the big computer. That's what *I* think. Cosmic computers. It will mean cosmic thoughts for *everybody*. We will have cosmic men and women, cosmic doctors. Everybody can be his own Doctor. Cosmic Professors and—"

"Cosmic whores," says Liz.

"Well, anyhow *that's* what I read," continues Dennis, "computers and electromagnetic rays. Now I have to go to Lugano to get Robin and the baby."

There is appropriate silence after Dennis's exit; Leary soon picks up the thread again. "Take me, for example," he says. "Let's say that *I* want to use this computer set-up —the one developed by some wild, inventive genius you don't happen to know—then, what would I do? Be specific. What really happens?"

Liz is stacking tea mugs against her bosom. She takes them out. Her son, Davie, grabs her hem again and waves good-bye to Eileen.

"Well," I say, "You would have this device called a 'terminal.' It looks like a TV set with a typewriter keyboard in front. You call the computer on the phone and then hook up the terminal to it. Words appear on the TV screen . . ."

"Now, *please*, don't you all agree with me?" Leary asks, looking around. "This description is not answering my question?"

No answer. The thin man slips out of the room.

"Tell me, Slack, what *can* this thing do for me? Can it solve problems? Can it give information? What?"

"I'm trying to describe it."

"Go on."

"Well, on the screen would probably appear some words. These can be anything at all, a question perhaps. You answer by pressing keys on the keyboard, *yes, no, maybe*. The computer can then act on the information you have provided . . ."

"What information?"

"Well, in one experiment, we asked psychological questions and the computer stored the answers and made a summary . . ."

"What questions?"

"Standard psychiatric questions. You know, *'Have you been feeling depressed?' 'Do you have trouble getting to sleep?'* "

"Go on."

"And the rest. You know. Standard psychiatric interview."

"Of *course* I know the standard psychiatric interview. *Both* roles. First I asked, then I answered. How about *'hallucinations'*? What about *'Do you take drugs?'*?"

"Yes, all such questions."

"My God, Slack, if the computer was any good, it would *know* Timothy Leary took drugs. It wouldn't have to ask."

Everybody has left now, except Eileen, who may be asleep.

"Lord, Tim," I whisper. "How did we ever get talking about this?"

He smiles. "You're tired, Slack. Get some rest. We have rooms up back. Sorry, no sheets. Or, if you want, there's a good inn."

"I think the inn," I say, looking at Eileen, whose eyes are closed.

"As you wish. I myself sleep outdoors." He pats my neck to show all is not lost. I smell that smell again. "There'll be a high time tonight. We'll come by for you about seven. You're just not a part of things here yet . . . and, Slack?"

"Yes."

"Stop pretending, Charles. You don't know anything about computers."

The Villa Carona turns out to be charming. Before sacking out, we look around: *Botanischer Garten, Schöne Spazierwege, Ristorante* and *Bar* (one bottle of Scotch). Eileen takes me off under an arbor at the end of the garden.

"There's Sam Stanley, for example," she says, giving me the eye of brown iron.

I search the view. "What about Sam Stanley?"
"Isn't *he* a computer-inventor?" The eye is still there.
"I guess so." The view is a valley of blue shadows.
"Certainly he's a computer-inventor," she says. "But isn't he a good one?"
"Many patents," I say, "but so what? Oh, do you mean . . . ? *I* know what you mean. He's *no freak*. Sam Stanley is *certainly* no freak. Very conservative."
"Right," she says. I feel the eye is gone. "Also about your writing. I just don't *like* people to make cracks like that. I can't even *read* Leary's stuff. And *another* thing, didn't your brother . . . yes he did! Your brother told us he met Leary. Leary is wrong about that, too . . ."
In our room, she undresses for the nap, but I just stand there with my pants down as realization creeps over me. "There certainly *is* something about that relationship, isn't there?" I say.
"You're different with him," she says. "You just seem to slip into some kind of one-down role. He rides over you. He becomes your teacher. *He gives you tests.*"
"He was, once, sort of, my teacher—my senior colleague, anyway." I get one leg out of the pants. "Old habits, I guess." The floor is shiny. They must polish it every day.
"But do you still want to take his course?" She stands there in her bathrobe pointing her little body at me and giving me what-for with the brown eyes. "He's a creep. I think he's a creep. He has let himself go. He needs a bath. He's trying to put you below him. And then telling you you don't know about computers!"
"Well, I certainly didn't stand up for myself, did I?"
"Maybe you were trying to protect him."
"Oh, I don't know. Our relationship goes back so far. I can't exactly say what I'm doing."

She steps over to me. "Do you want to 'become a part of things' with them tonight? He is a dangerous man, involving all those young people in bad drugs."

"I've been thinking about going," I say, kicking off the pants. "The answer is definitely no, but, then, also I thought maybe we should at least go and observe . . ."

"Haven't you seen enough of his parties? Don't you know what happens?"

"Pretty much."

She turns right around and goes down the hall to the bathroom, where she takes her own sweet time.

At seven forty-five, Dennis calls from the lobby and I answer. They are all down there waiting for us to go with them to a "castle" to have the party. Eileen shrugs: It's as I please.

"You know, Dennis, I think we're too completely tired to even get up. Eileen is, um, asleep and I just can't bring myself to wake her. You know how it is. See you in the morning, OK?"

When I hang up, she moves around behind me, breathing on my neck. "I'll show you what a high time is," she says.

Next morning, we walked over to their place but the door was closed and the motorcycle gone. I wanted to find out what happened at the party, I was also relieved to escape without facing them. I left a note that we were sorry to miss, etc., but needed to go to Lugano to find lodgings and rent a car. I said we would call in a few days.

It was more like a week. In the Arizona, we had that one expensive night with its insight (or perhaps delusion), then moved on to a good but cheap third-floor Zimmer in an old pension on the outskirts of town. Eileen turned out to have the patience, luck and skill for great boardinghouse finds. She never gives up, compares everything to everything else, *always* looks at just one more and then takes her time chosing the best of the lot. That's how we got Pensione Morf on Via Tesserete. Madame cooked delicious stew and the little Italian guy who polished floors saved a garden table for me every morning so I could write. I wrote nothing of value, but that wasn't his fault, or the garden's.

Instead of calling Leary, I brooded about him. Lugano is a great place to brood. Besides the gardens, there are easy-climb hills for scenic brooding, sunny cafés where you can brood all day over wine or ice cream or beer and watch the town girls, who have black hair and somber black eyes. When it rains, you can move under a shop awning and brood on the jewelry. When it gets chilly, you can take your *Herald Tribune* inside and brood over fine hot chocolate. And if it's really cold *and* rainy, you can dash back to your pension and climb the stairs to your room and close both the outside and inside shutters and creep under your featherbed for some totally serious brooding in absolute warmth and darkness.

After four or five days of this indulgence, I finally did call him one evening, but the phone didn't answer. At last, we rented a car, a Volkswagen, and drove up to Carona to have another try.

Leary was out but Dennis welcomed us anyway. He took us to the second-floor kitchen, surprisingly modern and adequate, where we made instant coffee. Liz came in and chatted briefly with Eileen. Robin and the baby were there.

"Do you work?" asked Liz of Eileen.

"Yes, I do," said Eileen.

"What do you do?" asked Robin.

"I work with pregnant teenagers," said Eileen, sounding just like a social worker.

"You mean they've slipped up and got knocked and need help?" asked Liz.

"Right," said Eileen.

"Well," said Dennis, "all I can say is, we have a lot of them around *here.*"

The thin fellow sat on top of the kitchen table with his chin on his knees. He said, in English with a Swiss accent, that the house was drafty. That was all he had to say. Dennis on the other hand, was filled with information which he was willing to share. Here are some of the points he covered:

Leary had gone to Bern for negotiations on an album he was making with a Swiss rock-and-roll band. There was considerable disagreement as to who should direct things. Dennis felt the band was less than adequate, rather corny ("musical," not "electronic") and only interested in Leary for his name. Leary, on the other hand, was into new, cosmic ideas about white noise, computers, ultrasound and drugs and had made important discoveries about subliminal stimulation and the value of electronically generated waves. The rock-and-roll group had not been catching on to all this. All they wanted to do was sing Swiss translations of American hits, and they were not up to feedback loops and ultrasonic vibrations. Not, that is, until Dennis spread wisdom around, "plenty of wonderful crystalline acid." After this, the rock band had a much more advanced sound. The resulting tape was still not to Leary's liking, because the engineer who put it together was completely straight at the time. He had, for example, entirely cut Leary's subliminal chorus of "Put opium into your arm," intended to be repeated at different frequencies and rates three hundred and sixty-four times (once for each day of Leap Year) during an entire side of the album.

I asked Dennis how, if the chorus was supposed to be subliminal, did they know it had been eliminated. Dennis replied that they just *knew* all right, they just *knew.* You couldn't fool *Timothy Leary* when it comes to subliminals. There was also trouble on the literary front. Author Clifford Irving was strongly admired by Leary for ripping off the Establishment press with his fraudulent biography of Howard Hughes. Leary, not to be outdone by Irving, was having his own fight with publishers. The way Dennis told it, I couldn't quite tell whether Leary was tricking them or they him. Either Leary had written one book and sold it twice to two different publishers (making him the victor over the capitalist-pig publishers); or he had written two books and sold them both to the same publisher for the price of one (making him temporary underdog in the battle for freedom from the New York money-grubbers); or both, in which case one publisher bought both books and another publisher bought just one of the same books sold to the other. Anyhow, the result was that one book, *Jail Notes,* was really just an early draft sent for approval and had never been properly honed down. The other book, *Confessions of a Hope Fiend,* was going to be *much* better if they only would allow Leary the time to do a good job. I told Dennis I could sympathize with that.

From records and books, we went on to people and events. What had happened to everybody? On this topic, Dennis was most knowledgeable. For example:

Leary's son, Jackie, was in jail but was soon to be released.

The house in Berkeley hills with its view had been sold to pay lawyers. The leftovers, four or five thousand, went to Jackie and Susan, who, with her husband, promptly left for India. Susan was worried they didn't have enough, but Dennis thought the money would "last for ever in India."

The Timothy Leary Defense Fund was in fair swing, with small sums coming in all the time from cosmic friends and neighbors all over the world.

Also, soon Leary and his group would have "all the money they would ever need." Presumably, this would be from books or records, but the source was not specifically mentioned.

Owsley had been arrested, had done time but was now out.

There had been an *"enormous* bust" in Orange County, California. Besides "dope and everything else," the sheriff also found equipment to forge passports. Copies of Leary's tract on "the honorable profession of drug smuggling" were likewise discovered on the premises. If Orange County ever got its hands on Leary again . . . well, the judge had already set bail, just in case they got him back, at five million dollars!

Leary had undergone fenestration operations on both ears and now could hear "like a teenager" without a hearing aid.

This house in Carona, the one we were in, as well as others they stayed in in Switzerland, was "provided by a friend." The name of the friend was not volunteered.

Leary had become great buddies with the son of author Hermann Hesse. Hesse, Jr., felt Leary was greatly responsible for the recent resurgence of his father's works in the States. "They" wanted Leary to play the part of Hesse in a movie of *Steppenwolf,* or, anyway, "they" were thinking about it. Hesse's son said so.

Rosemary was living with a Swiss nobleman of some

kind. The reason for her break with Leary was circumstantial: She just couldn't take any more of Leary's absences in lockup. There was a long story about how Rosemary had always wanted to bear Tim's child but needed special medical treatment. That was the last straw for Rosemary. The rich Swiss was handy, so she split.

Leary was "in close" with several rich Swiss of his own, who found him stimulating and charming. Leary's charm never faded. Only the other day he had had an accident with a bike and when the police came he had no license, no identification, no passport and no proper command of the language. His charm alone had gotten him off scot-free. Everybody who knew him well, liked him, except, of course, people with some kind of ax to grind, like Eldridge Cleaver in Algiers.

"Oh, yes, Dennis, tell us about that," I asked.

Dennis obliged, with the observation that Leary and Cleaver just had different "philosophies." Cleaver's motto was "Shoot to kill," whereas Leary's was "Aim to live." It was as simple as that. Leary believed in internal freedom first, Cleaver in external revolution. Leary knew there wasn't going to be an external revolution; Eldridge knew he knew. Eldridge couldn't take it, had him kicked out.

"How did he get here, I mean into Switzerland from Algiers?"

"Just got on a plane."

"No passport or anything?"

"That's right. He just got on a plane with Rosemary and got off in Zurich. Of course, the Swiss had to arrest him for having no papers, but they let him out eventually."

"How long can he stay in Switzerland?" I asked.

"Well, *that* doesn't look too good. He hasn't been arrested for any crime committed *here*, but still, if you have no papers—which, of course he hasn't . . . Actually, he was given until August first to get out of the country."

"August *first* has passed!"

"Of course, but then they don't actually come and get you for a month or two after that."

"My God, where will he go?"

"Well, there aren't too many places, actually. First of all, it has to be someplace with no extradition treaties with the U.S. Second, it has to be a place you can *get* to from Switzerland without landing in any place *with* an extradition treaty. Then, it has to be a place where it is possible for him to live. And, of course, it has to be a place that will accept Dr. Timothy Leary."

"Name one," I said.

". . . Um, well, to tell the truth, we believe our best hope is that the Swiss will change their minds."

Eileen asked, "Dennis, how was the party? The one we missed last week?"

"Marvelous. It was a *fabulous* party. Cosmic. You two really missed an unusual experience."

"What exactly happened?"

"Well, we went someplace different, saw some people and turned on."

"Did Leary sleep outdoors?"

"I don't know, I was too stoned to really know."

And lastly, what about Leary and us?

"I don't know," said Dennis. "You should have called him."

"But I *did* call him, just a few nights ago. No answer."

"That was probably the night we went out to dinner. He seems to want to go out to restaurants now, now that . . ."

". . . Now that his days here are numbered?"

"Oh, I don't know. Yes, you should have called him. Maybe he felt hurt."

And it was true. Dennis's theories were cosmic but his facts were solid. To make things worse, Leary tried to call us a couple more times, but *we* were out (taking the Volkswagen to St. Moritz on an impulse).

"It's like a honeymoon for us," I tried to explain when we finally got on the phone together, "the one we didn't get in Alabama." The connection was bad and I was shouting.

"Of course," said Leary, "but it looks like your chances with us are gone. We move again today. North to Lucerne."

"We can see you later on—say, in Lucerne?"

"I'm afraid that would be impossible."

"Tim, don't hang up. Let me just say this. I think we have behaved rudely, but the main reason is Eileen and I seem to need to be alone together. Also, truthfully, we are afraid of the scene, the drugs and all." I was talking loud and fast. "*Also,* I want you to know that I think it was very considerate of you to make this call now. You didn't *have* to. You could have just left for wherever you are going without calling. But you didn't. I want you to know that, if there is *any* chance we might see you again, we want to take the chance up. I mean it, Tim, I really do."

"Well," he said, "OK, but I don't think so."

Time might heal the wound but nothing could be done about it for now. We packed the Volkswagen and moved north toward Lucerne, but before we got there, I veered us off to the right, ending, luckily, in a charming spot called Immensee where audacious swans hogged the lake shore waiting for a boatload of children to come feed them twice a day. The swans didn't like American bathers to obstruct their symbiosis with the children, and when the boat came, the swans would attack me. They would honk and I would splash and the children would stamp and cheer. (Many rooted for the swans, I'm sure.) Twice a day, after this marvelous exercise, I retired to my typewriter to await the muse.

The muse didn't come. I didn't know what to do but move us on again. So I drove high into the mountains at the far end of Lake Lucerne, up to a hiker's paradise called "Seelisberg," where, all day long, no matter how you turn, the mountains slap your eyeballs. Everywhere, an edge, a ridge or a railing invites you to peek down and have your orbs sucked out and washed in the lake below.

We woke to cowbells every morning and slept to the tune of walking-club folksongs from a beer hall next door. In between . . . nothing. No work done. There was no use even trying to write.

"Why not send him a letter?" asked Eileen.

"He'd never answer."

"Give him a call."

"What will I say?"

"I know what to do," she said. "Invite him to dinner."

"He won't come," said I.

But he did. I sent a telegram, care of his attorney in Bern, saying he should pick the restaurant, the companions, the wine, the date and the time. I would pick up the tab. He bit on this.

We were to meet him in Schwartzenberg, a little farm town south of Bern. He said they had rented a farm there. We drove to the inn in town, which was closing for the winter, but they gave us a room for one night only. We weren't checked in more than forty-five minutes before the barmaid called up to say our friend was waiting.

He didn't want to show his face inside but waited, hidden, near the door until we came to him. Then he led us straightaway out, across the street, to a spanking new, four-seater, stop-sign-yellow Porsche parked at the curb. The car was spotless, obviously powerful—a lump of streamlined dynamite.

Eileen sat in back. "This beautiful machine," I said to her as I buckled my seat belt, "must have cost eight thousand dollars."

"Ten thousand," said Leary.

The dashboard was equipped with American dials, and Leary drove with his seat belt fastened under his fanny to keep the buzzer off. The car obviously fascinated him and made him pay more attention to his driving. Still he lectured.

"You may know by now," he said as we rolled along over the little roadways, "Switzerland is Disneyland. This is where Disney got all his ideas. The *purpose* of Switzerland is pleasure—especially for the rich. And the, ah, decadent rich." I thought I saw him wince, perhaps thinking about Rosemary and her new boyfriend. Out the window, a glider plane circled above us. "What you must do with Switzerland is discover how to crack it open to get at the goodies."

"But where do you get the money?" asked Eileen.

She meant, I think, "where would anyone get the money," but he thought, I think, she meant him personally. He didn't answer.

"And what do you do?" he asked her.

"I work with pregnant teenagers," said Eileen, sounding again like a caseload Lola at the social-work shop. "I am developing a project to open a school for neglected young mothers-to-be in Alabama." Why tell *him* about it? My heart sank. Now, *they* weren't going to get along.

"A worthy cause, I'm sure," he said. He drove in silence for several minutes. "And so you think a school is what they need, eh?"

"Yes."

"They may want something else besides school. Maybe they should be free. Maybe they should drop out."

"Well, that's what the county board of education thinks. It makes them leave when they get pregnant. They have nowhere to go."

"You think they should all come to your school?"

"I don't think they should come to yours."

Tie. Truce.

"Even if that's what they want to do, eh?" asked Leary. This time, she didn't answer.

No thank you. I'd rather not this time. Sorry. Thanks but no. I am running out of ways to decline.

"Toke?"

"Not just now."

"Pipe?"

"Sorry."

"Hashish-oil ball?"

"Uh uh." *Hashish-oil ball!*

"It's a ball of hashish oil." Robin smiles. "They're marvelous." She holds out this little brown, muddy thing, rolling it around in her fingers. "You *eat* it. Like this." Down it pops like Cracker Jacks at the movies.

Leary smiles benignly at Robin, who sets about rolling up some more hashish-oil balls. If Leary is annoyed at Eileen and me for non-participation in his afternoon drugfest, he isn't letting on. Leary is becoming the inner Leary, smiling, silent, eyes half shut, noticeable breathing, getting *there*. Now he has it. He is focused. Fused and fixated on nothing but his own interior point of concentration. It's a cool nobody can bust. No square plebs from Alabama are going to cross this mountain pass to spoil this Swiss-autumnal, dusky high.

We are all huddled in one little backroom of this old, windowless farmhouse with ceiling beams like battering rams and floor planks the size of diving boards. Candles flicker from every nook. Incense wafts from unseen crannies. We all sit motionless on mattresses—what else?—digging the heavy ambience. Eileen and I are not smoking, eating, shooting or in any other way injesting any stuff, including hashish-oil balls. However, it becomes necessary for us to breath in every now and then. That act alone is quite enough to get us well into things even without partaking of the quantities of dope of all kinds which, at Leary's unspoken bidding, Dennis and the ladies dish out like grits at a Baptist breakfast. Everybody is fairly zonked but Eileen and me. Everybody is *so* generous. They keep offering us things.

"Hashish?"

"Not right now."

"Pot?"

"None for us."

"Strudel?"

"No, I really . . . strudel?"

"Yes, apple and yummie," says Liz. "Baked this morning in our old, old oven, *outdoors*. You'll *love* it." She plonks a slice of wet agate on my plate next to the cup of green tea and the brown hashish-oil ball, of which I have been lately wondering how to divest myself of possession. I look at the strudel and the strudel looks at me. It *seems* innocent enough but, man, it had *better* be strictly strudel with *no* surprises. *Are you legal, strudel?* Yes, Charles, I am legal: There is nothing in here but us apples. Bite . . . and apple seeds, and cores, and apple stems, and skins. *Crunch,* man, hippie strudel, *crump!*

Everybody chomps strudel. Even Leary, who usually disdains such snacks, and who is also, no doubt, saving room for his free restaurant dinner. *Chomp.* Man, this is some heavy strudel.

The gang's all here: Liz, the thin man, Dennis, Robin, Silver Shoes, Baby Orion, seven-year-old Davie.

"Hi, Davie!"

"Mister, I am not going to say 'hi' to you."

"Why not, Davie?"

"I don't say 'hi' when I'm down."

"How's that again?"

"Well, you see, you *think* there is *one* Davie, but there are really *two* Davies. There is Davie Uppie and Davie Downie. Right now, I am Davie Downie and I don't say 'hi' to people."

"OK with me, Davie."

But not OK with Eileen. She gives Davie Downie the long look of brown iron. "Davie, I want you to come over here and say 'hi' to me."

Davie walks over to Eileen and says "hi." "I have crayons," he tells her.

"Let's draw something," she says.

Eileen is a big surprise. She has taken on the hippie girls as her clients and, low and behold, they appreciate it and *love* her. They *like* the fact that her mind is clearer than theirs. They listen to everything she says. She dispenses nutrition information to Liz and talks home remedies with Robin.

Baby Orion is sick with a cough. He won't take his medicine. After checking the label (no opiates), Eileen briefly pinches Baby Orion's nose. When he opens his mouth to breathe, she slips the cough medicine in.

Robin and Liz watch in admiration. "We really need somebody like you around here. We're isolated in this life," says Robin.

Liz thinks Davie may have a problem. Is he overly dependent on her?

"Well, Davie told *me,*" says Eileen, "that he was *sure* you loved him because you had come from England to get him at last."

"Right!" says Davie.

"I was away from him too long," says Liz.

"I think he is afraid of something," says Eileen.

"I'm afraid of *this,*" says David, holding up a record album. The album is inscribed "To Timothy Leary from Erika." On the cover is a full face of a screaming woman with white lips, white nostrils, and black cheeks, eyeballs and teeth. The pupils of her eyes are red. It is an LSD-trip recording by some German singer.

"That's just an LSD picture," says Dennis. "You better get over being afraid of *that.* When you grow up, you'll take it like we all do. You shouldn't be scared of it."

"But I don't *like* the picture," says Davie.

"I think *that's* the problem," says Eileen.

"You mean this *picture?*" says Liz.

"No," says Eileen. "The problem is LSD. David is scared of LSD."

"Do you think that really could be it?" asks Liz.

"Yes, definitely, I think that is it," says Eileen.

"Well, my, my," says Liz.

As if on cue, a thin, nondescript little guy in a brown beard wanders in, loaded on acid. We saw him first sitting on the ground as we approached the farmhouse in the Porsche.

"This is one of *our* clients," Leary had said then to Eileen. "He has come to us to have his experience."

All afternoon the little guy has been wandering around the farm on his trip. It is a bad trip and, to Leary's annoyance, the guy keeps coming in and saying so.

"Man, this trip is *awful.* Just *terrible.* I don't think I *ever* want to do this again. I never felt so *bad* in my life. I just want to *die.* Can't any of you *do* anything to make it any *better* for me?"

"Come here," says Leary.

"Where?" asks the guy.

"Over here on the mattress," says Leary. "Now, look me in the eye, please."

"Where?" asks the guy.

"In the eye," says Leary.

"Where?"

"Here, in my *face.* See my eye? OK, look me in my eyes. Deep. Now, One, two, three . . . *boom!*" Leary claps hands, *smack!* "You are cured! You are cured! Now, don't you feel better?"

The guy is silent for a minute, making up his mind.

"I said, *'don't you feel better?'* You are *cured!*" repeats Leary.

"Yes," he says. "Yes, yes, yes. You mean, I am all better?"

"Yes," says Leary, "you are *all better.*"

"And it *feels* all better, too," says the guy. "I mean, *pretty much* better . . . although, although, although . . . not *entirely* better, not *completely.* No, no. Gee, I don't know. I just don't know. I *just* don't know. No, man, I don't think so. I don't think so . . . It is still pretty bad. Awful, in fact. Damned awful. *Terrible.* Worse than before. Oh, my God, it is really worse than before. Help. Help. I'm suffering, dying. This is the worst thing that ever happened to me, the very worst. Can't you do anything to help? Anything at all?"

"Why not go outside and get some air? It will help," suggests Leary. The fellow leaves, shaking his head.

Dennis says, "Let's dig *sounds,* man, let's *do* something. Go back to the electronics room and listen to the tapes."

"Excellent idea," says Leary.

A new girl joins us. She takes a shawl off her head, and her hair is pitch black. She is dressed in shawls. While Dennis fiddles with the electronic gear, the girl and Eileen talk about where they come from. Her name is Patricia and she is half Swiss and half Spanish. It may be bugging Leary that Eileen gets along so well with his girls.

"Of course, one is supposed to listen to this while under LSD," says Leary to Eileen, "or some other appropriate substance. Do you and Charles take LSD together?"

"No," says Eileen.

"She's right," I tell him, "and we aren't going to do it."

Dennis is ready with the tape player. It is a huge machine, with speakers big as coffins. The coffins produce a sound somewhere between a siren and a sneeze. Dennis makes it louder. It lasts for at least twenty minutes. "Now, to *me*," says Leary, breaking the silence at the end, "that was a religious experience." He turns to Eileen. "Are you interested at all in religious experiences? Because if you are, you would see the importance of LSD. But perhaps you are not concerned with religious values. Maybe . . ."

"I'm coming *down*," says Dennis. "Let's *do* something. Let's go back to the other room and smoke some more dope—or *something*."

In the other room, Leary starts again to talk about the religious life and what it means. He is looking at Eileen, "I don't suppose you know what I'm talking about but—"

"Tim." I lean over to whisper to him. Some candles have gone out, and I have a hard time finding his ear. "Tim, I must tell you. Eileen is really *into* religious values."

"Oh, so?" he says.

"Yes." I am still whispering. "That's the reason I wanted you to meet her. She is a very unusual person. She has had a very unusual career. Tim, for fifteen years Eileen was a Roman Catholic nun, a member of a strict order, prayed five hours a day."

There is, for a minute or two, a stony silence. Without the candles, the room seems colder. With the silence comes a little fear, a leftover tinnitis from the electronic sounds like the boop-y-oop of the police.

"Let's go for a walk," I say to Eileen. As I get off the mattress, Leary gives my hand a pat. He is smiling again. "That's nice," he says. "Lovers to walk."

Outside was silent, starless, absolutely black. We walked. Water dripped somewhere.

"Let's stop," Eileen said, "or we will lose the way back."

"I think it's a trough," I said.

"I keep worrying the police will come in there," she said.

"He'll get hungry soon and we can go to dinner." I could touch the water now. We hugged each other against the barn.

"All those drugs," she said. "Where do they *get* all those drugs?"

"If they're not smuggling or dealing, I don't know."

"It's awful for the children."

"Do you love me?" I asked.

"Yes."

"Will you always be with me and help me be a good person?"

"Yes. Will you do the same for me?"

"If you need it, I will. Will you do it for me every day, no matter what?"

"Yes, no matter what."

At last he did get hungry, left the room and went and dressed himself for dinner in his handsome white sweater. He came back in the doorway to adjust the sweater, folding and unfolding the cuffs. He was showing off for the girls and making up his mind. Patricia got the nod.

Patricia, Eileen and I all got in the Porsche, set to go, but Leary was fumbling around. My God, I thought, he's too stoned to drive.

"The angels will guide us," he said, "because I can't

find my glasses," and tracked the yellow line between his headlamps all the way to the Schwartzenberg inn while angels diverted the oncoming traffic.

The inn was closed, but he woke the chef and rummaged up a waiter. He put his arm around the chef. Yes sir, there would be fine *entrecôte* and good wine and everything else very good for special people.

The waiter loved him at first sight and dressed up in full uniform to serve us.

He hardly touched his wine. "Well, am I different?" he asked me. "Have I changed any since sixty-eight?"

"Yes," I said, *"this* is different." I gestured at my arm with an imaginary hypodermic. "You said then that you never would."

He hung his head to the side in mock shame (or pretend mock). "It was my last tie to civilization. When they put me in jail, they broke that tie."

"What was it like in prison?" I asked. He had written two pretty good books about it, but I didn't know that yet.

"I wasn't there," he said.

Eileen and Patricia talked about religious highs. They agreed that special states of consciousness were possible through despair and resignation. Patricia said she had once come to Lucerne, broke and friendless, with no place to stay. She was desperate at first, and frightened, but then she grew submissive, and eventually her state of mind transcended all concern. It had opened into a beautiful high. She might want to get there again.

"We meditated on the crucifix for that," said Eileen.

"I guess that would be a good image for it," said Patricia.

Eileen said, "It works."

"You see," he said to me, "with them, there is hope. They know it all. You and I spend our lives trying to find out what they already know."

"Yes," I said, "that's the truth."

"So, Slack, where do you go now?"

"Back to Alabama, and what are you going to do? You will have to leave Switzerland. Where will you ever go?"

"There are no plans for that," he said.

On January 18, 1973, Leary was returned to California after being abducted by American agents in Afghanistan, taken to London and thence extradited to the U.S. Since the U.S. has no extradition treaty with Afghanistan, the capture was specially arranged and involved snatching away Leary's passport and then pacifying him with a First Class ticket and the company of a pretty young lady-friend, Miss Joanna Harcourt-Smith, on his trip back to jail in California. At this writing, Leary is interred in Folsom Prison, serving up to fifteen years for possession and escape.

In mid-September of '72, Eileen and I returned to Birmingham, Alabama, where I fought (and won) a tenure battle with the university. In May of 1973, Eileen was appointed Superintendent of the Alabama State Training School for Girls. Since then, we have lived in a cottage on the grounds of the school.

Notes

1. Timothy Leary, *High Priest.* New York: NAL, 1968, p. 286.
2. Ibid., p. 8.
3. R. Metzner, ed., *The Ecstatic Adventure.* New York: Macmillan, 1968, p. xiii.
4. *Playboy* Magazine, September 12, 1966, p. 102.
5. Ibid., p. 100.
6. Ibid.
7. Ibid.
8. Thad and Rita Ashby, "Yoga, Sex, and the Magic Mushroom," in *The Underground Reader.* New York: NAL, 1972, pp. 40–46.
9. Timothy Leary, *The Politics of Ecstasy.* London: Granada, 1972, pp. 182–193.
10. Ibid., p.293.
11. *High Priest,* pp. 6–9.

Bibliography

BOOKS:

Brecher, Edward M. and the editors of Consumer Reports, *Licit and Illicit Drugs*. Boston: Little-Brown, 1972.

Brown, Norman O., *Love's Body*. New York: Random House, 1966.

Ebin, David (ed.), *The Drug Experience*. New York: Grove Press, 1965.

Firestone, Ross (ed.), *Getting Busted: Personal Experience of Arrest, Trial and Prison*. New York: Douglas Book Corporation, 1970.

Hayes, Harold (ed.), *Smiling Through the Apocalypse: Esquire's History of the Sixties*. New York: McCall, 1969.

Hesse, Hermann, *Siddhartha*. New York: New Directions, 1951.

Howard, Mel and Forcade, Thomas King (ed.), *The Underground Reader*. New York: New American Library, 1972.

Leary, Timothy, *High Priest*. New York: New American Library, 1968.

Leary, Timothy, *The Politics of Ecstasy*. New York: Putnam's, 1970.

Leary, Timothy, *Jail Notes*. New York: Grove Press, 1970.

Leary, Timothy, *Confessions of a Hope Fiend*. New York: Bantam Books, 1973.

Louria, Donald B., *Overcoming Drugs*. New York: McGraw-Hill, 1971.

Metzner, Ralph (ed.), *The Ecstatic Adventure*. New York: Macmillan, 1968.

The Editors of Rolling Stone, *The Rolling Stone Interviews*. New York: Paperback Library, 1971.

Roxon, Lillian, *Rock Encyclopedia*. New York: Grosset and Dunlap, 1969.

Solomon, David (ed.), *The Drug Experience*. New York: Grove Press, 1965.

Wolfe, Tom, *The Electric Kool-Aid Acid Test*. New York: Farrar, Straus, & Giroux, 1968.

MAGAZINES:

Leary, Timothy, "In the beginning, Leary turned on Ginsberg . . . ," *Esquire*, July, 1968.

Levy, Alen, "Tim Leary, Won't you please come home," *Penthouse*, March, 1973.

Neff, Renfreu, "Tim Leary: Canterbury Tales on the Swiss Riviera," *Changes*, Dec./Jan., 1973.

"Playboy Interview: Timothy Leary," *Playboy*, September, 1966.

Pearce, Donn, "Leary in Limbo," *Playboy*, July, 1971.

Slack, Charles, "An Evening With Timothy Leary," *Eye*, March, 1968.

Slack, Charles, "How to Get Angry Without Actually Killing Anyone," *Eye*, April, 1968.

Slack, Charles, "Tim the Unsinkable," *Psychology Today*, January, 1973.

Zwerin, Michael, "Revolutionary Bust (3)," *The Village Voice*, Feb. 11, 1971.